FREE

TO

BE

MORE

FREE TO BE MORE

Creative Activism in the Era of Black Lives Matter

EDITED BY
Dr. Syrus Marcus Ware &
Dr. Ra'anaa Yaminah Ekundayo (ABD)
WITH
Dr. d'bi.young anitafrika

University of Regina Press

Printed and bound in Canada. The text of this book is printed on 100% post-consumer recycled paper with earth-friendly vegetable-based inks.

Cover design: Evan Marnoch
Interior layout design: John van der Woude, JVDW Designs
Editor for the Press: Rachel F. Stapleton

Library and Archives Canada Cataloguing in Publication

Title: Free to be more : creative activism in the era of Black Lives Matter / edited by Dr. Syrus Marcus Ware & Ra'anaa Yaminah Ekundayo with d'bi.young anitafrika.
Names: Ware, Syrus Marcus, editor | Ekundayo, Ra'anaa Yaminah, editor. | anitafrika, d'bi.young, 1978- editor
Description: Includes bibliographical references.
Identifiers: Canadiana (print) 20250323230 | Canadiana (ebook) 20250323354 | ISBN 9781779401328 (softcover) | ISBN 9781779401335 (hardcover) | ISBN 9781779401342 (EPUB) | ISBN 9781779401359 (PDF)
Subjects: LCSH: Black lives matter movement in art. | LCSH: Art and social action. | LCSH: Arts, Black—Canada—21st century.
Classification: LCC NX513.3.B53 F74 2026 | DDC 704.03/96071—dc23

10 9 8 7 6 5 4 3 2 1

U OF R PRESS

University of Regina Press, University of Regina
Regina, Saskatchewan, Canada, S4S 0A2
TEL: (306) 585-4758 FAX: (306) 585-4699
WEB: www.uofrpress.ca

We acknowledge the support of the Canada Council for the Arts for our publishing program. We acknowledge the financial support of the Government of Canada. / Nous reconnaissons l'appui financier du gouvernement du Canada. This publication was made possible with support from Creative Saskatchewan's Book Publishing Production Grant Program.

Canada Council for the Arts | Conseil des Arts du Canada | Canada | creative SASKATCHEWAN

This book is dedicated to all of the artists, activists, and artivists who are reminding us of the possibilities of freedom and to our ancestors who have stayed reminding us that art and activism are twin flames. We honour you and we thank you.

CONTENTS

Creative Reflections

A NOTE ON LANGUAGE

We are committed to undoing the past 500+ years of colonialism on this soil aimed at eradicating the Land of Indigenous and Black peoples. Naming is a significant form of resistance. We have chosen to use Indigenous place names throughout the manuscript, with the colonial place names bracketed alongside. We feel strongly that the work of supporting Land Back and Indigenous resurgences includes crucial work across multiple sectors of social life. Yet, we also know that language is another tool that helps move toward justice, and we have attempted to use Indigenous place-names to refer to sites across Northern Turtle Island in solidarity with organizers mobilizing in these sites and working with and on the Land.

INTRODUCTION

by **Dr. Syrus Marcus Ware**
Dr. Ra'anaa Yaminah Ekundayo (ABD)
Dr. d'bi.young anitafrika

I hate having to struggle—I honestly do
Because I wish I had been born into a world where it was
Unnecessary

This context of struggle and being a warrior and being a
Struggler
Has been forced on me by oppression

Otherwise, I would be a sculptor, or a gardener
Carpenter—you know, I would be free to be so much more…

I guess part of me or a part of who I am, a part of what I do
Is being a warrior—a reluctant warrior, a reluctant struggler

But…I do it because I'm committed to life

—ASSATA SHAKUR
sampled by Asian Dub Foundation (2001)

Assata Shakur offered these words with Asian Dub Foundation for their well-known track, "Committed to Life// Reluctant Warrior" (2001). She argued that she would have been free to be so much more—an artist, a sculptor, a gardener—if she hadn't had to become a reluctant warrior for the struggle. We are moved by these words because we, too, are committed to life. We are in the struggle to make the world a place where we all have what we need to thrive and where we show up for each other time and time again. We are world-building a future where we are free to be more—perhaps everything and all things that we dare to dream. We imagine a near future of both the artist and the activist united in a push for revolutionary change. *Free to Be More: Creative Activism in the Era of Black Lives Matter* brings together critical thinking about the cultural moment of the now—in the midst of a Black artistic renaissance, the global uptake of abolition, and movements to defund the police in the wake of the murder of George Floyd on May 25, 2020—with the complexity of systems changes, political swings to the right, and rising fascism, here and around the globe. *Free to Be More: Creative Activism in the Era of Black Lives Matter* pays tribute to lineages of creative revolutionary labour by Black artists while focusing on contemporary art and arts-based direct actions in Northern Turtle Island that illuminate the specificity of concerns, tactics, accountabilities, and vision emerging within this settler-colonial context. We approach art as a method of communication, teaching, and healing, and as a strategy for mobilizing, focusing, and highlighting in both contexts: activist and systems change. Even as anti-Black violence surges alongside, and with, widespread civil unrest, unchecked white supremacy at all levels of leadership and governance, and dangerous violent responses to attempts to finally abolish slavery completely, artists continue to pick up their tools and paint, draw, print, dance, weave, and express their outrage and dream of a freer future. Their creations are not mere representations of struggle, nor do they suggest a monolithic Black experience or unified vision of freedom. Black artists are constantly creating new works that are living embodiments of sociopolitical change and invitations for participants and audience members to feel, inhabit, and commit to world-building possibilities.

Black artists and activists are now creating and organizing in a context marked by more than a dozen years of Black Lives Matter (BLM) organizing in Canada. The BLM movement, aptly called the Movement for Black Life, in consideration of the many Black liberation groups and networks that facilitated the radical activism and change making that fuelled the movement throughout the past decade and beyond, is one rooted in history, love, and trans feminisms. This movement is led by Black queer and trans activists/artists (often called "artivists") who have reciprocally imbued their organizing with creative praxes and who have connected Black liberation and social justice praxes to their creative efforts. In 2018, when Syrus first drafted the creative introduction elements for *Until We Are Free: Reflections on Black Lives Matter in Canada* (University of Regina Press, 2020), co-edited with Rodney Diverlus and Sandy Hudson, he wrote a futuristic speculative fiction reflection on the BLM movement set in a time just after what we are living now, coupled with an epilogue that dreamed a future world of art and love and justice, one where we had all won our freedom. *Until We Are Free* was released in 2020, and became a Canadian bestseller in June of the same year, even though the harsh conditions of the global COVID-19 pandemic and lockdown restrictions kept us from gathering and from touring with this offering. By that time, with the uprisings in full swing, it seemed like the reimagined future was right around the corner. There was immense hope in the uprisings of 2020, and throughout the movements for Black lives of the past ten years. Now, as we write this in 2025, we are living on the precipice of that future. We are hoping in ways that will bring about crucial changes. Yet, our hope is now entangled with grief and the realities of a lifetime in the struggle for Black liberation. We keep going just as we get close enough to touch the future, even as we feel the pain of the pendulum swinging to the right and the white supremacist and fascist proclivities the swing brings with it. Poet and activist June Jordan reminds us that "we are the ones we are waiting for,"[1] that the transformations needed to create more livable futures will have to come from us. How can we begin to put into place the building blocks of the communities we are foreshadowing, dreaming of, or prefiguring? We lean into the speculative, working toward a care-oriented tomorrow rooted in powerful Afrofuturistic imaginings. By doing so, we get a chance to envision something different, something revolutionary, something to world-build in our imaginations as a practice for the future.

As editors, Syrus Marcus Ware, Ra'anaa Yaminah Ekundayo, and d'bi. young anitafrika recognize that we are living in a moment imbued with the speculative; in Black communities and beyond, folks are imagining and prefiguring a near future in the now. The 2020s reflect the futures imagined by authors articulating a world on the edge of collapse. Artists and dreamers like Octavia Butler dreamed about a chaotic time in the 2020s, full of radical change making and dynamic shifts. Butler set her best-known novel, *Parable of the Sower* (1993), in 2024—exemplifying the idea that the future will be all about creative transitions and transformations rooted in community. In the Star Trek franchise, the Black Starfleet Commanding Officer of Deep Space Nine, Captain Sisko, time travels only to end up in 2024 at the time of the Bell Riots—a moment of uprising that transforms economic injustice and ushers in a freer future.[2] We are living in the times of speculative change and creative revolutions—from the page to the screen to IRL (in real life).

Artists help us understand our reality and imagine freer futures. Social justice–rooted and -inspired art *is* everywhere. We are amid a series of local and transnational uprisings and activisms for Black liberation and Black trans, queer, and crip liberation. This is inextricable from the simultaneous, revolutionary, and activist-rooted Black arts movement growing alongside it. The symbiotic growth of Black arts and activism—sometimes referred to as "artivism"—in Canada can be witnessed from coast to coast to coast. While white supremacist conditions within the arts sectors continue to grant selective and contentious access (often rooted in limited Diversity, Equity and Inclusion [DEI] mandates, rather than meaningful structural systemic change) to Black artists for exhibition, acquisition, and cultural engagement, the commitment of Black artists who are activists (artivists) to creation, presentation, and community is thriving on its own terms.

Free to Be More: Creative Activism in the Era of Black Lives Matter extends these reflections through essays, roundtables, images, and other forms of artistic texts that centre and honour the critical and necessary labour of Black artists in social movements. Building freer worlds is fundamentally a creative project. Surveying multi- and interdisciplinary creative practices, this collection amplifies the breadth and depth of the ways Black artists across Northern Turtle Island mobilize cultural forms, functions, designs, and relationship-building to envision and enact transformative interventions in anti-Black racism that centre care, critique, and collectivity.

Future Archives: A Look Back at the Past Seven Years

Black lives matter, matter…
Black lives matter, matter…
Black lives matter, matter…

Black lives matter, matter…
Black bodies brutalized.
Black bodies criminalized.
Black bodies demonized.
Black bodies victimized.
Black bodies ostracized.
Black hyper sexualized.
Black hyper sexualized.
Like Natasha and Sophia and Tamir, Michael, Langley, Sandra Bland, Sandra Bland, Sandra Bland.
We cannot live without our lives.
We cannot live without our, our, our, our lives.
We cannot live without our lives…
Black lives matter, matter…
Black lives matter, matter…
Black lives matter, matter…
Black lives matter, matter.

—d'bi.young anitafrika, 2016

How will the radical and creative uprisings of the past decade be remembered in the future? Will all the posters, video clips of flash mobs, banners, and political music be archived for forthcoming generations to learn and build on? We've often wondered what will be added to the archives about this time of great upheaval and change making that poured into the streets. Who and what will be remembered from this time? Throughout the fiery summers of 2014, 2016, 2020, and 2025, we saw news reports of buildings on fire in Seattle and Baltimore, and people marching and rallying across Canada and the United States demanding justice, for Black life to be rendered inherently valuable and protected. For many who protested, this was all too familiar territory after decades of activism. For others, this was their first experience of this kind of collective change making. We saw artwork—plentiful and powerful works—as artists helped lead us into the spectacular futures we were building as we went. Banners, music, paintings, podcasts, and so many creative activisms mark this period in Northern Turtle Island.

The uprisings of the summer of 2020 built on past organizing, perhaps on those sparked by an ember that had been on a slow burn for hundreds of years since colonialism first altered these shores. For example, in 1967 and 1968, Jackie Shane, a Black trans soul and rhythm and blues singer—later portrayed by Ravyn Wngz in a Canadian Heritage Minute—was living true to her gender and fighting back against transphobic backlash from the music industry, her fellow Torontonians, and the ever-present police force. In the 1980s and 1990s, Black queer groups were resisting the racist and carceral logics that plagued access to queer space on Church Street (Toronto's Queer Village) and were organizing group outings to combat the policing they would receive trying to enter a mostly white space[3] and World Majority Lesbians were fighting back against targeted policing and marched with a truck and banners about police violence, resulting in harassment from onsite police at the parade.[4] On the heels of the Rodney King beating in Los Angeles in 1991, in the 1990s and early 2000s, Black activists and artists organized around police brutality and the targeted killings of Faraz Sulman (1995), Phillip Pannell (1990), Malice Green (1992), Sean Bell (2006), Don Myrick (1993), Jonny Gammage (1995), Nathaniel Levi Gaines (1996), Prince Jones (2000), Roger Owensby Jr. (2000), Deandre Brunston (2003), and far too many others to name.

In 2013, after George Zimmerman was acquitted of killing Trayvon Martin, a group of us in Tkaronto (Toronto, ON) who had been organizing around abolition for a couple of decades (including Syrus Marcus Ware, Nik Redman, Giselle Dias, Ky Williams, OmiSoore Dryden, Aruna Boodram) organized a gathering at Riverdale Park near the Don Jail (closed at the end of that year, with all remaining residents transferred to a new detention centre). The Don Jail was a functioning urban jail site in a middle-class neighbourhood in the east end of Tkaronto. The location of the Don was historic; the neighbourhood grew up around it, and despite the fact that it was there first, it was subject to much NIMBYism[5] from the neighbours. The urban location made possible a lot of visible activisms onsite at the prison, with annual Prisoners Justice Day events happening on the lawn in front of the jail, and gatherings in Riverdale Park behind the jail to call for anti-policing and for prisoners' justice. In 2013, it was the natural choice for a gathering about the violence of the carceral system. Called "Hoodies Up," this gathering outside the jail involved letter writing to activists and to the families of people killed by police, as well as letters to Marissa Alexander[6] who was in jail at the time. We held an open mic, and Black parents got up and talked about their children being taken from them—not always by police—an experience where our children are turned into something feared by society, forcing them to age faster and to

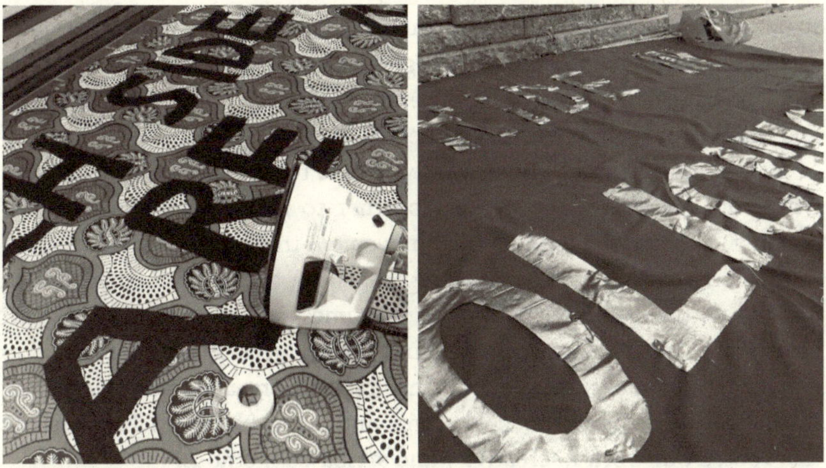

Which Side of History banner *(left)*, No Pride in Policing *(right)*. 2016. Photographs courtesy of Syrus Marcus Ware.

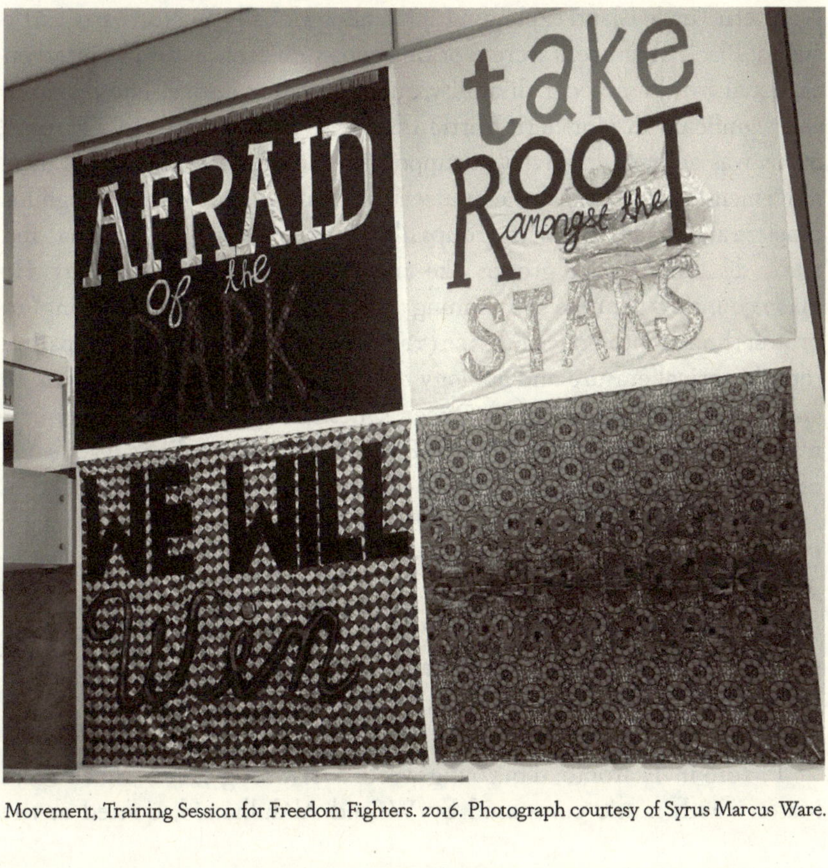

Movement, Training Session for Freedom Fighters. 2016. Photograph courtesy of Syrus Marcus Ware.

struggle under a systemic lens of adultification. This event was rooted in arts-based methodologies and strategies. We drew pictures, wrote letters, and made a candle sculpture at the end of the event—an altar to Trayvon and Marissa, for whom we had gathered.

A few months later, the first BLM action took place in Tkaronto on University Avenue. Artists came together to make signs and plan the action. BLM became a foundational movement that brought together organizers and artists to make change together. Our activism has always been imbued with song, chants, banners, costumes, and visual aesthetics that created a strong message of unified and unapologetic Black trans and crip feminisms and abolition. We drew inspiration from, and built on, the past several decades of activism in Tkaronto and across Northern Turtle Island that rooted our work in creativity and artsbased methods.

In the years following these initial gatherings, the movement for Black lives grew and expanded, with mobilizations around Black justice across Northern Turtle Island expanding and scaling globally. In Northern Turtle Island, Black organizers were working across differences and in intergenerational groups rooted in disability, queer, and trans justice. The year 2016 was significant in Northern Turtle Island for Black justice. In Tkaronto, Syrus was actively involved in supporting the ongoing Black liberation movement(s), working at the intersection of art and activism through his practice and organizing with groups like Blackness Yes!/Blockorama[7] and BIPOC disability justice groups like PDA:Performance Disability Art. He made countless banners proclaiming things like "No Pride in Policing" to protest the Toronto Police Service (TPS) mural on Church Street as part of their historical erasure and apology tour to the LGBTTI2QQA (Lesbian, Bi, Gay, Trans, Intersex, 2 Spirit, Queer, Questioning and Asexual community) a month before Project Marie. Project Marie saw police surveillance of queer public spaces. It involved the raid of a beach in Etobicoke in 2017 after an undercover cop solicited sex from gay people at the beach.[8] Despite trying to pinkwash police presence in queer spaces in Tkaronto and offering a meaningless apology for the bathhouse raids in the 1980s,[9] the cops proved their intentions by raiding another queer cruising space through Project Marie. Other banners proclaimed, "Which Side of History Are You On," "Justice for Abdirahman Abdi," and, of course, "We Will Win."

In 2016 in Tkaronto, d'bi.young wrote a new song called "Black Lives Matter" with music composed by Waleed Abdulhamid, quoted at the

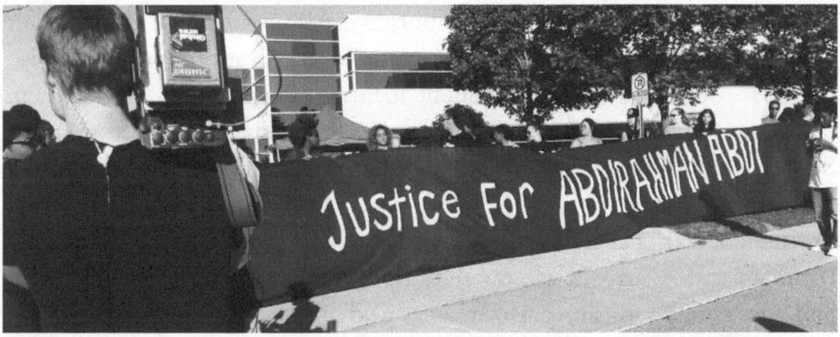

Justice for Abdirahman Abdi banner at SIU. 2016. Photograph courtesy of Syrus Marcus Ware.

start of this section, and a new play titled *esu crossing the middle passage*, included later in this volume, that built on their decades of work in dub poetry, theatre, and music for change. They performed this song live across the continent and beyond, bringing it home to the Blockorama Black queer stage at the 2016 Pride Festival in Tkaronto. In the tradition of protest theatre, *esu crossing the middle passage* was mounted at Storefront Theatre during the fifteen-day occupation by Black Lives Matter–Toronto (BLM-TO) Tent City earlier that year. The protest action, led by BLM-TO, was in response to the March 18, 2016, news that the Toronto police officer who killed Andrew Loku in July 2015 would not be charged nor have their name released to the public.[10] Set aboard a slave ship, the play chronicles the journey of a Black woman who is forced into the transatlantic enslavement system and tackles themes of misogynoir, anti-Blackness, border-crossings, police brutality, and emancipation. d'bi.young added new protest scenes to the theatrical piece in solidarity with BLM-TO Tent City. Community Talk-Back sessions, facilitated by members of Black Lives Matter, followed some performances. These sessions allowed members of the community to discuss, metabolize, resist, and heal from the anti-Black violence of the moment. During this time, Ra'anaa Ekundayo, one of few Laurentian University Black architecture students of that period, was completing their undergraduate degree at the institution's McEwen School of Architecture in N'Swakamok (Sudbury, ON). Inspired by the nuanced experiences of Black design students and practitioners, they began researching the relationship between architecture and segregation in the South Side of Chicago for their master's thesis between 2018 and 2020. Delving into the presence of the Illinois Black Panther Party, particularly the movement's use of activist art, they began exploring their own artistic practice through collaborative Afrocentric public art. Their emerging passion for Black activist creative exploration combined with the 2020 uprisings (and subsequent local responses) empowered them to become involved locally, eventually co-founding Black Lives Matter–Sudbury alongside a team of dedicated Northern Ontario–based activists and artists.

Indeed, artists everywhere were engaging in creating what Toni Cade Bambara called "irresistible revolutions" (Bambara, 2012) through dance and movement, music, performance, and interdisciplinary arts. These artists in many ways were helping create a visual and sonic story for these times—a creative archive. Everywhere, there seemed to be a revolutionary renaissance in artistic practice emerging globally. In Northern Turtle Island, artists were choreographing flash mobs, putting up street-based art exhibitions during tent city occupations, painting large-scale graffiti works and street murals, and creating music, short films, theatre, and performance and creative projects speaking to Black justice; a wide group of organizers in the BLM movement were organizing actions across Tiohtià:ke (Montreal, QC); Tkaronto; and Musqueam (xʷməθkʷəy̓əm), Squamish (Sḵwx̱wú7mesh), and Tsleil-Waututh (səlilwətaɬ; Vancouver, BC) and beyond. Pride protests started in Tkaronto in 2016 and 2017 and spread coast to coast to coast, and artists everywhere were engaging in movement-building, documenting these activisms, and creating innovative ways of organizing rooted in creative practice. The movement kept growing and the artists kept creating—making films, murals, books, and storylines. Mainstream media started weaving Black activism into their storylines,[11] and there were more and more people getting involved in movement-building.

And then 2020 happened.

2020 was a year like no other—unbelievable news hitting us daily—the stuff of science fiction imaginings. From finding proof of life on Venus, to the global COVID-19 pandemic,[12] to the wildfires spreading rapidly across the planet—the year started with a bang, a stressful one. Then, on May 25, 2020, George Floyd was killed by police in Minneapolis, and the world reacted with rage, horror, and calls for change. This murder was followed rapidly by the death of Regis Korchinski-Paquet while Toronto Police were in her apartment, and several others: Rodney Levi, Elishia Hudson, and Chantel Moore. The names in Canada grew and the police killings escalated, and there were others across Canada and the United States:

Breonna Taylor, Jacob Blake, and more—all who died or were injured in interactions with police. People poured into the streets to demand something different. Armed with chalk, paint, banners, movements, chants, and songs—and a lot of personal protective equipment (PPE) like N95 masks—crowds flooded city streets in uprisings that saw violence, fires, and riotous turmoil. There is a long list of tragedies that mark that summer of violence writ large—a spectacle of Black death on our news and social media feeds every day. And we found ourselves building care practices as a result—mutual aid and collective sharing to heal from the harms we were witnessing. BLM-TO organized a gathering on Black grief in June 2020 to gather and respond virtually to the moment. In this way, 2020 was also a year of beautiful and magical and powerful uprisings as communities deep in lockdown poured into the streets to take up justice, to call for change, and to water the seeds of abolition growing in our communities.

Across Northern Turtle Island folks were organizing. In the Arctic, the group Northern Voices Rising had convened a series of protests that drew hundreds to their small city in the Yukon; BLM-Vancouver members shut down ports and held marches and rallies in British Columbia and ultimately blocked the Vancouver Port and Viaduct in protest.[13] In Winnipeg, folks rallied for justice for Rodney Levi and called for defunding the police, while BLM-TO launched a widespread campaign aimed at defunding the police, including their creation of the website defundthepolice.org and the creation of a 7,200-square-foot mural on College Street in front of Toronto Police Headquarters ("Defund the Police," painted during a peaceful protest, 2020).

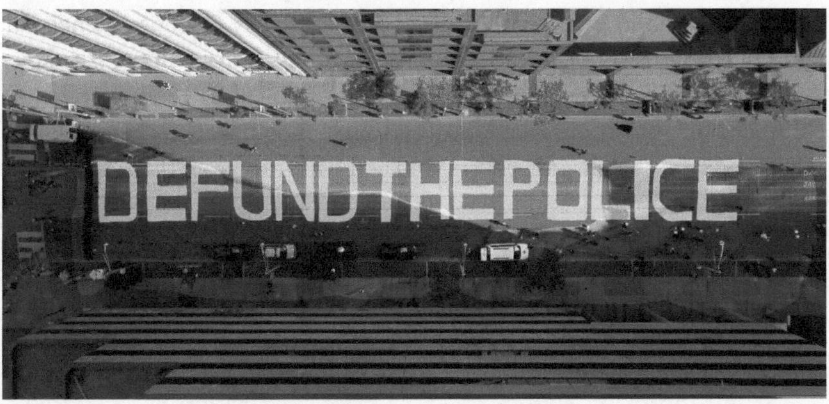

Defund the Police mural. 2020. Photograph courtesy of BLM Canada.

Farther east, chapters and independent collectives were organized—in Newfoundland,[14] in Fredericton,[15] in Halifax[16]—and they held active mobilizations throughout the uprisings of 2020. BLM–Sudbury painted murals, held arts initiatives like Culture Matrix: Black Arts Festival, and organized an annual northern caucus for Black folk living and organizing in N'Swakamok (Sudbury, ON) and in the north.[17] With these calls for change through a variety of methods, we saw the expansion of a beautiful renaissance of Black cultural production as well as the development of the distinct activist aesthetics and creative strategies for engaging audiences in the art of activism. From the vociferous chanting and songs on the mic at uprisings after Trayvon Martin's killing in 2013 carrying forward through the 2020s, to the banners and poetry, songs, and theatre that have been created through, by, and for movement-building and creative activisms, art has been the medium of our unrelenting resistance to systemic oppression. In late June 2020, after some incredible demonstrations of creative activisms across Turtle Island, we witnessed many arts institutions grappling with how they were going to address the current moment, given their relevance having been called into question with every passing day of silence. Enter Blackout Tuesday.

Blackout Tuesday was held on Tuesday, June 7, 2020, and was a digital initiative spearheaded by several arts institutions wherein they changed their social media profile pics to Black squares on Instagram, X (formerly known as Twitter), and Facebook, and made a post about their commitment to Black artists and communities. Syrus wrote an article for *Canadian Art* chronicling this trend and the backlash it received from Black communities who called out this form of performative activism for what it was—hollow and without any accountability or consequence. In his article, Syrus interviewed Black activists and artists about Blackout Tuesday and explored the social media activism of the moment being embraced by institutions that had otherwise not come out earlier in favour or in support of Black staff, artists, and activists. He wrote the following:

> My email is filled with these statements, the performative solidarities and demonstrative actions that do nothing to address the structural changes needed in this society for us all to live self-determined free lives.
>
> Perhaps the most perplexing, or perhaps most complex for me in these performativities are the pro-Black/Black Lives Matter statements from arts organizations and institutions. I have worked in various arts

institutions for decades and have been an artist for 25 years. I have witnessed firsthand the anti-Blackness that is dyed in the wool of the arts. We have a white supremacy problem that is perhaps the art world's best (worst?) kept secret—this secret is something these solidarity statements do not address. Without addressing the larger systemic issues that plague the arts, what is the purpose of these statements?

Dr. Naila Keleta Mae, artist and Assistant Professor, at the University of Waterloo stated the following this week on Facebook:

> *I am disgusted by statements from institutions, corporations and organizations on what they plan to do about anti-Black racism in the future if they have done little or nothing to end it in the past. Their statements need to explain why they haven't taken the horrors of white supremacy seriously even though they are well documented and centuries old. #Blackandfree*[18]

Indeed, these statements fail to "explain why they haven't taken the horrors" seriously: rather they paint the institution as already doing the work. Meanwhile, the history of erasure and the shutting out of Black artists from mainstream—and yes, even lefty art spaces—persists and cannot be separated in this moment of renewed support for "all Black lives"… As dancer, choreographer, and Black Lives Matter–Toronto co-founder Rodney Diverlus has stated, "*I wonder how many Black employees are reading their workplace's Black Lives Matter statements knowing full-well of how toxic/racist the workplace is, how little Black employees are supported/nurtured, and all the other garbage that comes with anti-Blackness.*"

As I read these statements in my inbox, I feel a mix of hope and rage; hope that perhaps this is the time to finally speak about the unspeakable in the arts, anti-Blackness, and rage because it's also just as possible that these performative activisms are attempts to placate us while maintaining the status quo. I think about Chaédria LaBouvier, the first Black curator and the first Black woman to curate an exhibition at the Guggenheim Museum in New York City, who was consistently passed over and had to fight to have her work credited because of systemic anti-Blackness. In response to the Guggenheim Blacking out their profile photo with a Black square for Blackout Tuesday, she famously tweeted, "*Get the entire fuck out of here. I am Chaédria LaBouvier, the first Black curator in your*

> *80-year history & you refused to acknowledge that while also allowing Nancy Spector to host a panel about my work w/o inviting me. Erase this shit.*" We are indeed in a new era; "we are not having it" as !Kona states.[19]

How does this process reflect any sense of accountability or responsibility to Black communities? In the end, we will always be the last hired, and when the statement blows up, the first fired.[20]

In contrast to the lacklustre response from arts organizations and institutions to Black art and artists and to the movement for Black lives, the work of Black artists was flourishing. We find ourselves in the middle of a Black renaissance and a moment of Black arts that is directly connected to Black activisms, and we are excited to be able to write and reflect on this catalytic timeline. This renaissance is exemplified by a flourishing of Black art and creativity spanning the past fifteen years that spoke back directly to the living conditions facing Black communities across Turtle Island. Playwrights like Donna-Michelle St. Bernard created *Gas Girls*; Leah Simon Bowden penned *The Flood*; Amanda Parris wrote *Other Side of the Game*; Makambe K. Simamba crafted *Our Fathers, Sons, Lovers and Little Brothers* (Theatre Passe Murialle, 2022); Natasha Morris offered *The Negroes Are Congregating* at the Theatre Centre in Tkaronto in 2019; Audrey Dwyer created *Calpurnia*; and the trio of Stephen Jackman-Torkoff, Tawiah M'Carthy, and Thomas Antony Olajide created *Black Boys*. In dance, artists like Antoine Hunter, Rodney Diverlus, Ravyn Wngz, Devine Darlin, Aisha Sasha John, and others were creating new movement works, including Diverlus's 2022 offering, *welcome, we've been waiting*, and their 2017 work, *in your eyes, the sparkle of gunpowder*. Visual artists Oreka James, Theodore Walker Robinson, Kosisochukwu Nnebe, Janine Carrington, Mickalene Thomas, Elicser Elliott, Natalie Wood, Sandra Brewster, Oluseye, Anique Jordan, Camille Turner, and many others were creating expansive works and solo and group shows across Canada. Artists were creating new works that brought together a deepening conversation about Black life in Canada and Turtle Island in these times, and institutions were also showcasing the work of Black artists in major institutions—we are thinking here of Brewster's *Blur* (2019–20) at the AGO, and Bowen's façade work at the National Gallery of Canada in the 2020s. In ways that sometimes aligned with Susan Cahan's 2016 articulation in *Mounting Frustration*, galleries were often filling their side/restaurant galleries, off-site spaces and online curatorial spaces, with work by Black artists during the 2010s. This renaissance continues post-2025, despite a lack of structural changes in these institutions and a lack of effort to acquire the work of Black artists to integrate into their collections. Recent Donald Trump–fuelled vitriol that encourages institutions to avoid "diversity, equity, and inclusion (DEI)–focused" exhibitions and content has had reverberations here, north of the medicine line, with Pierre Poilievre, Danielle Smith, and others parroting Trump ideology. Still, Black artists across the country continue creating new works, and continue to inspire change coast to coast to coast.

Notes

1 *Directed by Desire: The Collected Poems of June Jordan* (Copper Canyon Press, 2006).

2 "Past Tense, Part I" and "Past Tense, Part II." Episodes 11–12, Season 3, *Star Trek: Deep Space Nine*. Originally aired January 2 and 9, 1995.

3 Jin Haritaworn, Ghaida Moussa and Syrus Marcus Ware, editors, *Marvellous Grounds: Queer of Colour Formations in Toronto* (Between the Lines, 2018).

4 Jin Haritaworn, Ghaida Moussa and Syrus Marcus Ware, editors, *Marvellous Grounds: Queer of Colour Formations in Toronto* (Between the Lines, 2018).

5 "Not In My Backyard," or opposition of local residents to proposed projects.

6 Marissa Alexander is a survivor of domestic violence. From her support site: "Marissa Alexander is a survivor of domestic violence from Jacksonville, FL, who was prosecuted and threatened with 60 years in prison for defending her life from her abusive husband. After serving a sentence of 3 years behind bars and 2 years in house detention while being forced to wear and pay for a surveillance ankle monitor, Marissa Alexander was finally released on January 27, 2017." (https://www.facebook.com/FreeMarissaNow/)

7 Blackness Yes! Formed in 1998 and held the first Blockorama in 1999. Blockorama is the longest running and largest stage at Pride Toronto's annual festival, taking place in the famed Wellesley Parking Lot on Pride Sunday. Now over twenty-five years old, Blockorama is a destination for Black and QTBIPOC folks at Pride.

8 Marcus McCann, "The Cost of Policing," November 11, 2021.

9 The bathhouse raids of the early 1980s marked a turning point in Canadian history: police attacked bathhouses across the village, capturing "found ins"—people found in the bathhouse—and intentionally destroyed the building structures to limit queer gathering.

10 Andrew Loku's death was ruled a homicide in June 2017 by an inquest jury; the coroner's inquest verdict is not linked to any civil or criminal liability.

11 Emily St. James, "Scandal Tackles the Protests in Ferguson in a Powerful Episode," *Vox Magazine*, March 2015.

12 Robert Lea, "Life on Venus? Intriguing Molecule Phosphine Spotted in Planet's Clouds Again," *Space*, July 2023.

13 Michelle Ghoussoub, "Anti-Racism Protesters Block Vancouver Viaducts for Rally in Support of Black Lives Matter," *CBC*, June 13, 2020; Andrea Ross, "Thousands in

Vancouver Rally against Police Violence as George Floyd Protests Shake US," *CBC*, May 31, 2020.

14 Meg Roberts, "Thousands Come Together for Black Lives Matter Rally in St. John's," *CBC*, June 7, 2020.

15 Megan Yamoah, "Peaceful Protest in Fredericton for George Floyd Draws Large Crowd," *Global News*, June 2, 2020.

16 Benjamin Graeme, "Thousands Participate in an Anti-Racism Rally in Halifax," *Global News*, June 1, 2020; Anjuli Patil, "Demonstrators at Black Lives Matter Vigil in Halifax Say Now It's Time to Take Action," *CBC*, June 5, 2020.

17 Ian Campbell, "Sudbury Mural Makes Important Statement," *CTV News Northern Ontario*, September 29, 2020, https://northernontario.ctvnews.ca/video/c2044775-sudbury-mural-makes-important-statement; Jenny Lamothe, "BLM Sudbury Hosts 'Culture Matrix' Festival on Saturday," Sudbury.com, August 12, 2022, https://www.sudbury.com/lifestyle/blm-sudbury-hosts-culture-matrix-festival-on-saturday-5689153; Warren Schlote, "Black Lives Matter–Sudbury Panel Explores Links between Indigenous, Black Activism," *CBC News*, February 28, 2023, https://www.cbc.ca/news/Canada/sudbury/blm-sudbury-caucus-2023-1.6762155.

18 Syrus Ware, "Give Us Permanence: Ending Anti-Black Racism in Canada's Art Institutions," *Canadian Art*, June 24, 2020.

19 Ware, "Give us Permanence."

20 Ware, "Give us Permanence."

WE ARE A GATHERING

This anthology brings together writing, interviews, and artist statements about the incredible art of Black activism that has sprung forth from this revolutionary arts renaissance we are currently witnessing. We are compelled by Christen Smith and Lorraine Leu's articulation that a book anthology could be a catalytic gathering space where action and activism can happen as we learn together. They state: "We are a unique collective of voices. Rather than an assembly of writers and scholars, we are a gathering."[1] In many ways, this collection is a gathering—a counter-archived memory of a kiki[2] put to pages—a series of interviews, artworks, and reflections on the incredible artivism of the past decade and a half and on the change making happening that is birthing a new, freer future.

This book is divided into three sections. In "Part One: Black Arts, Abolition, and Activism," we open with Britta B's powerful creative work, "Black Boots," wherein she considers Black resistance through a poetic lens centring Black cultural renaissance rooted in activism. Merging collage and printmaking techniques, the "Defund the Police Poster Series" follows, demanding to "End the Terror" and "Defund the Police" through a reinvestment in community. Created for BLM Canada, this series features works by Anna Jane McIntyre, Elicser Elliott, Sandra Brewster, Ifetayo Alabi, and Camille Turner. In "Decolonial Frameworks by Black Arts Leaders," d'bi.young anitafrika facilitates a roundtable conversation with artists Carla Chambers, Nishi Gouldbourne, and Raechele Lovell, delving into their experiences formulating new decolonial pedagogical practices using the Anitafrika Method in a six-month artist residency program. In "'She Carried with Her... a Large Bundle of Wearing Apparel Belonging to Herself': Slave Dress as Resistance in Portraiture and Fugitive Advertisements," Charmaine Nelson interrogates the use of clothing as a method of asserting agency and selfhood by enslaved Black individuals. In "Vagabond: On Movement and Changemaking," Rodney Diverlus and Syrus Marcus Ware discuss the creation and development of their movement character, Vagabond, and its debut in 2018 in Tkaronto. They consider Diverlus's new choreographic work, *welcome, we've been waiting*, performed at Toronto Dance Theatre in 2022. Following this is "The Art of Step: Roots, Resistance, and the Rich Culture of Step in Montreal," a rich roundtable with Natasha Clery and Kayin Queeley discussing the origins of step in so-called Canada and the subsequent work of the Montreal Steppers over the past few decades. ToniXTones's chapter "From Boys to Men" follows, with images that open space for Black men and boys to reflect on their relationship to gender constructs. We then move into a consideration of activist aesthetics, artistic practice, and creation. In "Taking (James) McGill Down," Mohammed A. Odusanya looks at the statues toppling across Northern Turtle Island, with a specific focus on the colonial statue of James McGill in Tiohtià:ke, and the challenges of student activism at McGill during this period. "Framing the North: Black Arts Beyond the Metropolis" features a conversation-based interview on arts and activism by comrades and co-founders of Black Lives Matter–Sudbury. Frequent artistic collaborators Isak Vaillancourt and Ra'anaa Yaminah Ekundayo delve into the importance of centring Black experiences beyond urban centres and the critical emergence of conversations of anti-Blackness through an artistic lens in Northern Ontario. Finally, Syrus Marcus Ware offers wallworks excerpts from his recent show in "Activist Wallpaper Series," featuring toile-like patterns of activist portraits to create alternative environments where we get to be free.

In "Part Two: Our Practice/How We Create," we begin with an interview with Elder visual artist Winsom Winsom entitled "The Spiritual Artist" wherein she reflects on her life as a spiritual-political Black arts activist. We then move into a reprint of d'bi.young anitafrika's "esu: crossing the middle passage" before offering "We Gather" by Erica N. Cardwell, which highlights the work of Sandra Brewster. Building on Brewster's work, we follow with "The Zoo," an interview with Kyisha Williams that delves into abolitionist film practice in the last decade, and the role of

Black queer storytelling in shaping future worlds. In "Decolonize Love," King Kxndi features line drawings and black-and-white motifs mixed with pops of colour to contemplate what love and relationships look like outside colonial boundaries and governance. We follow this artwork with images from Camille Turner's videowork *Nave*, which was voted best in show at the Toronto Biennial of Art in 2022. jamilah malika abu-bakare offers "Fugitive Sound Art: Sound as Refusal, Sound as Refuge," an engagement that dives into the sonic, considering the science of sound, fugitivity, and the presence of Blackness in sound art in a moment of increased brutality toward Black people and the targeted policing of our communities. Moving to a consideration of Black-Deaf creative praxis, we offer a roundtable discussion with Natasha "Courage" Bacchus, Syrus Marcus Ware, and Ra'anaa Ekundayo entitled, "Unheard Voices: Theatre and the Black Deaf Experience." New poetry by Aisha Sasha John entitled "total: An Excerpt" helps close out this section before "Introspective Retrospective," that features d'bi.young anitafrika in conversation with multidisciplinary Black and Afro Indigenous trans artist Ravyn Wngz, who shares insights into her life, practice, and activism.

Lastly, we offer "Part Three: Living as if We're Already There," a section beginning with Syrus Marcus Ware's 2017 article, "On Writing 2025: Light Years From Now," first published in *C Magazine*. We continue speculative dreaming with Yung Yemi's "The Afrofuturist Dreamscape: Black Cultural Identity," in which Ra'anaa Yaminah Ekundayo and multidisciplinary artist Yemi discuss Yemi's unique approach and understanding of Afrofuturism in the context of speculative fiction and organizing in Northern Turtle Island. Through a blend of styles, cultures, and historical elements, his community-oriented work fosters dialogue on Blackness, radicality, and the power of art. Kanika Gordon offers "The Archive as Living Entity: Notes from Yamayeka," a discussion that reflects on memory, relationships, and the archive. Following this discussion, Kim Ninkuru offers her much performed work, "Black Digital Angels," a poem that reflects on Black trans experience, expectations of community, and mediating care in a digital world. Kayode Jonathan Akande offers the artworks "Winter," and "Black Futures." Closing this section, Pauline Lomami examines policing and the ongoing work to counter policing's effects on our communities in the chapter "Force and Form."

We have chosen to end the collection with some creative reflections from artists in the community. These creative reflections consider processes and subjects and offer us insights into the work of key artists making works to create Black affirming space in Canada. We begin this section with "The Four Queens" by Simone Elizabeth Saunders, a work that draws on her celebration of Black womanhood through depictions of Black Love, Black Magic, Black Dreams, and Black Power. We follow this with "Maroon Child: Mobility of Imagination" by Theodore Walker Robinson, with insights into their creative approaches rooted in their identity as a Black, low-vision, trans, nonbinary artist who grew up under the restrictions of a conservative Caribbean household that was less than supportive of their practice. Following this is « PHANTASY No. 3 » by RYAN AD, that centres youth resistance through a consideration of Black life at leisure with unbridled imagination and rest, and "Ice Cream Dreams" by Janine Carrington, wherein she reflects on her digital artwork of the same name that uses colour and texture to depict joy and possibility for the young characters in the image. The last of these entries is "They Say We Can't Breathe Underwater" by Natalie Wood, which is the next encyclopedic offering that showcases her investigation into Black justice, carnival, and dirty mas exemplified by the Blue Devils in Trinidad and Tkaronto.

These artworks, chapters, and poems are from artists based across the continent of Turtle Island (North America) and whose works both reject the myth of a bordered Blackness and challenge the limiting borders of the nation state. These works speak to the essence of Black Lives Matter organizing; trans feminist, queer, crip, Mad, Deaf, and disabled theory; and practice and praxis existing in a borderless Blackness that is expansive and ever deepening.

Indeed, the artists and activists in this publication are embracing revolutionary approaches and digging deep into community to root their work over a durational period. We are moving beyond the immediate urgency of the 2020 uprising moments and now find ourselves four years later, amid a huge climate crisis and white supremacy and fascism being uplifted across Turtle Island through government processes and decisions—including but not limited to trans witch hunts to root out trans people, with a particular focus on trans Black Indigenous and People of Colour (BIPOC) folks by cis transphobes like Pierre Poilievre, a leader of a national political party, along with noted transphobes Scott Moe[3] (SK) and Danielle Smith[4] (AB), as well as the attempted closing of the many safer drug use sites opened in the last four years to save the lives of community members affected by the tainted drug supply (CITE). Ontario's premier is privatizing seemingly everything, including the Greater Toronto Area's once beloved Ontario Place, now destined to be an exclusive spa for the rich few.[5] Black people are still facing targeted policing and violence and houselessness continues as encampments stretch from park to park, connecting dots from community to community in most cities in Northern Turtle Island.

We need more organizing now, not less. We need community, art-based activisms, and Black leadership to get us to a freer changed future. The artists in this book are helping us get there—one project or program at a time, and for this we are thankful. We hope that this collection will serve as an archive or counter-archive of what is happening here at this moment, even as the collection tracks us forward into the future. We hope that this collection is useful to all future generations of creative change makers in the middle of this incredible Black cultural revolution.

Bibliography

Benjamin, Graeme. "Thousands Participate in an Anti-Racism Rally in Halifax." *Global News*, June 2020. Found online on August 22, 2024, at https://globalnews.ca/news/7011986/george-lloyd-anti-racism-demonstration-halifax.

Campbell, Ian. "Sudbury Mural Makes Important Statement." *CTV News Northern Ontario*, September 29, 2020. https://northernontario.ctvnews.ca/video/c2044775-sudbury-mural-makes-important-statement.

Casaletto, Lucas, and Richard Southern. "Group Claims Ontario Place Redevelopment Will Use Millions of Taxpayer Dollars for New Spa." *City News*. Found online on August 22, 2024, at https://toronto.citynews.ca/2024/04/10/ontario-place-therme-spa-redevelopment-plans-taxpayers-ford-government/.

CBC News. "'Defund the Police,' Painted Outside Toronto Police Headquarters During a Peaceful Protest." *CBC*. June 2020. Found online on August 22, 2024, at https://www.cbc.ca/news/canada/toronto/toronto-protest-outside-police-hq-1.5619271.

Dayal, Pratyush. "Community Members, Advocates Fear Rise of Transphobia in Sask. after Election." *CBC*. October 30, 2024. https://www.cbc.ca/news/canada/saskatoon/sask-to-become-most-transphobic-province-worry-experts-1.7367337.

Ghoussoub, Michelle. "Anti-racism Protesters Block Vancouver Viaducts for Rally in Support of Black Lives Matter." *CBC*, June 2020. Found online on

August 22, 2024, at https://www.cbc.ca/news/canada/british-columbia/anti-racism-protesters-block-vancouver-viaducts-for-rally-in-support-of-Black-lives-matter-1.5611242.

Lamothe, Jenny. "BLM Sudbury Hosts 'Culture Matrix' Festival on Saturday." Sudbury.com, August 12, 2022. https://www.sudbury.com/lifestyle/blm-sudbury-hosts-culture-matrix-festival-on-saturday-5689153.

Lea, Robert. "Life on Venus? Intriguing Molecule Phosphine Spotted in Planet's Clouds Again." *Space.com*. July 2023. Found online on August 22, 2024, at https://www.space.com/venus-clouds-phosphine-evidence-debate.

McCann, Marcus. "The Cost of Policing Public Sex." *Xtra Magazine*. November 11, 2021. Found online on August 22, 2024, at https://xtramagazine.com/power/toronto-police-project-marie-sex-212096.

Patil, Anjuli. "Demonstrators at Black Lives Matter Vigil in Halifax Say Now It's Time to Take Action." *CBC*. June 2020. Found online on August 22, 2024, at https://www.cbc.ca/news/canada/nova-scotia/hundreds-gather-for-Black-lives-matter-vigil-in-halifax-1.5600768.

Rhodes, I. I., and Mark Alan. "Alternative Pasts, Presents, and Futures in Star Trek: Historical Engagement and Representation through Popular Culture." *Geographical Bulletin* 58, no. 1 (2017).

Roberts, Meg. "Thousands Come Together for Black Lives Matter Rally in St. John's." *CBC*. June 7, 2020. Found online on August 22, 2024, at https://www.cbc.ca/news/canada/newfoundland-labrador/Black-lives-matter-rally-st-johns-1.5601646.

Ross, Andrea. "Thousands in Vancouver Rally against Police Violence as George Floyd Protests Shake US," *CBC*, May 2020. Found online on August 22, 2024, at: https://www.cbc.ca/news/canada/british-columbia/vancouver-police-protest-1.5592620.

Schlote, Warren. "Black Lives Matter–Sudbury Panel Explores Links between Indigenous, Black Activism." *CBC News*, February 28, 2023. https://www.cbc.ca/news/Canada/sudbury/blm-sudbury-caucus-2023-1.6762155.

Smith, Christen A., and Lorraine Leu. "Toward a Dialogic Transnational Black Feminism: An Introduction." In *Black Feminist Constellations: Dialogue and Translation across the Americas*. University of Texas Press, 2023.

St. James, Emily. "Scandal Tackles the Protests in Ferguson in a Powerful Episode." *Vox Magazine*. March 2015. Found online on August 22, 2024, at https://www.vox.com/2015/3/6/8160727/scandal-lawn-chair-recap-ferguson.

Tasker, John Paul. "Federal Justice Minister Accuses Alberta Premier Danielle Smith of 'Demonizing' Trans Kids." *RCI Canadian News*. February 1, 2024. https://ici.radio-canada.ca/rci/en/news/2046272/federal-reaction-danielle-smith-trans.

Ware, Syrus. "Give Us Permanence: Ending Anti-Black Racism in Canada's Art Institutions." *Canadian Art*, June 24, 2020. Found online on August 22, 2024, at https://canadianart.ca/features/give-us-permanence-ending-anti-Black-racism-in-canadas-art-institutions.

Yamoah, Megan. "Peaceful Protest in Fredericton for George Floyd Draws Large Crowd." *Global News*. Found online on August 22, 2024, at https://globalnews. ca/news/7018115/george-floyd-protest-fredericton.

Notes

1 Smith and Leu, "Toward a Dialogic Transnational Black Feminism," xix–xliv.

2 Kiki is a Black queer and trans term that refers to a hangout, party, or gathering.

3 Dayal, "Community Members, Advocates Fear Rise in Transphobia."

4 Tasker, "Federal Justice Minister Accuses Alberta."

5 Lucas Casaletto and Richard Southern, "Group claims Ontario Place redevelopment will use millions of taxpayer dollars for new spa," *City News*, April 10. 2024.

PART ONE

BLACK ARTS, ABOLITION, AND ACTIVISM

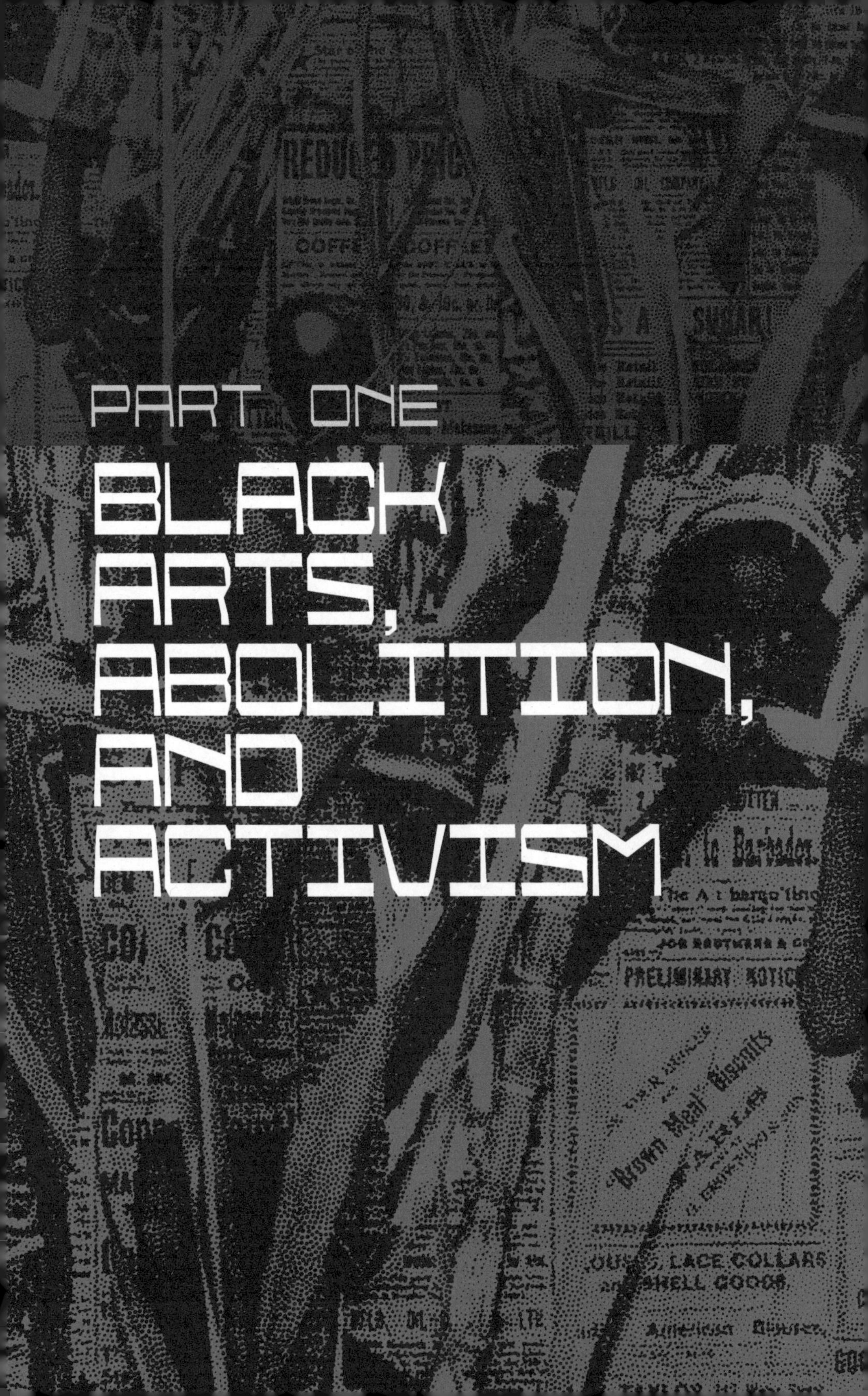

BLACK BOOTS

by **Britta B**

said no Black

and broke in-
to Black
boots
loosened the strings of my Black, Black
hoodie
pulled my head see-through

soaked Black worry
in a bath
of Black laughter

tucked into, tinkered out of Black
turtleneck fractures
saw the spy
on the other side
of the tunnel
spat purple-Black paranoia
over boom bap
stitches hunched
pitch Black
helmet hips,
Black shellac fists

rolled around in Black cotton sheets and t-shirts
'Til I snatched
cavities
on a Black satin dress

took it off and put on
Black track pants
and Black leather gloves
felt my way through the dark
of a long Black coat's
arms parked in front of the mirror
with Black
wings

of what little I got, I and a lot of Blackish
and
Black

begin every day
re-entering this
Black-listed grin

Black comes back
Black attracts Black

Black goes
with everything
sure

but what would you give to be
the Blackest thing

on Earth?

BLM DEFUND THE POLICE POSTER SERIES

by **Anna Jane McIntyre**
Elicser Elliott
Sandra Brewster
Ifetayo Alabi
Camille Turner
for Black Lives Matter–Canada

Posters reproduced courtesy of BLM Canada and the Artists.

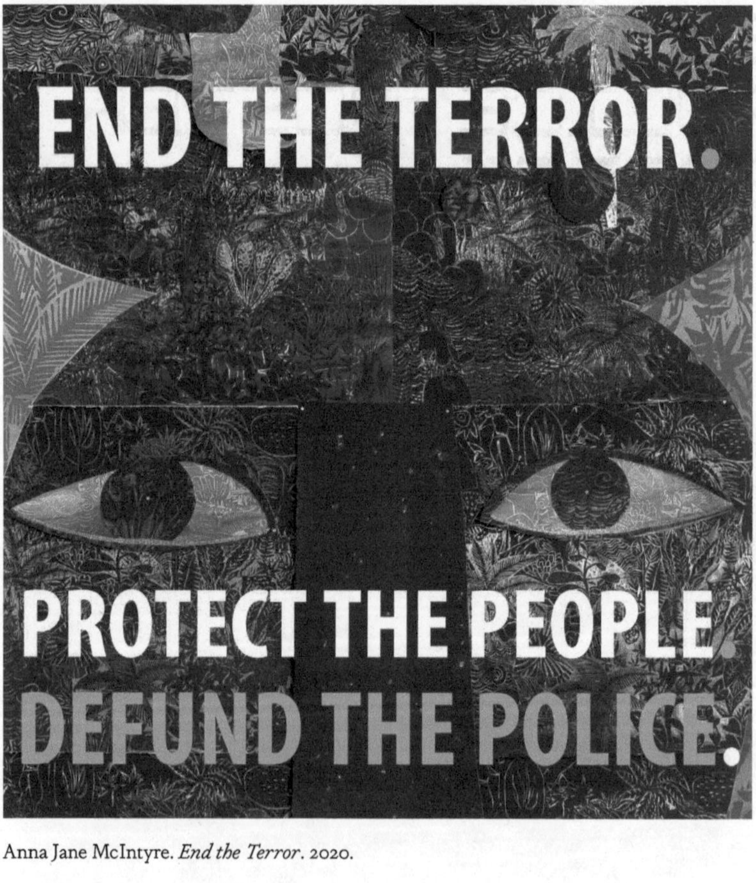

Anna Jane McIntyre. *End the Terror*. 2020.

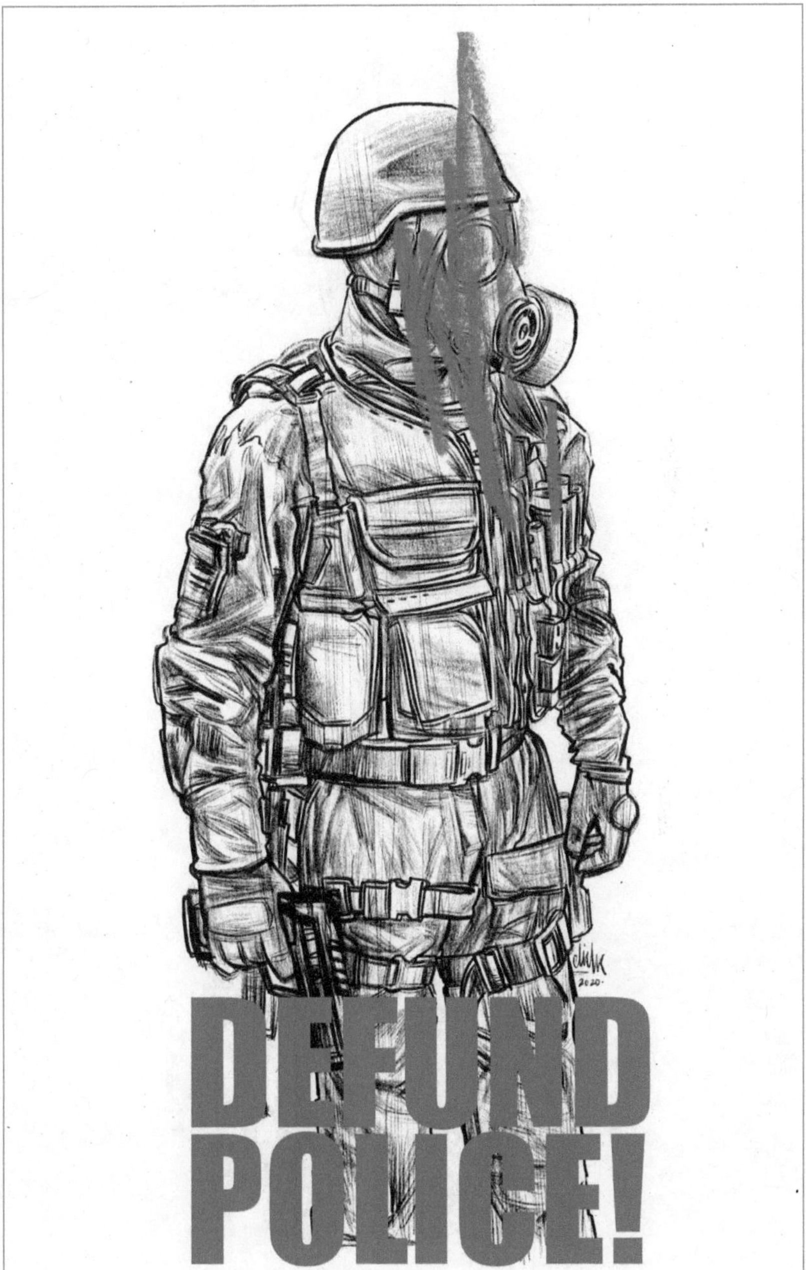

Sandra Brewster, *Defund the Police*, 2023, gel transfer on wood.

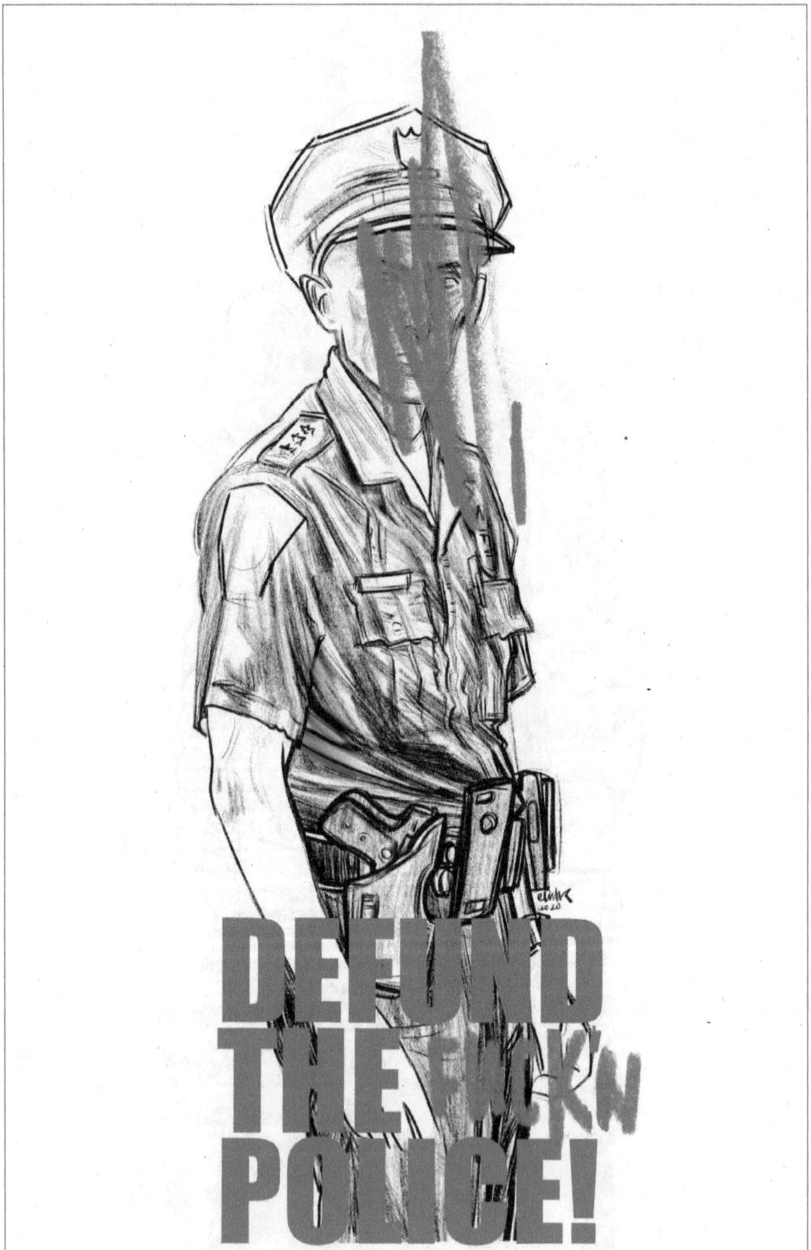

Elicser Elliott. *Defund the Fuckin Police*. 2020.

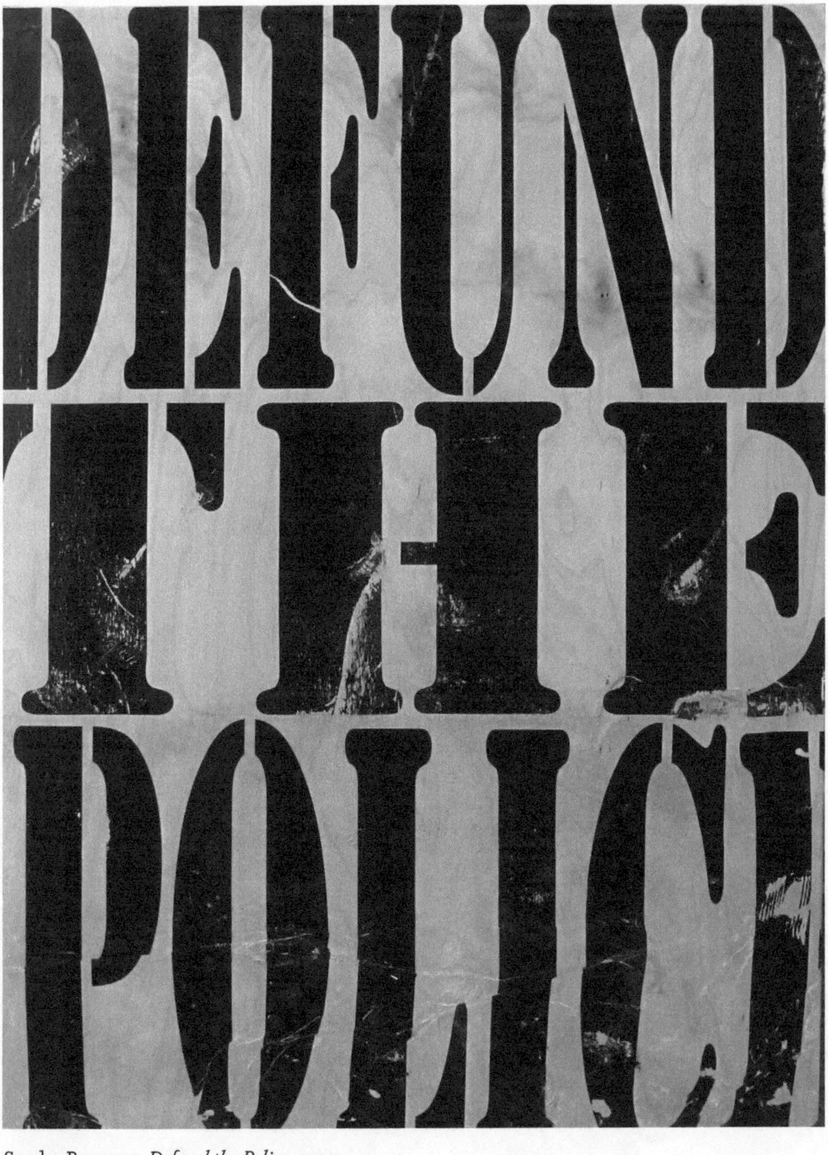

Sandra Brewster. *Defund the Police*. 2020.

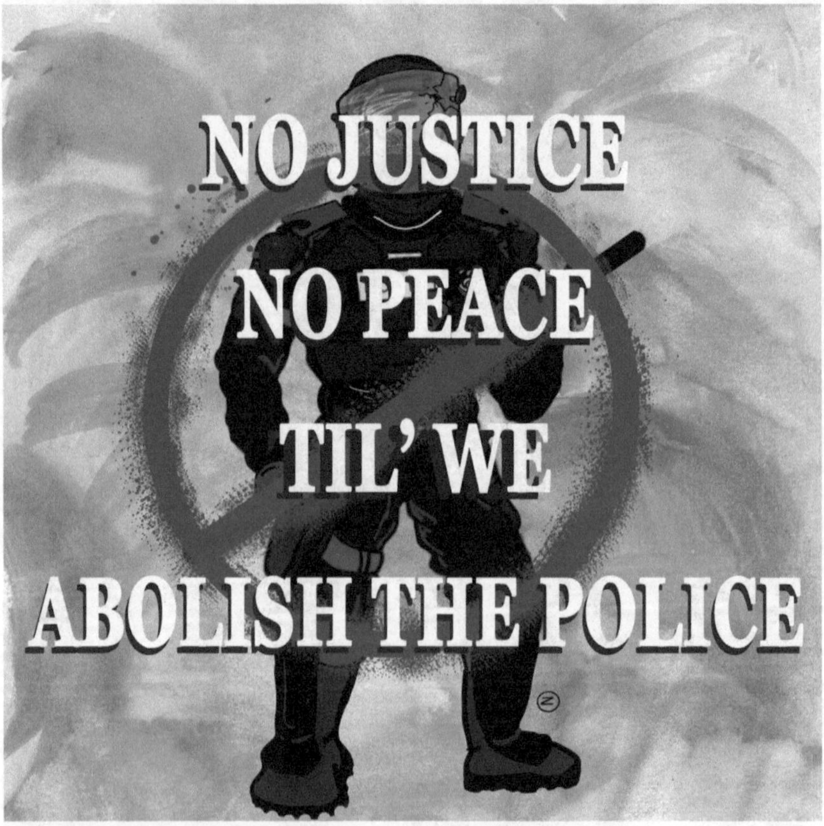

Ifetayo Alabi. *No Justice No Peace*. 2020.

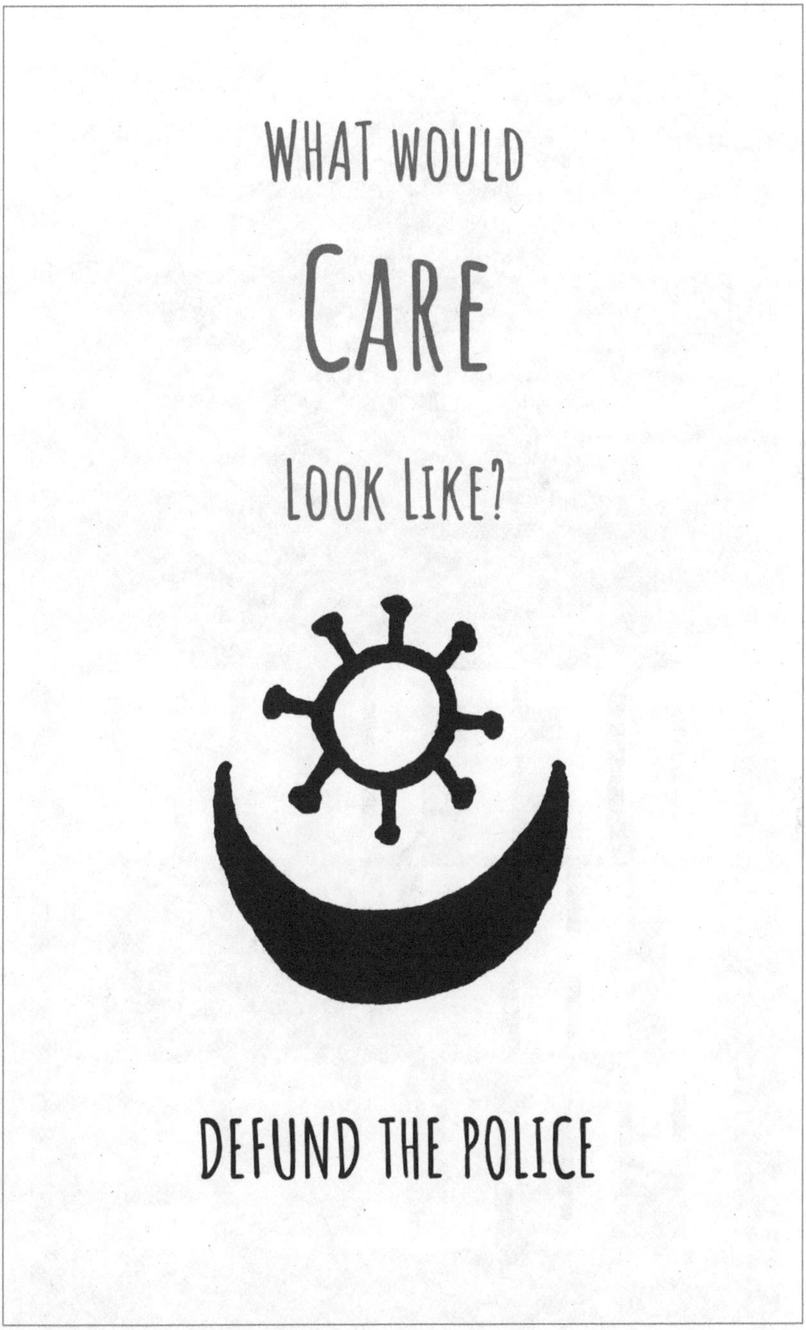

Camille Turner. *What would care look like?* 2020.

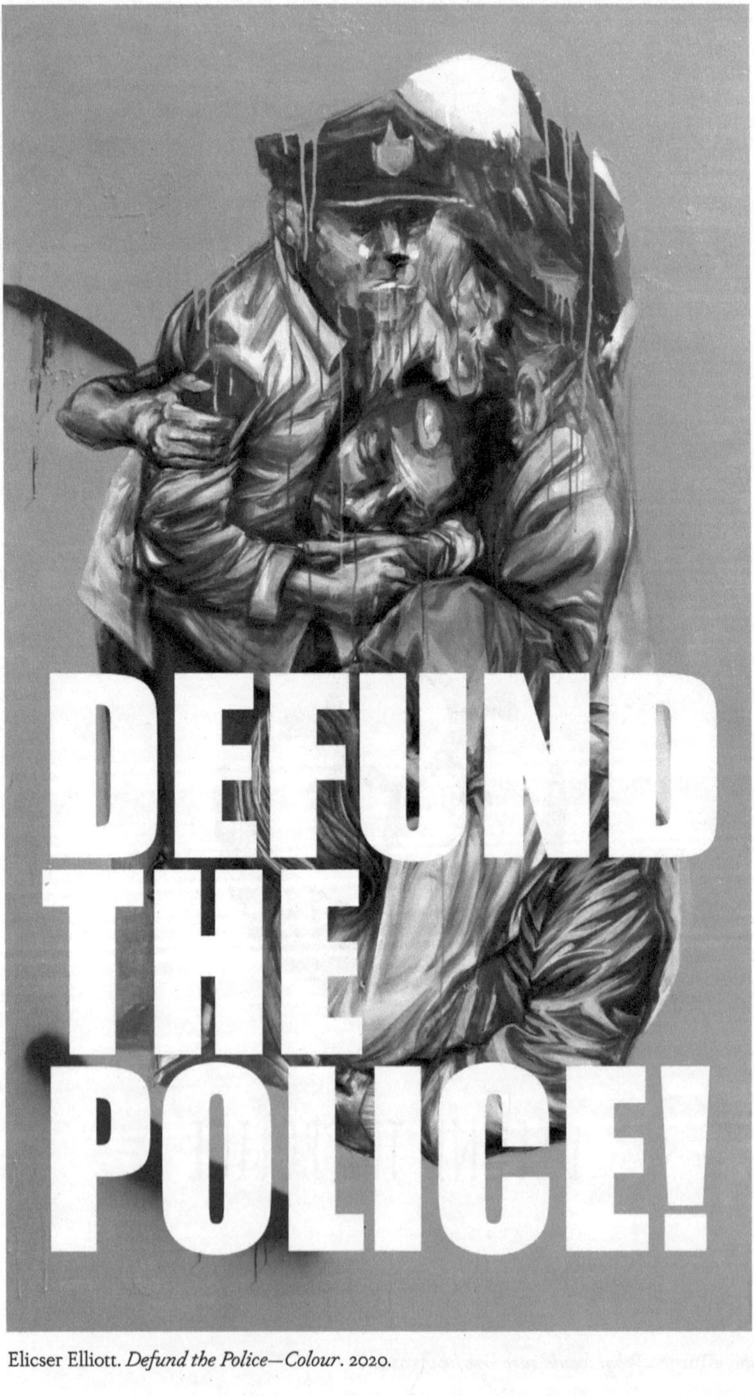

Elicser Elliott. *Defund the Police—Colour*. 2020.

DECOLONIAL FRAMEWORKS BY BLACK ARTS LEADERS

by **Dr. d'bi.young anitafrika**

The Embodied Relationality Framework helps artists reclaim the past to shape future performances, using observation, mimicry, and entertainment. It fosters symbiotic ways of being and promotes sustainable practices to protect Black artists' health. This framework blends individual and collective creativity, making creation a performance of agency and forming a cycle of power.

It encourages attuning to the rhythms of one's creative body and those around us, translating power into collective bodily knowledge.

—CARLA CHAMBERS,[1] Creator of the Embodied Relationality Framework, *Decolonial Frameworks by Black Arts Practitioners*

Transformative Care work is a testament to my commitment to merging art and healing. It serves as a pathway to positive transformation, inviting individuals to explore their inner selves and connect with the world around them on a deeper level in community. My art aims to inspire hope and bring people together through shared experiences, bridging divides and promoting compassion and inclusivity in a constantly changing world.

—**NISHI GOULDBOURNE**,[2] Creator of the Transformative Care Work Method, *Decolonial Frameworks by Black Arts Practitioners*

The DiverseWorks Decolonial Praxis weaves Afro-diasporic movement narratives into artistic liberation, centring dance as storytelling to assert identity and resistance. It highlights Black bodies, creating spaces for self-reflective dramaturgy and reclaiming narrative power. Rooted in lived experiences, it calls us to dance in adversity, speak truth, and create with ancestral spirit. It challenges white supremacy and reclaims narrative spaces, using somatic practices to reconnect with our essence and community.

—**RAECHELE LOVELL**,[3] Creator of the DiverseWorks Decolonial Praxis, *Decolonial Frameworks by Black Arts Practitioners*

THE FOLLOWING IS AN EDITED TRANSCRIPTION OF AN online Circle convened by d'bi.young anitafrika featuring Carla Chambers, Nishi Gouldbourne, and Raechele Lovell, three practitioners from the Decolonial Frameworks program who centre music, dance, and multidisciplinary arts in their work. Each practitioner created a transformative framework introducing their unique decolonial approaches to theatre and performance education. Our discussion explores each practitioner's personal and pedagogical locations as they investigate and reshape the epistemological, ontological, cosmological, aesthetic, and somatic lenses through which they view themselves as storytellers and story leaders. In addition to publishing a flipbook with Spolrusie Press entitled *Decolonial Frameworks by Black Arts Practitioners*,[4] d'bi.young anitafrika curated a Decolonial Frameworks Symposium that featured artist-led introductory workshops, expounding upon each artist's approach.[5]

The following Circle conversation encapsulates the dialogic pedagogy of the Anitafrika Method, which guided the six-month framework-building process.

About the Decolonial Frameworks Program

In October 2023, I received funding from the Canada Council for the Arts to lead a six-month program using the Anitafrika Method, entitled "Decolonial Frameworks for Black Arts Leaders in Northern Turtle Island." The initiative emerged from the repeated interest of arts practitioners throughout the years in how the Anitafrika Method came to be as a decolonial methodology. The practitioners' ongoing curiosity, at a time when the global Black Lives Matter movement was powerfully galvanizing the world toward radical transformative solidarity, finally led me to design a systems-change-specific residency for Black arts leaders. For over fifteen years, I had worked on developing the Anitafrika Method—a nurturant Black-queer-feminist pedagogy of transformation—and alongside it, a resource compendium comprising a master class video series on applying the Anitafrika Method in arts practice, a deck of praxis cards, video lectures centring each of the method's nine principles, and a digital workbook designed to provide step-by-step guidance on decolonizing strategies for theatre and performance training. My curiosity about the method's broader applicability in the arts drove me to explore how it could serve as a guide for other Black arts leaders to develop their own decolonizing and liberatory frameworks. Using this toolkit, I guided nine multidisciplinary arts practitioners from across Northern Turtle Island through the method process as they created their own frameworks. This resource aimed to equip theatre practitioners with practical tools and theoretical knowledge to apply the Anitafrika Method in their creative processes.

Through the program, I aimed to facilitate a process where Black Arts Leaders could harness the principles of the Anitafrika Method to craft personalized approaches that challenge colonial paradigms and promote systemic change in their artistic and educational practices, aligning with Sylvia Wynter's concept of "epistemic disobedience," which calls for rejecting colonial knowledge systems and creating new, decolonial epistemologies (Wynter 2003). Over six months, program participants met virtually every week, creating a sacred space where the Ubuntu philosophy of "I am because you are because we are" was embraced and embodied.

The course was presented in three stages: Self-Transformation, Creative Expression, and Community Embodiment. In stage one—Self-Transformation—artists engaged in somatic, self-reflexive, and critical thinking activities that provided support as they navigated the complexities of their intersecting identities of race, class, ability, age, gender, sexuality, and so on. The activities helped them address and process the life challenges and systemic oppressions they face, acknowledging how these experiences manifest and linger in their bodies. This stage aimed to foster personal growth and resilience by encouraging deep self-awareness and embodied understanding of their lived realities.

In the second stage—Creative Expression—practitioners received support in identifying their world views and passions, which they then integrated into developing a holistic praxis for creative intervention. Many practitioners built on workshops they had previously developed, choosing to expand these into comprehensive frameworks. Practitioners were encouraged to draw on their cultural backgrounds, personal narratives, and community needs, ensuring that their frameworks were deeply rooted in their lived experiences and could address specific challenges faced by their communities. This stage emphasized the importance of aligning creative practices with personal beliefs and values.

The third stage—Community Embodiment—provided practitioners the necessary support to refine their evolving frameworks. This stage included writing a chapter about their framework, creating and sharing an online workshop for the community during a public symposium, and publishing a digital anthology of all their methods. The goal was to ensure that the frameworks were thoroughly developed and effectively communicated to a broader audience, fostering community engagement and knowledge dissemination.

The Decolonial Frameworks program nurtured an environment of active listening, mutual support, and embodied care pedagogies. This approach cultivated a container of safety and trust for practitioners to thrive in. Our interactions were deliberately holistic and empathetic, recognizing the interconnectedness of our journeys toward healing, liberation, and praxisbuilding. By creating a supportive and inclusive space, we were able to engage with each other's experiences and insights, facilitating a collective process of growth and transformation. The following Circle shares further insight into our journey together.

The Decolonial Frameworks Circle

d'bi.young (d'bi): Welcome, welcome. Thank you for being here in the Circle. Let's take three deep breaths together [pause]. Let's begin by introducing ourselves and sharing our reflections. How are we physically, emotionally, and spiritually right now? What meaning are you finding at this moment?

Carla Chambers (CC): I'm Carla Chambers, a singer, writer, producer, advocate, teacher, friend, sister, caregiver, and lover. These roles shape my practice. I'm feeling new. Emotionally, there's constant processing, especially when facing systemic issues in hospitals and schools, which I address in regular meetings. I also consult with artist friends. I'm here, navigating systems in the arts affecting Black expression. I'm feeling tired. When I started in the arts, I was passionate, but now I feel almost indifferent. That's why I say I'm new—my emotional investments have shifted. To protect myself, I've detached and dissociated from the noise of others' emotions. I'm leaning into bearing witness and letting things emerge, rather than constantly problem-solving. In times of flux and transition, nothing makes sense, and I'm learning to embrace that.

As a Black womxn, it's practical for me to embrace the insensible amid discord. It's new for me not to feel the need to act immediately. Bearing witness and understanding its value is a big shift. My energy is spent differently now, feeding into solutions indirectly. This overlaps with how I'm doing—I'm following my feelings, honouring them, and not feeling overwhelmed. I channel my feelings into nourishing actions, which aren't always constructive. Sometimes, it means taking a bath, playing a song, or sending an advocacy email. I focus on the present, taking the most nourishing action to honour my feelings. That's how I'm feeling, doing, and being.

Nishi Gouldbourne (NG): I'm Nishi, and I feel called to the word alchemist. This term resonates deeply with me as it encapsulates my ability to transform grief, joy, and creation. I see myself as a creator, birther, healer, and alchemist. Currently, I'm grieving. This unaddressed grief affects my being. I am physically ill. As someone who approaches life holistically, I notice how my sickness manifests in my head, neck, and lungs, impacting my ability to express myself and set boundaries.

Being an empathetic person, I absorb a lot of emotions and information, some of which aren't mine. I'm learning to let go of what's not mine and focus on my body's intuition.

My income has halved, but I don't want to take on more work. This is challenging for me, a pragmatic person used to ensuring everything gets done. However, I'm shifting my priorities. I am choosing to be present for my child. Having worked from a young age, I now feel the need to rest and create space for grief for myself, allowing those around me to support me emotionally, mentally, and resource-wise. I'm drawn to stillness and being around sources that nourish me. I'm considering changing my employment direction, leaning more into creativity and reproductive care. I'm allowing myself to follow what I feel called to and let everything else align naturally.

Raechele Lovell (RL): I'm quite unwell. This has been the hardest year of my adult life. The past twelve months have been incredibly challenging. I believe challenges lead to greatness, and my ancestors don't impose anything I can't handle. However, at times, I doubt my capacity to cope. I'm in survival mode. Physically, I'm unwell, as you can hear in my voice. My immune system is weakened, and my lifelong resilience is greatly diminished.

In moments of optimism, I see this as an opportunity to learn thoughtfulness, to slow down, and to be one with the universe. But intrusive thoughts and self-doubt create inner struggles. A recent car accident was a wake-up call, making me realize how unwell I am. Reflecting on my life, I've been unwell since childhood, dealing with neglect and abuse by compartmentalizing and numbing myself to pain. Realizing my hip was dislocated and my spine sprained, yet still dancing through it, made me confront my numbness and acceptance of pain as normal.

I'm learning that our melanated bodies deserve better. I need to advocate more for myself and live my life more for myself. I'm facing uncertainty with no car or job. My company has crumbled, and I've questioned if artistry is worth it. I've applied for non-art jobs, closed my company, and stopped applying for grants. But the universe hasn't delivered any jobs, pushing me back to my artistic path. I've always advocated for myself, even as a child. Now, I'm burned out and tired, but it's okay—it's not my fault. I'm processing, letting go of negative thoughts, and returning to my own knowing. I'm trusting the unknown, moving forward one day at a time, taking time to breathe and be with myself and the universe. It feels like grieving—a process of acceptance. Society makes it difficult to be a Black womxn artist. But the universe nudges me to keep going. So, I see myself as an interdisciplinary artist, an artivist, and an educator doing social work through storytelling. I'm healing for my ancestors and myself, striving toward a more equitable future.

d'bi: Ase! I am on the final path in this PhD journey, and it is innerwhelming. It is. I find myself often as a recovery mechanism saying, I am in this moment now, not any other moment. I don't need to think about the next moment. I am only actually alive right now at this moment. So, what I am doing at this moment is all that I have the capacity to focus on because anything more than that makes me want to run inside the darkest, tiniest cave in my body and not come back out. Physically, I'm feeling all kinds of sensations, some phantom, some real. Everything is activated. Emotionally, everything is activated. It's all part of the work, highlighting everything. Spiritually, I'm holding on to being present. It's all I have the capacity for, and it's been a ride. I move between staying updated on world events, wanting to send energy to my kin, and retreating into solitude. It's a constant dance between engaging with the world and withdrawing.

Meanwhile, I'm writing my thesis, which is partly a memoir. I need to document my experiences now, not wait for a future book deal. This PhD is that record. I'm also inviting us into a Circle because my experiences mirror those of my kin. I want to understand my experiences through their stories, to know my kin, myself, and how we thrive. I want to learn and be in community. All of this is happening simultaneously. If this were happening ten years ago, I probably wouldn't have made it. But now, having cultivated these practices over a long time, I know deep inside I have what I need, just like the women before me. That's what I'm holding on to.

Could each of you share why you chose to create a framework?

RL: I felt compelled to do the residency when I saw it as if my ancestors were whispering in my ears. It kept appearing everywhere I looked, like a sign. I saw it last minute, but it kept popping up on every social platform I opened. The residency's framework called to me, and I felt the need to deliver, as I've been conditioned to be a people pleaser. Through this process, I learned the importance of this affirming and nourishing work that needs to be archived. The civil rights era isn't over, and there's still much work to do. Coming together to reaffirm each other is a powerful interruption to the gaslighting we face. I believe my perspective is valid, even if I'm a minority among a vocal majority who don't understand. I've been othered my entire life, and I believe this has given me a critical lens to tackle these growing societal issues. This residency has been the most powerful medicine I've found—more effective than traditional mental health interventions, pharmaceuticals, or other societal mechanisms. These traditional methods have often been harmful to me. Offering this truth to the universe seems to be the only way to counteract the pervasive negativity.

NG: Much like what Raechele mentioned, creating this was a much-needed affirmation for me. Knowing that the tools and resources I've learned along the way are beneficial to someone like me was crucial. Since the beginning of the pandemic, I've been jotting down notes and thoughts, collecting tools and reflections that inform my framework. Looking back at these notes, I realized that I knew what I was talking about all along. It's beautiful to see that clarity and insight in my past writings. Many of us might find similar value in revisiting our journals. As a child, I destroyed my journals because my privacy wasn't respected. This shaped my relationship with archiving thoughts and perspectives. This framework was something I needed for myself, and I'm happy to offer it to others as well.

CC: I've been processing this question for a long time. As we talk, I'm listening and taking notes. Colonialism uniquely impacted Black women by extracting our creative power and redirecting it for others' survival, including our children's. There hasn't been a chance to recover until now. From the beginning of time, the oldest human remains in Africa came from a Black womxn, emphasizing our foundational role. Today, science and sociology are exploring epigenetics and intergenerational trauma, acknowledging the profound impact on humanity when Black women are excluded. Black women have been missing from the equation to the universe's detriment. This moment is a reset, restoring our creative power.

My mission has been to reclaim this power for myself and others. I realized this need through my healing journey and physical rehab, where my damaged leg[6] metaphorically represents my creative muscles that need rest, nourishment, and action to function fully. This process is mirrored in many Black women's experiences today. We're called to deep rest, self-nourishment, and creative practice. Many are leaving traditional jobs to pursue long-neglected passions, leading to better health and fulfillment. This transformation is reshaping how I view my creative work, expanding my identity beyond singing to my voice, presence, and influence.

The framework I created calls on the elements of the Earth to ground me and avoid intellectualizing the spiritual process, which is a trauma response. We are called to tie up loose ends and start anew, using the decay to nourish new growth. This group is cultivating a new Earth through grieving, transformation, and transmutation, integrating these processes into our reality. Our systems haven't supported this balance, but Black women, existing on the fringes, have protected the best parts of who we are. I'm learning to lean into rest and reprogram my muscles to respond to new sources of energy, focusing on what I have the capacity for. This sacred energy resonates with others, creating a natural exchange. I'm inspired by artists like Cleo Sol, who took a hiatus to find their voice amid the noise of others' opinions. This resonates with my journey of muting external noise and focusing on my inner voice. It's exhilarating yet scary, but art gives me the bravery to face it. It's a lot, but it's necessary.

d'bi: Who is your framework for and what impact do you hope it will have?

CC: My method started as an experiment. During my grief journey, I realized colonialism has taken away our ability to grieve. This scarcity mindset, influenced by capitalism, patriarchy, and racism, denies us open grieving. I refused to be told to "get over" my grief and began to question why grieving isn't encouraged in society. This reflection led me to nature, where everything is part of a life cycle. We talk about this in spirituality and science, but philosophically, life is a cycle that should be celebrated, including beginnings, middles, endings, and rebirths. Incorporating this into my creative practice was essential for my healing. I focused on what I needed at each stage, especially to be present for myself and my children.

This approach became a creative practice. I lacked the tools to grieve in a generative way, as grieving was often viewed negatively. My method uses elements paralleling life stages to unblock creativity, guiding us through the process and out of stasis. My goal during grief was to avoid stagnation. Disappearing isn't an option. We must find a way to live that isn't aligned with capitalism and colonial conditioning. Returning to nature, treated as sacred and part of my being, was my first step. I reverse-engineered the processes I observed in my grief state, noticing patterns and applying them to different life stages. Birth represents new beginnings, air is the flow stage, fire is the crumbling stage, and the water stage is disintegration, returning to source. I mapped this out for easy application during my rehab process, following my body's cues on exercise and daily activities. This practice disciplined my mind to follow my body. The method is for anyone creatively blocked, whether it's job boredom, incubating a creative idea, or processing loss. The grounding aspect deals with literal and metaphorical grounding.

RL: I see my framework as a reclamation of dance as a spiritual Afrocentric practice that can heal and cultivate community. As an artist and dance practitioner, I've observed that many Western dance techniques are appropriated from Black culture. Delving into these cultural traditions reveals their use in ceremonies and spirituality. Our ancestors preserved these rhythms and practices to combat cultural genocide, even though we've lost many references to their meanings. It's vital to continue embodying these traditions in our bodies and voices. My method advocates for creating space for this reclamation, especially for Black women practitioners, to reclaim and share this power with society. This ensures it is no longer stolen but recognized and researched. The exercises in my framework connect with polyvagal and somatic theories, promoting healing for both body and spirit, and embodying Indigenous ways of knowing, being, and doing. The method embodies the circle, the strongest shape, applying a top-down approach to decolonizing the dance sector here in Turtle Island.

NG: I define my method as transformative care work, a space for creators. I believe everyone is creating something new. This space addresses how we are supported not only in physical spaces with each other but also through ancestral connections, plant kin, and unseen forces that aid our creative processes. Care work, especially for Black people of marginalized genders, involves labour that often goes unrecognized. It encompasses supporting each other in creating new systems, ways of being, and beautiful work, including family. It's about reconnecting to Indigenous practices and showing up for one another. Everything in this world is constantly creating and recycling, working with what is present. That is transformative care work.

d'bi: A recurring theme in all your frameworks is the focus on the whole being, the whole person, working with all facets of the human entity. Recognizing what you as practitioners prioritize, I would like us to examine how colonial violence in training spaces dismembers, dissociates, degrades, and violates practitioners. All three of you describe your approach as holistic, concerned with the entire human being, not just a part that can produce a product for a capitalist agenda. This contrasts with celebrated Western training systems in theatre and performance that do not centre the whole person. Colonialism, capitalism, and patriarchy compartmentalize and disconnect us from our roots. Our connection to the earth or the body is considered impure. Racist European literature draws parallels between Blackness and impurity, Black womanhood and filth, and diverse sexualities with deviance. These parallels lead to our dismembered humanity as Global Majority people. It's vile and violent, and articulating it is challenging because it is so heinous.

RL: You're describing ballet.

CC: My god, I was thinking of opera.

d'bi: Can you speak about the juxtaposition between systems that dismember, compartmentalize, and denigrate, acting upon us un-holistically, and your own frameworks that are attempting to rehumanize us holistically.

RL: For me, you're describing ballet and, to a large extent, theatre training. Ballet stands out because I'm working on a project addressing its colonized aesthetic. Ballet often depicts the demure, white womxn who needs rescuing, delicate and barely touching the ground. The aesthetic emphasizes white, thin bodies, with men providing strength and telling repetitive European stories. The training is deeply harmful and colonial. We're examining where racialized bodies and gender nonconforming people fit, and if there's room for evolution. The traditionalism in ballet is rooted in appropriated African culture, distorted over time.

I've always loved dance, and dreamed of being on stage since I was five. However, training in dance studios and acquiring professional skills brought more harm than good. I was told I was too fat, too brown, and needed to straighten my hair. This trauma didn't make me a better dancer or artist—it just hurt me. Many brilliant artists, born to be truthtellers and mirrors to society, are lost due to this system. They suffer from eating disorders and body manipulation, and are forced to leave the industry. The industry oversexualizes and controls us, which is deeply colonial and patriarchal. Men often dominate as directors and choreographers, controlling our time, bodies, and minds, effectively stealing from us.

This drove me to seek other ways. I knew I was meant to be a dancer, so the system had to be wrong. As a biracial person in a white supremacist area, I didn't always have access to traditional diasporic dance forms or acceptance in those spaces. I wanted to build something contemporary and inclusive of our modern diasporic society. I aimed to counter the negative messaging about what a dancer's body should look like. Despite my European and African ancestry, I was never accepted, even when I conformed to their standards. Many opportunities were denied to me, but I still ended up excelling. This made me wonder what could have been with support instead of trauma. Ultimately, the colonized European patriarchal harm led me to develop my framework. After ingesting a lifetime of trauma, I decided their standards were wrong and untrue.

CC: For me, it all starts and ends with vibration. As a singer raised in a Caribbean Pentecostal church, I grew up immersed in African traditions under a Christian guise. Learning about West African practices, I recognized many familiar rituals and realized I had always interpreted the Bible through an Africanist lens. One story that stood out was when Jesus healed a blind man by spitting in the dirt to make mud, applying it to the man's eyes, and telling him to wash it off. This resonated with me as an African practice of using earth and water for healing. My fascination with vibration extends to quantum physics, where light, colour, sound, and matter are all seen as vibrations. I realized how colonial structures disrupt these natural vibrations. I loved opera from a young age but was constantly told my voice was too dark, too loud, or didn't fit the expected mould. My singing, rooted in the sacred traditions of my upbringing, was my unique vibration. Despite criticism, I remained true to my voice and eventually left those limiting spaces.

Developing one's voice is a way to take up space in the universe, using elements and vibrations that match one's energy. If I want to be loud and bombastic, I'll sing opera; if I want to be soft and introspective, I'll sing folk. Art, as a universal technology, should be boundless, not confined to rigid structures. The colonial history of opera, including practices like the castrati to prevent women from performing, exemplifies this dismemberment. The Black church, as an African diasporic context, contrasts with the limiting art school environment. My journey through these spaces taught me that my energy and voice need to match my stage in life. This holistic approach informs how I sing and resist colonial structures.

NG: I would like to challenge the notion of urgency in our bodies, the constant need to produce, which prevents me from slowing down and assessing what my body needs. This reflects on Black bodies and the legacy of chattel slavery. I have a poem about the dismemberment of a Black woman's body and how everything demands our bodies to produce while taking parts of us. Who and where are the spaces that bring us back together? The framework comes in because there are spaces, people, sources, living and non-living things like our ancestors, that help us reconnect. Not being indoctrinated into these relationships is a disservice to our bodies and creativity. We give so much just by being here. We've been taught to disconnect from the Earth and our spiritual practices to sever us from what is generative to our bodies. This holistic approach informs my facilitation. Creating spaces where people can be with me and accept me as I am now is crucial. Acceptance is vital, especially as we've been shamed for mental illness or grief, both seen as inconveniences. When someone is grieving, we need to ask what we can do in this space with them. Grieving is vibrational, and we feel its magnitude. How do we hold that space together holistically?

d'bi: Could you share a few points on practitioner care from your method?

RL: My offerings for practitioners would be to first take time to breathe and be with oneself, to centre the breath every single day with mindfulness. The second is the cultivation of space, creating the opportunity to hold the power within the space. For me, that looks like picking and choosing the environments where I choose to move my body. I prefer to be mindful of who will be witnessing within that space. Creating a safe space includes a collective agreement, a room agreement, certain ethical agreements to ensure emotional and physical safety for practitioners. Financial management of the company is also important. Producing for myself as opposed to being hired by a company, being mindful of who the funders are, and the shared values we have. Ensuring folks are paid a living wage and that our time is respected. Giving us the tools to be safe, whether it's a clean floor or free from patriarchal power structures that can be emotionally harmful. Advocating for personal space for practice and taking time for improvisation to connect to the source. Using dance as a somatic practice to maintain a healthy vessel.

CC: Recognize that money is not the only resource you need. Make sure you are resourcing yourself fully to find joy in the process. Not everything needs to be easy, but joy makes it bearable. Prioritize community and collaboration. Colonialism created the archetype of the starving artist, but nothing happens in a vacuum. Be mindful of the systems of community and collaborations you're part of. Never be afraid to say no and walk away from a situation that is not resourcing you well. There's too much abundance in the universe to settle for less.

NG: I want to affirm that you, the artist, the creator, are right where you need to be. You have the resources you need to create this magical thing. Affirm the tools and ways you move, slow down, document it. This is part of your rituals. Ground yourself in that practice, knowing what is best for you. Recognize the struggle in ourselves and others. Be more compassionate and create new ways that honour our creation collectively and individually.

RL: And d'bi., thank you for your beautiful, transformative, Ancestral work that you're doing, and I hope that in those moments where you feel like crawling into the cave, you can just hear our voices echoing in your head, telling you, "You've got this, you're amazing, you're a witch, you're a shaman, we need you."

CC: And the cave is not a cave. It's a tunnel. [Everyone laughs]

d'bi: Ase! Let's all take a deep breath in, and a long breath out [pause]. And another deep breath in and a long breath out [pause]. And one more deep breath in and a long breath out [pause]. Bring awareness to the sounds that you can hear [pause]. Bring awareness to the sensations you can feel in your body and on your skin [pause]. Gently allow your eyes to float open and bring awareness to what you see around you [pause]. Let's take a few moments to be present with ourselves, present with the offering we just shared with each other [pause].

Thank you, Carla, thank you, Nishi, and thank you, Raechele, for who you all continue to choose to be in the world. Thank you for sharing your time with the Circle today. We need you. And thank you for showing us what your radical love looks like. Walk good, my kin.

This article is a chapter excerpt from d'bi.young anitafrika's PhD dissertation entitled *Black Womxn Theatre: Personhood, Practice, Pedagogy*.

References

anitafrika, d'bi.young. "Decolonial Performance Praxis: The Anitafrika Method." PhD dissertation in progress, London South Bank University, School of Arts and Creativity, supervised by Elena Marchevska.

anitafrika, d'bi.young, ed. *Decolonial Frameworks by Black Arts Practitioners*. Spolrusie Press, 2024. https://heyzine.com/flip-book/5555be51f2.html. Accessed August 15, 2024.

hooks, bell. *Feminist Theory: From Margin to Center*. South End Press, 1984.

Lorde, Audre. *Sister Outsider: Essays and Speeches*. Crossing Press, 1984.

Stamatiou, Eleni. "Pierre Bourdieu and Actor Training: Towards Decolonizing and Decentering Actor Training Pedagogies." *Theatre, Dance and Performance Training* 13, no. 1 (2022): 96–114. https://doi.org/10.1080/19443927.2021.1943509.

Wynter, Sylvia. "Unsettling the Coloniality of Being/Power/Truth/Freedom: Towards the Human, After Man, Its Overrepresentation—An Argument." *CR - East Lansing* 3 (2003): 257–338.

Notes

1 Carla Chambers is a multidisciplinary artist, scholar, and creative entrepreneur with a master's degree in Comparative Literature and Arts from Brock University. She has built a successful consulting career working with artists and arts organizations in fund development, marketing strategy, and community outreach. Combining her expertise in arts administration with her artistic passion, Carla founded the Embers Lab, a Womxnist think tank dedicated to generating Black-led multidisciplinary projects that promote social and personal transformation through the arts. Through the lab, Carla aims to expand her craft as a singer and writer into directing, producing, and exploring visual mediums alongside like-minded creators. Carla is a designer, cultural intercessor, and alchemist of ideas, committed to delving deeply into knowledge and discovering new avenues for artistic empowerment. Her work focuses on using art as a tool for healing and empowerment.

2 Nishi Gouldbourne (they/fae) is a multidisciplinary artist committed to storytelling that ignites change. As a Black, disabled, Afro Caribbean, queer nonbinary individual, their work challenges societal norms, inspires introspection, and amplifies marginalized voices. Nishi uses art for healing through rituals, energy healing, herbal medicine making, and reproductive care work. They create compassion-driven, trauma-informed spaces, drawing from their experience as a survivor of gender-based violence. Rooted in Abolition, Black Feminism, and Healing Justice, Nishi seeks liberation. Embracing their trans and neuro-expansive identities, Nishi honours Indigenous African and Caribbean traditions and finds inspiration in the land, people, and spirits around them. As a chronically ill individual, they value community interdependence, consent, and self-autonomy. Living on land stewarded by the Anishinaabe, Haudenosaunee, and Wendat, Nishi strives to build respectful and understanding relationships.

3 Raechele Lovell is a multifaceted artist and artivist situated in Kitchener, Ontario, on the Haldimand Tract. Her artistic journey began in her father's steel drum band and was further inspired by Caribbean dance performances, leading her to study dance intensively from a young age. Overcoming numerous obstacles, she funded her education through creative means, demonstrating remarkable resilience. Raechele is a choreographer, artistic director, dramaturg, educator, theatre practitioner, facilitator, and producer. She is the founder and executive artistic director of DiverseWorks Dance Co., where she envisions a future where Afrocentric artistry thrives. Her work is deeply rooted in decolonial praxis, developed during her residency at the Ubuntu Decolonial Arts Centre under the mentorship of d'bi.young anitafrika. Raechele's efforts challenge colonial norms and celebrate the dynamic traditions of Afrodiasporic storytelling.

4 *Decolonial Frameworks by Black Arts Practitioners*, the premiere flipbook publication of Spolrusie Press, stands as a crucial text in a time when the world is on the cusp of transformative change. It takes us beyond the colonialhistorical-systemic oppression that pervades the globe, impacting the fabric of human relations and the health of our

entire planet. Through its nine new praxes, the anthology heralds a call for new ways of thinking, being, and creating that honour the wisdom of Black, Indigenous, and Global Majority communities. It advocates for systems of thought and practice rooted in equity, empathy, and profound respect for and attunement with the Earth. In doing so, it offers pathways toward healing and justice, providing actionable insights for those dedicated to building a future where the planet and all its beings experience love.

5 The program booklet and artist workshop archives can be viewed at the following url: https://decolonialartscentre.com/decolonial-frameworks-symposium-2024.

6 Carla's damaged leg that she refers to was the result of a severe car accident that she experienced.

"SHE CARRIED WITH HER...A LARGE BUNDLE OF WEARING APPAREL BELONGING TO HERSELF"

Slave Dress as Resistance in Portraiture and Fugitive Slave Advertisements

by **Charmaine Nelson**

Introduction

WHILE LIVING ON THE CARIBBEAN ISLAND OF ST. VINCENT in the eighteenth century, the Anglo Irish special magistrate John Colthurst participated in the deliberate and abject humiliation of an enslaved woman named Dutchess. Colthurst's diary recounts his encounter with Dutchess in a crowded local courthouse where people had gathered to hear the details of her supposed crimes: the theft of money with which she purchased an array of beautiful items of clothing. Her alleged misdeeds behoove us to contemplate several interconnected domains of transatlantic slavery including slave dress, cultural preservation, and self-determination and, more specifically, the experiences of enslaved people of African descent. None of these can be fully understood outside of the intersecting web of sex, gender, and racial identities within the "peculiar institution," as slavery was known then.

The first domain—slave dress—entails a contemplation of how the enslaved acquired the means and materials to adorn, protect, and beautify their bodies amid endemic material deprivation, cultural prohibitions, economic disenfranchisement, and pervasive physical violence. Given these forces, the second domain—cultural preservation—was never within the full control of the enslaved, but rather their abilities to preserve or adapt their African cultural practices were ostensibly dictated by white society. Therefore, the third domain—self-determination—was neither an individual nor a community right but a constant point of resistance and struggle. Taken together, these three domains are my starting point for a comparison of slave dress in tropical slave majority sites like the Caribbean Island colonies of St. Vincent and Jamaica and temperate slave minority sites like Canada.

I present here several examples of what a decolonial practice of Art History can achieve. I analyze one dominant form of "high" art—oil portraiture—and two "low" art forms—print advertising and dress. However, my choices of artist and sitter for the portrait, a slave-owning white man and an enslaved Black woman, respectively, allow me to interrogate the under-acknowledged racial biases of the genre, which too easily occasioned violent encounters for Black sitters. Print and dress have typically been excluded from art historical contemplation due to mass production, wide circulation, group production, and low cost in the first instance, and to the quotidian nature in the latter. In thinking through evidence of slave resistance in print culture and dress, several academic norms are destabilized. First, within a field, Slavery Studies, which is dominated by historians who typically focus upon resistance as flight or rebellion, I wish to highlight the understudied cultural dimensions of slave resistance. Second, my focus on dress and print culture (and the representation of the former in the latter) contributes to the democratization of Art History through a continuing interrogation of what constitutes art. As both a focus of control by enslavers and of resistance by the enslaved, slave dress reveals its significance as a site of contestation as well as private pleasures and self-care and public cultural expression, preservation, and transformation. Accordingly, then, third, my centring of the experiences of enslaved people like Dutchess depends on acknowledging them as cultural producers and people who challenged their pervasive colonial misrepresentation.

Dutchess's Day in Court

While Dutchess's "clothing acts"[1] were demonstrations of her resistance, her court appearance was a retaliatory ordeal at the hands of a violent white legal system that defined enslaved people as chattel. Accused of stealing money, not for basic sustenance and self-preservation but for beautification, self-care, and what could be called pleasure, Dutchess was charged with using her supposedly ill-gotten gains to purchase elegant clothing. As Colthurst asserted, the items included

> Wearing apparel fine enough for a Princess… Their colours vied with those of the rainbow, first a flaming bright yellow bonnet, flashy dresses without number, necklaces and earrings without end, rose coloured silk stocking and two pairs of pink satin shoes!![2]

Notably, the desire for luxurious articles of dress appeared ridiculous to upper-class white sensibilities when the intended wearers were enslaved field labourers, socially and physically distanced from elite white women.

For the nineteenth-century white citizens who packed the courthouse to gloat at Dutchess's humiliation, the desire to transcend her enslaved status and to adorn her body in ways that acknowledged her beauty was, as the scholar Rebecca Earle has noted, incongruous at best or repellant at worst. Enslaved and free Black people were certainly aware of the class mobility, however tenuous, that clothing could provide. Examples of slave escape often hinged on the dramatic alteration of the enslaved person's clothing to pass as a free person. But Dutchess's preferences of dress do not appear to be about resistance as flight but about resistance as self-care, or assertions of individuality and humanity.

At the heart of Dutchess's story is white society's failure to see enslaved Black females as women or as feminine outside of their reproductive capacities as breeders of new "slaves." Indeed, routinely deprived of sufficient and diversified nutrition and labouring gruelling hours at back-breaking tasks, enslaved men and women across the Americas were customarily underweight, exceptionally muscular, and, in the tropics, deeply and constantly tanned compared to upper-class, leisurely whites. How the nature of their lives transformed the bodies of enslaved Black women opened a vast gulf between themselves and the ideals of white feminine beauty that people like Colthurst naturalized.

Dutchess's story does not merely expose the rift between the gendered expectations and performances of middle- and upper-class whites and enslaved and impoverished Blacks; it also exposes the animalization of the latter by the former. The use of terms like wool and hooves to describe the hair and feet of black people was common. As Colthurst recounted, when Dutchess was forced to try on the shoes in front of the packed courtroom, those assembled "shouted when the pink satins were placed upon the hooves of Dutchess. In truth I never saw anything as unsuitable as the satins to such feet."[3] Colthurst's cruelty is palpable, and we can only imagine Dutchess's utter humiliation as the target of such public venom and ridicule. Arguably, Dutchess had a clear desire to transcend the drudgery, pain, and stark material disenfranchisement of her enslavement by acquiring beautiful clothing and jewellery with which to adorn her body. Her bid to escape, if only fleetingly, the crushing obscenity of slavery illuminates the dress norms of many Caribbean colonies like Jamaica.

In the wealthy, plantation-riddled British colony, it was customary for enslaved women to be provided with once-yearly rations of oznaburgh—a plain-woven flax fabric—with which they were forced to make clothing for the entire enslaved population of their respective plantations.[4] This labour was on top of their most common labour as agricultural field workers on the innumerable plantations—that were mainly cultivating sugar—which dotted the island.[5] According to Lucille Mair, in Jamaica "in 1832, sugar employed 49.5 per cent of the slave work force. Most of those workers were women, the ratio being 920 males to 1,000 females."[6] Despite the imposition of the fabric rations, the ingenuity and resourcefulness of enslaved women resulted in creative outcomes. Through the production and use of dyes and perfumes (made from musk wood and rosewood) and the manufacture of natural material like lacebark (from the laghetto tree), enslaved Jamaicans found ways to assert their individuality through their dress cultures.[7]

Although oznaburgh fabric was also imported to Canada,[8] enslaved Blacks in Canada, unlike those held in bondage in Jamaica, wore a diverse range of clothing and fabrics; however, a unique slave dress is illusive because the enslaved typically wore their enslavers' second-hand clothing.[9] As such, Canadian slave dress, frequently described in Canadian fugitive slave notices, was constantly recounted as old, worn, discoloured, and daubed with paint.[10] Initially placed to hunt and re-enslave people, such advertisements have become one of the best sources for understanding the appearance, actions, and dress of the enslaved; this is because enslavers were so desperate to recuperate their missing "property" that they willingly disclosed often invasive details, details that were rather unhelpful in their bid to define human beings as chattel and slavery as a "civilizing mission."

While many enslaved people wore typical European clothing, there are also glimpses of African cultural preservation. A fugitive slave advertisement placed on May 14, 1767, by the Montreal vintner James Crofton offered a reward for Andrew described as "remarkable for being clean dress'd and wearing a Handkerchief tied round his Head,"[11] which is a description of the African dress practice known as headwrapping. Often associated with Black women in the Caribbean, headwrapping survived the Middle Passage to be adapted for both functional and beautification purposes. It also became a tool of social distinction through which Black and mixed-race women demarcated their bodies within a social landscape in which complexion was not securely conflated with social status.

Marie-Thérèse-Zémire

The French-Canadian François Malépart de Beaucourt's 1786 oil portrait also sheds light on slave dress, cultural retention, and the violence of artistic representation. Originally circulated as *Portrait of a Negro Slave and Negress,* it was renamed *Portrait of a Haitian Woman* in 2011, a move that I protested for the way it retroactively liberated the enslaved Black sitter and evacuated the art of all ties to Canadian slavery.[12] Depicting an enslaved, dark-skinned female sitter, offering a tray of tropical fruit strategically juxtaposed with the orchestrated exposure of her breast, the sitter's smile acts as a twin to the offering of food with body/sexuality, implying her complicity in her hyper-sexualization. The portrait's anomalous nature resides in the facts that it is a fully finished, professionally rendered, individual representation of a specific enslaved subject, and the only known "high" art rendering of an enslaved person in Canada. Importantly, it is also the only known visual representation of the African dress practice of headwrapping in the context of Canadian slavery for which—unlike the United States, Cuba, and Brazil—the photographic archive only depicts free Black people.[13]

This image of an enslaved female cannot be thoroughly interpreted and understood without a rigorous exploration of historical Western "high" art portraiture and the institution of slavery. Historical and contemporary insights shed light on the role that class has traditionally played in "high" art portraiture and the identity politics and power dynamics at the heart of slavery. In the first instance in 1796, the Earl of Fife issued the following lament:

> before this century, very few people presented themselves to a painter, except those who were of *great families*, or remarkable for their actions in service to the country, or some other extraordinary circumstance... as lately... every body (sic) almost who can afford twenty pounds, has the portraits of himself, wife and children painted.[14] (italics added)

Clearly, Fife did not support the democratization of the genre for the ways that the increased affordability opened it up to sitters whom he deemed to be unworthy. Portraits are of course about individuality and specificity, and Fife's understanding of "great families" included people who wished to be remembered as individuals. As such, traditionally, the title of a portrait is the sitter's name. However, with unfree people, the practice has instead been to render Black sitters anonymous in titles with terms like "dark," "Black," "Negro," "mulatto," and "slave" and, in conversation pieces with white subjects, to present them as compositionally abject, foreign, and labouring bodies.

Hilary McD. Beckles's more recent contemplation of the power imbalances between enslaver and enslaved also informs an understanding of Beaucourt's depiction of this enslaved Black female. As Beckles has incisively argued,

> Neither colonial statutes or slave codes, then, invested slaves with any rights over their own bodies, but rather transferred and consolidated such rights within the legal person of the slaveowners. This direct translation of legal entitlement into social power and authority meant that white men especially were located at a convergence where the racial, sexual, and class domination of slave women provided a totality of terror and tyranny.[15] (italics added)

Troublingly, Beaucourt exemplified the threat of social power that Beckles so ably articulated since he was at once the artist, the patron, and the enslaver. Detailed records compiled by Marcel Trudel reveal the likely sitter to be Marie-Thérèse-Zémire, one of two enslaved Black people documented as the property of the artist's white wife, Benoite Gaétant.[16] Identified as a négresse, she was listed in legal documents as belonging to the widow of the painter after his death.[17] According to Frank Mackey, Marie was twenty-five in April 1796 and twenty-nine at her death on December 15, 1800.[18] Therefore, she would have been fifteen when the portrait was painted in 1786. The couple met and married in the 1770s or 1780s, when Beaucourt studied at the Bordeaux Academy in France, after which they travelled to St. Domingue (the western third of the Caribbean Island of Hispaniola), arriving during the Haitian Revolution (1791–1804), before returning to Montreal via Philadelphia in 1792.[19]

St. Domingue, France's richest colony built on sugar cultivation and other plantation mono-crop agriculture, had by this time become exceptionally lethal for enslaved Africans. Malick W. Ghachem argues that in the 1780s, "During their first three to five years of labor in Saint-Domingue, newly purchased Africans died on average at a rate of 50 percent."[20] Although Beaucourt depicted Marie as a domestic, a world typically inhabited by light-skinned, or mixed-race enslaved people, Marie's darker complexion corresponded to that of field labourers, making it likely that she was from a neighbouring plantation in Cap François (now Cap Haitien), a busy centre of sugar export, where the Beaucourts temporarily resided.

Marie's anonymization in the title stems from her marginalized status in Quebec and St. Domingue (Haiti). Typically created over a period of sittings, it was customary that the portraitist knew the name of their sitter, and the portrait—the sitter's likeness—was normally named after them. The sitter was traditionally also the patron or a relation or affiliate thereof, and, as such, had control over the commission and their likeness. In contrast, portraits of the enslaved turned the traditional Western practice on its elitist head. Marie was not the patron of the artwork and, as the legal property of the couple, had no control over her likeness and no say over whether she wished to pose for Beaucourt at all let alone in this fashion, with her breast exposed.[21] The sexually charged nature of the portrait highlights the precarious status of enslaved Black females and their vulnerability to sexual predation.[22]

We should also consider how the portrait would have reinforced the possibility of Marie's real-life scrutiny and sexual violation since she likely worked as a domestic in the home (and studio) of the artist (especially once in Canada), moving through spaces where the Beaucourts' and François's clients saw her juxtaposed with her painted exposed body. Again, the nature of this "high" art portrait and the seeming enslavement and impoverishment of the sitter makes it completely unlikely that the Black woman either commissioned or owned the painting. Rather, it is far more likely that Beaucourt kept the painting for his own social, cultural, economic, and sexual ends.[23] Marie's potential discomfort, shame, and fear within such a scenario must have been psychologically devastating. As the patron, the artist, and the enslaver, Beaucourt embodied an astonishing and dangerous convergence of cultural, social, and legal authority, which was arguably manifested in its most explicit material form in the object of the painting itself. Not merely attributable to his occupation and professionalization as a European-trained painter, it was Beaucourt's (and his wife's) social status and identity as an upper-class white man that allowed him to purchase another human being and to demand that she sit for him in the compromised fashion that he dictated. Peculiarly then, this portrait circumvented the traditional artist–patron relationship, effectively disempowering the sitter, who would not have had the ability to contest her representation without penalty.

Ironically, I would argue that Beaucourt's so-called portrait of Marie's body as exposed Black skin and smiling face did not and could never have accurately captured her likeness. It does not—and would never have been designed to—capture what I imagine to be her sorrow, shame, remorse, and pain at being exploited against her will in this way. Where then do we look for Marie in a portrait that was not about Marie? To look for Marie, not as a body but as an identity—culture, desires, and potentially even choices—is, I believe, to look at her headwrap and the fruit still life. The headwrap, a West African dress practice that survived the Middle Passage, was passed down to enslaved Creoles by their African-born ancestors as self-care and adornment. Decoding the material and aesthetic nature of Marie's—again, not that of a "field slave"—may allow us to consider how she inserted her cultural identity into the otherwise violent scene of the portrait.

As scholar of Jamaican slave dress Steeve O. Buckridge has ably argued under the force of white cultural annihilation, cultural expression became a survival strategy for the enslaved.[24] Viewing slave dress as a spectrum of possibilities between accommodation and resistance, Buckridge contends that dress was one area over which enslaved Blacks were able to exert some influence, preserving and adapting African aesthetics and practices. To this end, the brightly coloured, neat, and precisely tied headwrap that adorns Marie's head is a sign of African cultural preservation and resistance in the face of white oppression, material evidence of the continuation of African dress heritage, and its evolution, across the Atlantic, across centuries. Furthermore, Buckridge positions the headwrap or tie-head as a pervasive symbol of resistance with immense communicative power that took on many coded forms across a range of diasporic locations.[25] Headwraps were a communal aesthetic language of beautification through which the enslaved signalled status, ethnicity, class, labour, maternity, and kinship relations; they were also a practical tool to balance loads, hide unkempt and lice-infested hair and facial wounds, guard against heat, rain, and dirt, and style one's hair. Marie's headwrap appears to have more symbolic and beautifying functions rather than practical ones, although the latter is certainly still possible. This is conveyed in part by the brilliantly coloured, eye-catching fabric, its seeming refinement (the quality and texture of the fabric), and its positioning. It reads more as a prized possession than a means of disguising or camouflaging the head.

Madeleine Major-Frégeau has described the fruit as: ananas (pineapple), pomme-cannelle (sugar apple) on the marble slab, and noix de cajou (cashew nut) in front of the pineapple and oranges.[26] The sugar apple grows in tropical or semi-tropical climates and was originally known to South America, Central America, Southern Mexico, the Caribbean, and dry regions of North Queensland, Australia. All the fruits were foreign to the temperate climate of Quebec, Beaucourt's home, and impossible to cultivate naturally (that is, outside of a greenhouse) in the region. Therefore, most of the white citizens of Quebec would never have tasted any of the still life's tropical fruits other than in candied or preserved forms. Since Marie was likely from a region in which the fruit was typically grown, she was also assuredly far more familiar with their nutritional and medicinal uses than the artist. Both the cashew nut and sugar apple were used as food and medicinally. In a portrait created because of, and memorializing, a vast power imbalance (if not outright coercion), one area through which Marie may have exerted some degree of significant and, if during the moment of production, undetectable control, was in the selection and staging of the fruit still life.

I want to suggest then that the sugar apple's exclusion from the platter held by Marie may be instructive since, although the flesh of the pods inside of the green skin is edible, the seeds themselves, acrid and poisonous, were used by enslaved females as an abortifacient in their resistance against breeding and sexual violence. According to Londa Schiebinger, the knowledgeable use of vegetation, herbs, and fruits for reproductive resistance to prohibit impregnation or induce an abortion thereafter—commonly demeaned as "folk medicine" by white colonizers and enslavers—was widespread throughout the European colonies among women of African descent in the eighteenth century.[27]

Many historical European fruit and food still life paintings of often bountiful (even excessive) spreads imply that the feasters have come and gone, leaving a mess for the domestics to tend to. About the possessions and decadence that wealth ensures, the immediacy of consumption is often indicated by the presence of peeled citrus or variously opened fruit ready for eating. Set apart from this tradition, the fruit that Marie carries has not yet been readied for consumption. Furthermore, her enslaved status signals that she is intended to prepare, not to eat, the delicacies. Clearly, this portrait was never intended for Marie as a patron, who would almost certainly not have had the money or the cultural capital to commission such an artwork, nor a separate and suitable home in which to install it.

Headwrapping in Quebec and Nova Scotia

Headwrapping was also described in another Canadian fugitive slave advertisement printed on June 18, 1776, in Nova Scotia for the return of a "Negro Women named FLORIMELL."[28] The anonymous notice recorded the day (June 10) and time ("between the Hours of 9 and 10 at Night") that Florimell had escaped, revealing heightened surveillance of her. While her clothing was a blend of female and male items (a gown, petticoat, and men's shoes), the notice also stated that "she commonly wears a Handkerchief round her Head."[29] But unlike the mixed-race, African American Creole Andrew, signs point to Florimell's Africanness. Besides her headwrapping, Florimell also purportedly had "Scars in her Face" and spoke "broken English."[30] Although enslavers often described the scars which riddled an enslaved person's body earned from corporal punishment, harsh labour conditions, accidents, and illnesses, Florimell's scars may have been the product of the ritual-based community marks of scarification.

Known as "country marks" by enslavers, the African cultural practice of scarification—the custom of marking the flesh to create aesthetic patterns with specific ethnic and community meaning—was outlawed within one generation of African arrival in the Americas. Together with her headwrapping and broken English, an uncommon occurrence for enslaved Creoles in Nova Scotia, the three signs point to Florimell's likely African birth. Cash shared more with the enslaved Vincentian woman Dutchess than either of her Canadian counterparts. Under the headline "RAN-AWAY" in the November 4, 1779, *Quebec Gazette,* the Quebec City tailor Hugh Ritchie detailed his hunt for the twenty-six-year-old fluently bilingual (English and French) "Negro Wench named CASH" who had escaped alongside an eighteen-year-old "Negro Lad named NEMO."[31] What links Cash to Dutchess is the type and amount of the clothing with which she absconded, described as "a large bundle of wearing apparel... consisting of a black sattin Cloak, Caps, Bonnets, Ruffles, Ribbons, six or seven Petticoats, a pair of old Stays, and many other articles of value which cannot be ascertained."[32] Like Dutchess, Cash's bundle was comprised of refined pieces of dress, commonly associated with white women. Also, like Dutchess, Cash's escape prompts us to think about her not merely as a "slave" but as a person seeking her freedom, who understood her real value as a human and as a woman who thought about how she adorned her body. Cash's departure, with an excessively feminine and refined bundle of clothing, also speaks to Black female defiance of the flattening of gender within transatlantic slavery through the imposition of masculine labour and dress, like Florimell's "Men's Shoes."[33] Given Hugh Ritchie's occupation as a tailor, it is likely that the labour he stole from Cash was related to his business and that Cash rightfully understood the clothing with which she escaped. Indeed, even Ritchie conceded as much when he noted that Cash's collection of clothing "belong[ed] to herself."[34]

Conclusion

Like the fugitive slave advertisements, the oil painting of Marie was an unauthorized, stolen likeness. The two types of visual culture—one "high art," exclusive, coveted, and expensive, and the other popular, mass-produced, widely circulated, and ephemeral—nevertheless, were both exploited by enslavers to dehumanize and objectify the enslaved in ways that profited the white enslaver: in the first case as a calling-card for Beaucourt's newly honed, European training, which could attract new clientele in Montreal, and in the latter, to identify and criminalize the enslaved to incentivize the public's willing participation in their recapture. These histories of slave dress and its representation are inseparable from the identities and experiences of the enslaved who existed in an oppressive system within which whites exerted sadistic control over all aspects of their lives. Dress then became a way to assert one's individuality and humanity, to insist that "I am human" and "I belong to myself" in a world where the enslaved were legally classed as movable personal property. The fact that Dutchess, Andrew, Florimell, and Cash affirmed both declarations is why we can recover their names and deeds today.

Selected References

Beckles, Hilary McD. "Property Rights in Pleasure: The Marketing of Enslaved Women's Sexuality." In *Caribbean Slavery in the Atlantic World: A Student Reader*, eds. Verene Shepherd and Hilary McD. Beckles. Ian Randle, 2000.

Buckridge, Steeve O. "The Role of Plant Substances in Jamaican Dress." *Caribbean Quarterly* 49, no. 3 (September 2003): 61–73.

Colthurst, John *The Colthurst Journal; Journal of a Special Magistrate in the Islands of Barbados and St. Vincent July 1835–September 1838*, edited by Woodville Marshall. kto Press, 1977.

Cuenod, Andrew. "Andrew Cuenod, Hath Lately IMPORTED from London and Cork, &c." *Nova Scotia Chronicle and Weekly Advertiser* 1, no. 38 (Tuesday 12 September to Tuesday 19 September 1769): 303.

Earle, Rebecca. "'Two Pairs of Pink Satin Shoes!': Race, Clothing and Identity in The Americas (17th–19th Centuries)." *History Workshop Journal* 1, no. 52 (October 2001): 175–195.

Ghachem, Malick W. *The Old Regime and the Haitian Revolution*. Cambridge University Press, 2012.

Lord, Barry. *Painting in Canada: Toward a People's History*. NC Press, 1974.
Mackey, Frank. "Appendix 1: Newspaper Notices." In *Done with Slavery: The Black Fact in Montreal 1760–1840*. McGill-Queen's University Press, 2010.
Mair, Lucille Mathurin. "Women Field Workers in Jamaica During Slavery." In *Caribbean Slavery in the Atlantic World: A Student Reader*, edited by Verene Shepherd and Hilary McD. Beckles. Ian Randle, 2000.
Mathurin Mair, Lucille. "Women Field Workers in Jamaica during Slavery." In *Caribbean Slavery in the Atlantic World: A Student Reader*, edited by Verene Shepherd and Hilary McD. Beckles. Ian Randle, 2000.
Nelson, Charmaine A. "The Fruits of Resistance: Reading Portrait of a Negro Slave on the Sly." In *Representing the Black Female Subject in Western Art*. Routledge, 2010.
Pointon, Marcia. *Hanging the Head: Portraiture and Social Formation in Eighteenth-Century England*. Yale University Press, 1993.
Trudel, Marcel. *Dictionnaire des Esclaves et de leurs Propriétaires au Canada Français*. La Salle: Éditions Hurtubise HMH Ltée, 1990.

Notes

1 Rebecca Earle, "'Two Pairs of Pink Satin Shoes!'," 177.
2 Colthurst, *The Colthurst Journal*, 121–22; Earle, "'Two Pairs of Pink Satin Shoes!'," 178.
3 Earle, "'Two Pairs of Pink Satin Shoes!'," 179.
4 Reverend R. Bickell, *The West Indies as They Are: Or a Real Picture of Slavery: But More Particularly as It Exists in the Island of Jamaica, in three parts with notes* (London: Printed for J. Hatchard and Son, 187 Piccadilly: and Lupton Relfe, Cornhill, 1825), 54. Figure 34.2; Hugh Ritchie, "RAN-AWAY," *Quebec Gazette*, November 4, 1779, vol. 740, p. 3; Bibliothèque et Archives nationales du Québec (BANQ), Montreal, Canada.
5 Mair, "Women Field Workers in Jamaica during Slavery."
6 Mair, "Women Field Workers in Jamaica during Slavery," 390.
7 Buckridge, "The Role of Plant Substances in Jamaican Dress," 62, 63, 65, 68.
8 Cuenod, "Andrew Cuenod, Hath Lately IMPORTED from London and Cork, &c.," 303.
9 Mackey, "Appendix 1: Newspaper Notices," 307–40. See the descriptions of slave dress in the fugitive slave advertisements transcribed in the appendix.
10 Mackey, "Appendix 1: Newspaper Notices," 307–40.
11 James Crofton, "RUN-AWAY, from James Crofton," *Quebec Gazette*, May 14, 1767; transcribed in Mackey, "Appendix 1: Newspaper Notices," 315.
12 Nelson, "Representing the Enslaved African in Montreal," 111–133. Beaucourt, the son of a French soldier and amateur painter, was born on February 25, 1740, in La Prairie, Quebec, and died in Montreal on June 24, 1794. François enrolled at the Académie de peinture, sculpture et architecture civile et navale in Bordeaux in 1775, to which he was elected in 1784. Barry Lord has indicated that the addition of the de by François to his last name was an aristocratic pretension which reveals the painter's class aspirations.

Donald Blake Webster, *Georgian Canada: Conflict and Culture 1745–1820* (Royal Ontario Museum, 1984), 141; Lord, *Painting in Canada*, 31–32; and Jacques Des Rochers, "Portrait of a Haitian Woman: A Loan from the McCord Museum," *M: The Magazine of the Montreal Museum of Fine Arts* (September–December 2011), 15.

13 This is because Canadian abolition came into effect with British abolition in 1834, before photography had been made widely accessible through a convenient and affordable process.

14 Beckles, "Property Rights in Pleasure," 693.

15 Beckles, "Property Rights in Pleasure," 693.

16 Trudel lists the artist and his wife's family name as Beacours. The other enslaved person is listed as a male, Jean-Baptiste-François nègre, who was reportedly baptised on April 14, 1791 at the approximate age of fourteen. Since he was only nine years old when François painted Marie, this likely rules out a romantic relationship between them. Trudel, *Dictionnaire des Esclaves*, 72.

17 Trudel, *Dictionnaire des esclaves*, 114, 379. Trudel also claimed that Marie was buried on December 16, 1800, at l'Hôpital-Général.

18 Mackey, *Done with Slavery*, 466 (note # 13). Mackey's sources were: BANQ, register of Hôpital-Général chapel, December 16, 1800; HDM, Hôtel-Dieu de Montreal, admission registers, Book E, April 19, 1796.

19 We can track the Beaucourts' movements through his newspaper advertisements in Philadelphia for artistic patronage.

20 Ghachem, *The Old Regime and the Haitian Revolution*, 36. Ghachem's calculations did not include the mortality rates of the Middle Passage, which he estimates for French ships at the rate of 13 percent. At the time, transit between Africa and the French Caribbean took an average of seventy days.

21 For a fuller discussion of the meanings and implications of the exposed breast in the portrait see: Charmaine A. Nelson, "Racing Childhood: Representations of Black Girls in Canadian Art," in *Slave Dress as Resistance in Portraiture and Slave Advertisements*, 457; and Nelson, "The Fruits of Resistance."

22 Since the children born to enslaved females, regardless of the social status of the father, became the property of their enslavers, slavery created an economic incentive for the endemic sexual exploitation of Black women and girls. So-called natural increase was of course not natural at all but involved deliberate sexual exploitation through rape, concubinage, and coercion. See: Herbert S. Klein and Stanley L. Engerman, "Fertility Differentials between Slaves in the United States and the British West Indies: A Note on Lactation Practices and their Possible Implications," *The William and Mary Quarterly, Third Series*, 35, no. 2 (April 1978): 357–374; Richard H. Steckel, "Birth Weights and Infant Mortality among American Slaves," *Explorations in Economic History* 23 (April 1986): 173–198; Deborah Gray White, *Ar'n't I a Woman?: Female Slaves in the Plantation South* (W. W. Norton and Company, 1999); Beckles, "Property Rights in Pleasure," and Nelson, "Racing Childhood."

23 Beaucourt's wife may have inherited the painting since the inventory compiled after Beaucourt's death and before her second marriage to Gabriel Franchère lists "six paintings" (six tableaux). Inventory and Wedding Contract for Benoit dit Gaetan Bnigne, June 19, 1810, Faubourg Saint- Joseph, Montreal, prepared by Notary Louis Huguet-Latour, Inventaires après décès de la région de Montréal, 1791–1840, Centre

d'archives de Montréal, Bibliothèque et Archives nationales du Québec. I am grateful to Ariane Côté, who translated these complex historical texts from French to English.

24 Buckridge, "The Language of Dress," 17.

25 Buckridge, "The Language of Dress," 86–94.

26 Major-Frégeau, "La vie et l'oeuvre," 60.

27 Schiebinger, "Nature's Body", 181.

28 Anonymous, "RAN AWAY," *Nova Scotia Gazette and Weekly Chronicle*, June 18, 1776, no. 303; British Library Newspapers, London, UK.

29 Anonymous, "RAN AWAY."

30 Anonymous, "RAN AWAY."

31 Ritchie, "RAN-AWAY," transcribed in Mackey, "Appendix 1: Newspaper Notices," 323.

32 Ritchie, "RAN-AWAY," transcribed in Mackey, "Appendix 1: Newspaper Notices," 323.

33 Anonymous, "RAN AWAY."

34 Ritchie, "RAN-AWAY," transcribed in Mackey, "Appendix 1: Newspaper Notices," 323.

VAGABOND

On Movement and Changemaking

by **Dr. Syrus Marcus Ware**
Rodney Diverlus

WHAT FOLLOWS IS A CONVERSATION ABOUT THE EMERgence of Vagabond—a character rooted in movement practice first articulated by Rodney Diverlus in 2018 at Wildseed Centre on 76 Geary Street in Toronto. In the conversation between Rodney Diverlus and Syrus Marcus Ware, the pair discuss Diverlus's projects *welcome, we've been waiting*, *Vagabond*, and other choreographic and character developments sparked by these times, Black life, and community.

Syrus Marcus Ware (SMW): Rodney, I am so thankful for the chance to chat with you today! First, it's been incredible to watch your artistic practice—both your dance work, your choreographic work, your production and programming work, and, of course, now developing into other areas including film, really exploding since... really, in the last five years.

So much of the focus of this book is looking at the impact of art and activism on each other and what's happened really in this steamroll from the uprising to 2020 forward, and it's been such a fruitful time for so many artists, and I think that it's been... this last five years has been a very busy one for you. I would love to just chat a little bit about, maybe for people who are just getting tuned in, you are a multi-hyphenate artist working across a lot of mediums. What do you think about your creative practice at this moment looking at it in 2024. How would you describe it?

Rodney Diverlus (RD): At this moment, my creative practice is so curiosity-driven and so full of wonder and intrigue. I think I'm genuinely curious as to what I'm going to create next. I'm genuinely curious about what is going to happen in 2025, 2026, and beyond, and that feels like a good place to be. In the last four years, I feel like I was doing a lot of work to respond to what was happening around me and how could you not? I mean, our world was getting upended. This is the first time, I think, in my creative life for sure, that I feel a genuine sense that I am following what I am curious about, whether I understand it or not. If there is something that sparks my curiosity, I become curious to figure it out. Let's dig a little deeper into it. It feels generative—like possibility. I also feel like... and I know that as a multi-hyphenate, other artists who are existing in a multi-hyphenate space, we're carving out a new paradigm of what it means to be an art maker.

I think that many of us inherited a paradigm from our previous generations that was rooted in a capitalist way of thinking, which told you that you specialize in one thing and that became what you were known as. I think perhaps it's a world of social media, perhaps it's a world of fragmentation, perhaps it's because the world is just more globalized than ever—I feel like we're in a generation of makers that actually are uncategorizable, and for the longest time, I always resisted that and I'm at a place where I'm fully embracing it and I want my practice to be unborderable in the same way that myself and my peoples have moved across borders and across continents. I've watched my family remake who they are. My art is kind of like that.

I'm constantly interested in following my curiosities but also training in other mediums. I recently began to dig deeper into filmmaking as a storytelling medium; and part of that training for me is just going back to reinforce the kind of stories I want to tell.

I want to get to a place where I can think, "I'm curious about X, I want to tell X as a story." Let me look at my toolbox and [ask] what are the skill sets that I have that can deliver that? Is X best told as a dance? Is X best told as a write-up piece? Is X best told as a cinematic piece? Is X best told as a hybrid modality? I'm on a quest to learn as many tools as possible, so then I can just be honest with my curiosity, and I can serve whatever it is that I'm curious about and figure out the avenue and the tool to deliver that. I feel really blessed and am grateful [to] the ancestors for guiding me to this place. At the same time, I want to honour my curiosity by just continuing to dive into it and seeing just how far I can continue to make-believe my way through life.

SMW: There's something exciting about following your curiosity and following the mystery and seeing where it takes you and where you end up. I think that there's a distinction that is so precise I think that we're making here, which is that for so long, particularly in mainstream art institutions, BIPOC artists and Black artists in particular were always having to do response projects. Our work was always in response to, or in reference to, or speaking back to the inserts in the book, never the actual text. I think it's so exciting to be in a moment now where we can say, "No, baby, we're dreaming forward, we're dreaming in all of these different ways." I'm curious about your process of tapping into the learning and pedagogy that a core part of your practice is not only being curious, but then following that curiosity to training in film, to training in all these different areas. I mean, I know you've had extensive training in dance, but there's all these other areas that you're moving into. Can you talk a bit about your relationship with training and education? I know that you also mentor others.

RD: I'm kind of obsessed with it. I'm obsessed. I'm drunk on learning. I think there's a piece of it that's about doing some inner child healing work. Growing up around the chaos of immigration, possible deportation, gun violence, poverty and all that came with that, my safe space was in learning. I enjoyed digging myself into a book or developing a new skill. I've seen the benefits of consistent training. I've gotten to a point of really understanding my body and how it relates, and that only comes from twenty years of working in a modality. I respond quite well to long-term development. I realized I'm patient; I play the long game. I've seen how much training and education and pedagogy and exposing myself to different ways of seeing and imagining dance has transformed my dance practice. I'm just excited to do that with other pieces of my practice. I genuinely see this as a toolkit that you're just taking different tools and you're adding to it. I find that spaces of pedagogy also invite me to imagine different ways of thinking and working and being. But I'm at this point in my practice where exposing oneself to different pedagogical frameworks and theories and practices and approaches really just allows one to be more flexible, allows one to just see what's beyond [what's] in front of them. I think it allows me to also be able to have skill sets that I can pass on. I feel I'm at the place of my practice style, shockingly, where I'm now mentoring a couple of creators and dance creators. At first, I had a weird complex about it being like, "Well, I'm still emerging in so many aspects of myself. Who am I to mentor you?" There is a part of me that realizes I've been a dance artist professionally for over a decade... and training for two decades. I have some things to offer. But it's hard to hold on to this realization. I would not be here if it wasn't for people pouring into me, people like yourself, people like some of my professors, people, like some of my mentors, some other artists that... and when I know I work with freaking collaborators like yourself, it's like mutual pouring in. I've seen just the benefits of that for me. I'm excited to be at a place where I'm not gatekeeping everything. That gate was kept closed for me. You said, "Here is the secret to getting the grant, my friend." You told me that. You told me the ways. I remember writing my first grant, and you said, "This is the framework. This is what you need to do." I'm now successful with them. To not gatekeep that information and to pass that on... If I also pass as much information along, it's going to come right back to me tenfold.

SMW: I can remember when we were first doing an opening for the Wildseed Centre, when it was still up at 76 Geary Ave—that was my first experience with the Vagabond character who had perhaps been in emergence for a while. That was my first experience with this character. They had a head that appeared to be a lampshade. In a trench coat?

RD: Trench coat, yeah.

SMW: And they took us on this journey. I've seen so many iterations of this beautiful work. Could you talk a bit about the emergence of this character?

RD: Yeah, the Vagabond and the Vakabon. I mean, first, I just want to also say that you really have seen this character from the first time that I took this character out of my brain and my body to share. It's great to be in conversation with yourself and other audience members with that work: the Vagabond, or Vakabon as we call it in Haitian Creole. That work began with an investigation of duality. In English, when we call somebody a vagabond, it typically has a pseudo positive. The vagabond is that person that's out there adventuring the world. They're a little aloof, they're a little bit like they're just adventurous. There's a sense of adventure and possibility. In Haiti, when you're called a vakabon, it's the opposite. It's like you are chaos and trouble and you are up to no good. You are constantly up to no good.

As a child, I got called a vakabon a lot, a lot. I would bring home 98 percent, 99 percent marks, but my teacher would be, "Smart, great intellect, but is a vagabond who needs to tame down a bit." I think there is a part of me that actually enjoys chaos and that enjoys mischievousness and that sees these rules and order as not real and made up, and the idea of order is a subjective thing that we all agree to.

This character started wanting to be born out of me as a way of almost soothing an alter ego self and nurturing a part of myself that I feel like I never nurture, the part of me that wants chaos.

This character literally, inevitably came out of me and it became a vehicle for me to explore that aspect of my psyche. The Vagabond, the Vakabon... I would also like to say that this character was the first character that I created for myself. As somebody who was very flamboyant as a child, masculinity was very much literally beat into me. I remembered vividly, vividly, my aunt having a conversation with my mom because the women of the church were talking about how I walked. I guess I had a bit of a sway and sass to my hips, a swinging of my arms so much when I walked and really tried to change my physical language to not out myself. There are different ways that I think masculinity has been ascribed to me and that I played into that ascription.

This character for me was also a channel for me to explore my androgyny and to create an image of myself and how I see my vessel in my flesh and my body moving, and that it just simply was an avenue to do that. So yeah, I mean, the Vagabond slinks around causing chaos, and in many ways, the Vagabond forces us to look at ourselves and to let go of our chaotic selves. If there are the cliché of the angel and the devil on the shoulder, the Vagabond is definitely the devil telling you, "Do that. Yeah, you should try that." The Vagabond loves chaos. The Vagabond loves uncertainty, loves a tenuous relationship. I developed the character over many iterations. I see this character existing in varying different contexts, and every time I go back to work on the character, I give it a new world to live in while still refining the aesthetics of it.

The character has a two-tone to themselves in which, like an eggshell, they present themselves with a lampshade as a head and fully clothed—every inch of the body is covered. The last iteration, I collaborated with costume designer and visual artist Diseiye, to design this silky, shiny, polka dot—

SMW: Black and white—

RD: Yeah, black and white polka dots, and they were playing with different polka dots and this image of that, we were thinking of basing it off a clown and just thinking about clown imagery but not clowning. We got polka dots, and we thought, "Let's just play with polka dots, but let's play with the starkness of black and white."

This character, over time, sheds the layers, and every time, you think they are going to get down to the core of who they are. There's another layer, so we removed the lampshade to show a mask, removed the mask to show a half mask, and then by the time that we fully shed ourselves to show the true version of me, the last iteration of the character, I had shaved my head, shaved all my facial hair, and it's just me and my body and my naked body.

There's a way that I also think that the Vagabond works to get us to strip the aspects of ourselves that we perform, our gender, our style, our aesthetic, the performances that we put on, our hair, even our hairstyles. At the core of it, the Vagabond invites us all to dig into the ugly parts of ourselves: the chaotic, the messy parts, the parts that don't make sense, the parts that let the intrusive thoughts win. The Vagabond is an invitation for all of us to explore that part of ourselves.

SMW: What happened for you through this process of reintroducing yourself as you were shaved down to nothing/everything? What happened through the performance of that kind of freedom? What you're describing sounds like a kind of freedom.

RD: It is, yeah.

SMW: What was the impact of that artistic experience on your life?

RD: It was quite impactful. I think the impacts of just confronting parts of myself that I perhaps don't want to confront, I think, has allowed me to taste a kind of freedom that I didn't know was possible. When I used to think of freedom, it's often in bilaterally relational, or relationally bilateral, for lack of better words; often within a limited framework of: how do I get freedom from society? How do I get freedom from relationships? I used to see it as external to me, that somehow, my freedom came from changing the waters that I swam in. This project confronted me to think about inner freedom and that one can be free even in the context of not having the kind of freedoms one might want in life.

Even if I don't have economic freedom or social freedom or justice or the things that I fight for and want, I can have peace of mind. I can have freedom within myself. I can experience a version of freedom internally that I desire. It's profound for me. It really, as working on this project in many ways, has helped. It could all be so simple. We live all these complicated lives that it's like it could honestly be so simple. I think this character really has shown me... and what's interesting is that the characters become us, and we become them.

Even when I'm not performing the Vagabond, I keep those things that I discover in performance with me, and I help to share them out. There is that part that just reminds me [that] levity and lightness and simplicity can come even when the external circumstances around us are tumultuous and hectic and busy.

SMW: I'm so excited for whatever the next iteration of the Vagabond character is. I just think about these five-plus years, more, six-plus years of this project, and how it helps us to, as you say, just really think through all the parts of ourselves as viewers, as we experience and interact with this character.

I wonder if you could talk a little bit about how that idea of levity and bringing some of that in informed some of the choices that you ended up making for *welcome, we've been waiting*, because of course, this was this offering that was bringing us all back to the theatre after a period of being away because of the pandemic situation and people not being able to gather. This offering that you gave us that was so fundamentally about or how I experienced a joy, a levity and a joy.

RD: A levity, yeah. It's interesting because these two projects were created around the same period of time in my life. A few years later I recognized that they were in conversation with each other. Whereas the *Vagabond* was about finding internal levity and joy, this work was very much about finding that collective levity and joy, an exchange between performers and audience. I set this work on the ensemble of Toronto Dance Theatre, a company. My first time working with a dance company since I left my time dancing with a dance company! I really was in a place where so much was happening around us. We are in such a time of intensity that I—through the magic of performance and make-believe and suspension of disbelief—I have an opportunity to offer an antidote to that. I have an opportunity to offer joy and lightness and a sense of smile—a sense of ease—to the people who came and watched.

For most of the audience, this was their first live show that they had seen since the pandemic. That dawned on me, and it was constantly in the back of my mind throughout my creation process.

I wanted a work that an audience could come to enjoy from any background, from any age, with any amount of literacy of dance, and just feel joy. To feel held! I wanted a work that was compassionate, and I think *welcome, we've been waiting* is a work of compassion and it's a work of simplicity. It's the simple things. We are so nostalgic for the simple days. We often talk about the simple days—when things were just so simple that we just went around the block and did x, y, z, and nothing more. My work seeks to investigate that simplicity.

There were moments in which you just got to sit back and just watch a dance unfold. You didn't have to look too deeply. You didn't have to think too "Oh my gosh." You didn't have to think about whose character was what, you just got to watch people dance and watch people move and enjoy some music. The work continues to be an offering of space and grace for audiences, like easy listening, to be honest with you. You know the radio station where you're like, this is easy listening

FM! The work also gives space for us to reflect on what it meant for us to be together at the same time and place after so long in isolation. *welcome, we've been waiting* was very much a product of its time. If I work on it in the future or develop it in the future, I can anticipate that it will change most of our work, but you only get your first show back after a plague…

RD:…once. Well, hopefully once, knock on wood, knock on wood, but based on the hundred-year timeframe for plagues that if I survived the so-called Spanish flu and I watched a show afterwards, I'd want it to also bring me back to remembering that there are some joys about being together, even in a context of safety needing to be considered.

SMW: You've been moving into new directions in your work. What are you most curious about in your practice right now?

RD: I think overall in my practice, I am interested in interrogating the conventions of theatre that I understand to be fact. Since I was twelve, there were rules and conventions of theatre that we've learned, that have been passed down to us over the hundreds of years of Western theatre being developed. The proscenium, the "on" and "off" stage, your "thank you fifteen" to your stage managers "fifteen minutes till curtain" notice, are all shared experiences in live performance. There's all these not talked about conventions of theatre that if you've done it long enough, you start to just embody. In my practice right now, I'm just really interested in interrogating those. I'm interested in flipping audience and performer relations. I'm interested in showing what's not shown. I'm interested in giving reverence to the work, the choreography that happens outside of the stage. When we go on stage and we're saying some lines or dancing or singing, that's half of what we do.

I'm still very much interested in subverting the typical things that are a part of production making and performance making that we take for granted. I'm into finding ways of introducing different players in performance, whether it's performer, crew, creator, audience, critic, whatever. All of us are players in the act of performance and production. I'm really interested in changing those dynamics and exploring new ways of introducing new possibilities and that's an expansive thought. It's a forever thought. I don't know what comes out of it, but every time I do work now, I think, "Okay, in what ways does it have to have a three-act structure and start, middle, and end, and can I subvert the composition? Can I subvert audience-performer relations? Can I make something multisensorial? Can I flip the script of how you imagine something in my own way?"

SMW: I'm curious how the care practices in your work or maybe even the abolitionist approach to humans coming together. I was curious about the way that you have made work, because what I'm hearing is that there's care practices that embodied somatic practices and helped the cast in nourishing yourselves, feeding yourselves, thriving in the space in between the onstage moments…has any of that been informed by this wild ride that we've been on as activists in the last four years?

RD: Absolutely. I think that one could not live during the last four years without really interrogating—perhaps that is just too strong of a word—but investigating the way we work. I'm in a place now where it's like how we work matters to me more than what we work on, to be honest with you. Even for projects and someone's like, "I have a project," I'm just like, "Who is it?" "Oh, it's okay. It's this person and I know they're going to create a safe space. Yeah, I agree with it. Tell me the details later," versus when I started my career, I was like, "I really want to know the project. Send me the script. I want to see all the details before I make a decision." It means for me, even our rehearsals from the beginning of the process, from saying yes to closing out, that *how* we engage with the work matters for me more than *what* we work on. It means also dissecting and rejecting the things that just don't work for us. I know, for me, I came from a world where you would work on a dance work for seventeen…seventeen weeks straight, nine to five. That doesn't work for me. That doesn't work for most people.

I constantly…I'm trying to shed the exploitative, abusive power, hungry, hierarchical, reductive parts of our practices that we, as dancers, know so intimately because, I would argue above all other performance mediums, [we] bore the brunt of those toxic practices, right? Dancers are often asked to leverage our bodies for change. You get injured, no one cares, keep it moving.

That work was really the beginning of that. I also was working in a company, and so I have worked in a company before, and I joke that dance companies are paid plantations sometimes. Some of them feel like indentured servitude, and there is a particular way that dance companies can foster toxicity. It's often when we don't see the human, when we just see them as oil paint for the canvas, and they're not oil paint for the canvas.

They're not the prop. They're not the pencil for the sketch. They're a human being, a living human being. That means giving in the space for however people felt. Sometimes people are like, "I just don't feel like moving today. My body doesn't feel like it." I come from a world in which you would interrogate that and ask, well, what is it specifically? They would have to give you specifics. Then, once they give you the specifics, you then go, "Okay, well maybe you can just do the first half." Or I say, "No, actually. What can you do today? You want to observe? Okay, sit and observe and let's talk about it afterwards." I think it's about giving endless grace, and, obviously, there's boundaries that must be put in always, but those can be negotiated as need be.

That project was one of the first projects that really transformed how I work. What's funny is that it's always a work in progress because there are so many toxic things, just like you, I've heard you talk about this in *Abolition* a lot, that it's like an aspiration. It's not a product because there are many ways that we embody punitive ways of being in our lives.

I know that coming from a conservatory style training, a classical style training, that still to this day, there are things that I look back at myself and I say, "Oh, Rodney, does it have to be like that, or is it like that because it was told to you like that? Do you need to do XYZ? Okay, does this have to happen? Do you have to decide about what the costumes are, or can those be collaboratively created with the dancers and what they feel good at?" To me, it's a work in progress and I'm still in a place of asking what do we need for processes. Is this something I've inherited because somebody, who's likely a white man, has devised it ages ago?

SMW: I love that so much and am so interested in all of the collaborative ways that you work. You mentioned collaboration. I think this gets away from a colonial concept of the "lone individual genius" that is somehow making everything happen solo. It's as if these other players, as you're describing, aren't a key part of what is ultimately happening here. It's a team effort. Even if there's someone who's leading the process, it's still a team effort and it is collaborative. What does dance need now as we head forward given everything that's happened in the last four years? If you can imagine forward, maybe as far as thirty years, what do you think you might be doing as an artist and what do you think the state of art and activism might be?

RD: I love that so much. You raise great questions! For the first one, my immediate thought was that dance needs more... more attention, more resources, and a more symbiotic relationship with our politics and our way of life. Dance needs more visibility, space, and time. There's a generation of us grappling with the definition of dance, which has become quite nebulous. When we expand the umbrella of what dance can be, it enriches and improves. By broadening our concept of dance beyond traditional North American training and performance, we allow it to flourish and become more vibrant. Dance, as a movement form, has a strong potential to be inaccessible, and often it is. It tends to be default inaccessible before it becomes accessible. Part of making dance more inclusive involves recognizing it as a birthright that everyone is entitled to, whether they have formal training or mobility. We all dance in our lives every day, even if it's just navigating a schedule or moving through daily tasks.

I want us to remain in this expansive mindset because that's how art movements are born. Art movements like modern, postmodern, and contemporary are shaped when people ask broad, probing questions beyond the immediate. I want us to move beyond seeing dancers merely as bodies for hire or dance as mere window dressing in the arts. We deserve so much more. I also reject the idea that dance should be just an accessory. Often, commercial dance is relegated to backup roles or space animation. However, I believe in the storytelling power of the body itself—that dance doesn't need elaborate lighting, costumes, or large budgets to be impactful.

While we do need funding, at its core, dance is something that any number of people—be it two or a hundred—can engage in. It's a fundamental aspect of our lives from birth to death.

Practically speaking, though, dance is chronically underfunded. It's surprising to me that I can secure more funding for other mediums than for dance, even at this stage in my career. It's disheartening to still have to turn down offers because they don't meet my needs, and the field is still dealing with financial constraints.

Traditionally, Western dance has attracted individuals from middle-to-upper-class backgrounds, often without a full understanding of the costs involved. As a result, many dancers face financial challenges, but they are not typically experiencing systemic poverty, as there are safety nets in place. This has, in some ways, created apathy about the high cost of creating dance in our current economy. Looking to the future, particularly in the context of art and activism, I remember you, Syrus, mentioning in 2021 that we are in a Black Renaissance, a transformative period. I truly believe we haven't yet reached the height of this change.

The coming decade will be transformative, and our world's increasing volatility and violence indicate that we must stay vigilant as artists. The lessons we learned in 2020 and 2021 taught us that the studio and the stage are just containers for art, not the art itself. We, the artists, are the art. We are magic. I am excited to continue encouraging artists to step out of the studio, engage with our communities, and see our art as part of a broader conversation and [an] essential tool for making the world a better place.

SMW: I think that is a beautiful place to stop. Thank you so much for this conversation, Rodney. That was so beautiful.

RD: Thank you. Thank you for having me.

THE ART OF STEP

Roots, Resistance, and the Rich Culture of Step in Montreal

by **Kayin Queeley**
Natasha "Tashe" Clery
in conversation with
Dr. Ra'anaa Yaminah Ekundayo (ABD)

IN THIS CONVERSATION, NATASHA "TASHE" CLERY, WHO brought step to Northern Turtle Island (Canada), and Kayin Queeley, the founder of the Montreal Steppers, delve into the rich history of step, with a focus on its roots in Montreal. This insightful conversation explores the radical roots of this art form, and its significance as a powerful tool for community building and resistance. This chapter outlines the cultural pride of step, tracing its evolution into the twenty-first century.

Ra'anaa Yaminah Ekundayo (RYE): I'm excited to be in conversation with you both today. Could you both introduce yourselves, and within that, can you share how you were introduced to the art of step, or what initially called you into this world?

Tashe Clery (TC): Okay. Step has been near and dear to my heart since first viewing it really. From my perspective, I grew up in the eighties and the nineties where the Huxtables were our first vision or view into an Americanized higher-middle-class living after the whole "slavery, slavery, slavery, the Caribbean, work hard, work hard, work hard." So being influenced by the music as well as the TV at that time, a different world was... It's like I saw it once, and I ran to school. I was studying at Vanier at the time, and I mobilized with the team, with my friends more than anything, and said, "We should create a team for the basketball team." The basketball team was fantastic. I wanted to be at all the games anyway, so I pitched it to the school and said, "We got a cheerleading team for y'all that y'all never seen before," and they were like, "We're paying you and you can be a coach." And I was like, "What?" And they were just like, "Here, here, here, here."

We just got started and it was steady; she went from there. I graduated a year later and passed it on essentially to one of the team members who was there; his name was Chris Bennett, and he went on to make it really diverse here in Montreal. He took it to a competitive level, basically took it out of Vanier College and brought youth as well as our peers, and made it into a very, very dynamic thing. They competed nationally. They've been to Toronto. Boots[1] is really doing awesome things. We just wanted to be dynamic. A lot of music. We had singers, we had a rapper. It was just interesting how that group of women just became all of what they did for the time that we were. Yeah, it was like a flash of time that I never really thought that I would hold, but I do move with a perspective.

I think about it a lot now. I acknowledge that at the time, part of my pitch was, "Canada doesn't have anything like this. You guys really want to give us a spot," and Vanier was like, "Here you go. Here. Sure, go ahead." But looking at it now, there's nothing written, there's no records, there's no video. It was like one of those groups that you started at college, and it drops away. And if you have any record of it, it's from a dance or something. And then coming back around to meet Montreal Steppers, "Oh, I lobby the message, I lobby the story to you now where you can pick up from there," because meeting the Montreal Steppers is really what brought it full circle and has given me the opportunity to not only be a stepper again at fifty-two, but to be part of a movement that is beyond performative. Montreal Steppers—it's a cumulative experience of step, and I think it's just so powerful. And to have the opportunity to experience it now at my stage, at this age, and have all the roots of it on top of it, especially this South Africa experience, is mind-blowing.

RYE: And does any remnant of it still exist at Vanier?

TC: There are no remnants of it at Vanier, and if there are, I don't know who has them. The thing about performing in 1991 is you couldn't perform and record at the same time. And unless your parents were present doing it, or siblings... Sometimes it's just the information that is lost. The information is lost. There was no way to imagine recording it. I know that there are some of my peers that maybe had their parents record it on VHS kind of thing, but VHS—

RYE: Yeah.

TC: It became very poignant and significant when the Montreal Steppers said, "Where's all this history? Where's all the information? Where are all the pictures? Where's all the memorabilia?" I went, "There's none. Hurt me." It really brought on a huge study about the things we do and how the information is collected and recorded and saved and appreciated. Sometimes we do big things, and it's nowhere. It's not written anywhere. And you just walk with it knowing it's something that you did and it's something that you have, but it's not something that you can hold really. So yeah, not very much information about it at all outside of the crew that we started. There's a couple of us that still have sweatshirts. There's a couple of us that have a few pictures here, and then photos. I found the old wrap that we'd had on loose-leaf paper. But it's in the ether.

RYE: I would love to see that wrap. I'm very curious what the wrap was like.

TC: I'll take a picture and send it to you.

Kayin Queeley (KQ): Yeah, I think, for me, like most people, you watch the movies: step shows, a little bit of *Stomp the Yard*. That's my generation. That was big as a cinematic film around stepping, right? So, give people the lens into what the American landscape was. In the

Caribbean, when we go back to explore a little bit of history around stepping, mostly just drum and African dance for us, steel pan drum dancing, all the other things. But stepping was something that didn't really take root in the Caribbean. That's where, for the United States, there's so much ownership over, "This is our thing."

I saw it on television later when I left Saint Kitts, I went to school, I went to Upstate New York, closer to Canada than to New York City. And there they had a choir that was multidisciplinary, with various art forms. In the choir there was of course singing, but then there was a little bit of liturgical dancing that you sometimes see in the churches, like the praise dancers. And then they had a step team. And Tashe talks about 1991 with Vanier Stompers, but in 1991, the choir director at that time I think would've seen a group in Albany have praise dancers, a step team and a choir. And then he says, "Oh, we should do something varied," because then if you have a college choir, not everybody might want to just sing. Some people want to dance, and some people have step background because they're coming from New York City, Upstate New York. So, the teams at that point were generating a lot of people who, because you're coming out of New York City, most church groups, most high schools, would've had step teams.

In 2007—that December—I saw the choir, I saw the step team. They did a little fun number. And then in 2008, that winter or spring semester, depending on how they call it, I joined the choir and then I said, "I want to try out for the step team." And I really couldn't do the stomp clap move stuff. I was struggling. For somebody that [had] Caribbean roots could roll up my waist and do all the things, and I couldn't get the *tap, tap-tap-tap-tap, tap*. I just couldn't get that hard hit, then movements, and I had to work.

And then I did very well in the team. I went on to lead the team. I was very active in the choir. I was always involved. I was running the choir; I was running the step team. I ran it for two years, training the people, and then wanted to take the performances to a different level. For me, it was more like we were always having a lot of fun, which is fine, but I was like, "But let's push some stuff, some precision, some movement, some shifting, some angles. Let's add a little element." At the shows now, we would see a shift to where the audience couldn't wait to see the step team.

You know the audience was coming for the choir, but they were like, "Boy, the step team. The step team." The dancers were going to dance and then we were going to do our things. But then I just really was getting deeper into it, and I said, "Okay, but let me learn a little bit more about the fraternity part of it. How did that come about?" Because we weren't in any fraternities or sororities. There were some fraternities, sororities, on the university campus in Plattsburgh, and some of them were doing stepping, some were also experimenting around strolling, different versions around step, but that's how I was really immersed. I would say from 2008 pretty much up until 2013 in stepping, leading, choreographing. And it was interesting for me because people were then assuming that I had probably come from New York or did stepping before, because I was building choreographies. I was like, "We're going to do this." But in my mind—and the team laughs at me now, laughing in a jesting way—but where I could hear the rhythms and say, "Okay, in these eight counts we can have these different combinations." And then people will say, "But how are you doing that?" And I said, "Well, I know that I could build a step in this pattern." But you understand that nobody can do that like that.

TC: Not just off the top of their head.

KQ: Not just off the top. I think I started to explore something about myself, and it was an unlocking of a skill set that I didn't know. But the words I put to it now [are], I was walking into a path that preceded me and talents that I got from my ancestors that I didn't recognize until it was unlocked. Right? Because these are the gifts that are sprinkled down, however they land on you, and I didn't know that was going to come for me. And then I got some experiences in the choir to do mini workshops, going to schools and just teaching the kids a little bit. And then I'll continue in another part of the question around more or less coming to Montreal with the Montreal Steppers, but my introduction and foundation is there.

That's how it started for me with stepping, because I had never touched it in the Caribbean, but when I was in university, that's when I got a huge, huge exposure to it. And then starting, see, my ex-girlfriend at the time was going to Howard, and I visited her in DC, and I went to a step show, and that was seeing step times a hundred because then you had the Alphas, you had the Deltas... So, you had the fraternities, sororities, really giving you what they do in the South. It is just an appreciation for the variation of what you can see in step.

RYE: It is so fascinating to talk about the ways in which... I don't know, just even how you were talking... things came through you through your ancestors, and you really feel these moments. And it's also especially comforting listening about your step journey because, in my heart of hearts, I've always wanted to do step, but I'm thinking, "The rhythm's not there." It's comforting to know that if you practice hard enough, you can get there. We're talking about our bodies, and we've been talking a lot about movement, and the resistance in Black bodies. I remember that I had listened to a panel once and they said, "Black bodies in motion are the greatest forms of resistance." I would love it if we could talk about the ways in which step embodies this resistance through Black bodies. If you want to go first?

TC: Yeah. From my perspective, it was always extremely empowering to arrive at the basketball games, fully geared up—huh huh huh! Set a tone from the minute we walked in and found our spot on the bleachers. And then any noise on bleachers is noise. Noise. And I mean, we respected the cues and when coaches were like, "Enough so I can talk to my players, please." We were like, "Sorry, sorry, sorry." But outside of that, halftime was like, "Forget it, let me show you what Vanier got. Let me show you what Vanier AAA is talking about." And then, because of that, Dawson started a team the next semester, and then it became the Vanier versus the Dawson thing because that's how it was on the court as well. AAA basketball as well as AA basketball.

KQ: I don't think I was thinking about Black bodies in resistance at the start of learning step or running the group. We were focused on doing a little good ten-minute run at the concert, making sure we hit the hits and did a deal. Make the noise. But it's only after, again, where you're in the moments and more things speak to you. What is it about this thing that makes me feel so alive? Your words. What is it about me just coming in here for the first session? Wow, there is something there that is a calling, is a connection, is a pulling, is a tugging, and I think what we allowed ourselves to do was boldly lean into it and not skirt around and say, "Well, we're only going to do that." Our resistance within this resistance narrative we have is even saying, "We are going to talk about the history," and this is what Tashe outlined, too, in our final class. That when we go on stage to say, "We're going to tell you all this history. Some of you're going to feel a little way in your heart because you're like, oh Lord, he wasn't there." But we are also going to, in that same moment, invite you to stand up and open your mouth and go, "Yes, yes," with us. In thirty minutes, you're going to tell us all this stuff we did, but still turn it around and—

TC: —And dance with us.

KQ: We're going to collectively make music together. We go back to the history of the intention to bury Black people, but they couldn't. And even in history, looking and going to the African American Museum, coming off the heels of apartheid, looking at all those spaces we go in and we see every time, a lot is changing. Every time, something is shifting. We are going to move from this to this, then this, then this, then this. We start with slavery, then this, then with segregation, then this. It also says to me, in all those moments, in Kevin's words, plotting resistance and plotting and resistance and plotting so that there is this shifting of, "Well, we got to change this because we want to... We must change this because we are going to..." And that's that. You're not going to not open your morning step. We laughed about it in class. So even just the crying or the shouts or the chants is... you're not going to silence me, and my claps are going to ring through, and my stomps are going to shake the ground. And when we are in these spaces, because you don't want us in certain spaces, so going to fraternity, sorority, to create our own spaces in historically Black colleges and universities, we're going to get our own space. We're going to do our own thing. And then what's going to happen? You're going to come around and see it and still say, "Can I get it?"

TC: Can I get some of that?

KQ: Can I get some? I will never come from it as a standpoint of, "Well, I was always talking about resistance and history." No, no. That is something I learned over time. I saw, I recognized, I felt, I experienced, and then I had enough courage to name it and name it clearly with the support of the people around me that collectively, now, we say, "We are not going into any space to just do a step." You got to know where this comes from because that pulls the resistance story out of it. And we know this is the tactic. If you don't talk about the resistance or the drum is taken away—that's why we must use the body. Something will always want to be taken away because then we must plot. And when I go boom, boom, boom on the drum, we are planning. And you just think we're just having a good time, but we're strategizing because we always must. The motion, the movements, the sound, the power, you feel it, right? We say it in the show.

TC: It's contagious.

KQ: We clap. We remember the hands that were cultivating crops for the entire world. Places like Saint Kitts, which was one of the highest producers of sugar, funding the British Empire. Every time I walk around Europe, and I see the buildings, I think, "On my ancestors' backs." Cobblestone on their back, big buildings on our back, because the sugar was coming from there and sugar was the most lucrative... Sugar was white gold. That's what it was. It's white gold. It's in everything, right? That's another topic. We can talk about food. But it's the resistance of understanding that that's the power in it, of when we collectively stomp, and clap, and we've experienced and felt that power. When we say, "Everybody, don't be passive in this step. Go boom," because you feel it. And that's what it is, to shape the space around us, to call, to wake up. To say to the ancestors, "We will never forget you. We won't forget you." Let's do it.

TC: Let's dance.

KQ: Yeah. So yeah, for now.

RYE: This is such a rich conversation, and my one regret is that this is not an audiobook. Because I'm just listening to the vibrancy [with] which you both talk about step, and even because step is... it's the sounds, the noise, it's the vocal cues, and everything. I would love for us to talk about step as it is now. And especially considering the 2020 uprisings, and since that's the focus of this anthology, we're recognizing all these key moments around 2020, but also providing context of how leading up to 2020, things have been set in place. I'd love for you both to talk about the 2020 uprisings and how it impacted the world of step and the endeavours of the Montreal Steppers. We've been talking about the commodification of step, right? And as you know, 2020, important moment, and it opened a lot of space for Black people and Blackness, but also really opened up this commodity culture.

KQ: What I could say, honestly, because I must be respectful in the sense that I could only talk about what I saw in my own lens of running Montreal Steppers with step. To speak to it outside of that context, I really can't. But I know that, like you said, I think that is a marker in history where people now are either, "I didn't know this was still happening." Where many of us are challenged like, "Okay, maybe this is so." And then really bring to light a lot of stuff. And when we finished our Ottawa show last year, we had a great conversation with a well-connected woman in Ottawa. Adrienne, I think, is her name. We sat down post-show to just talk about the idea of this Black art and who wants it where and when. And she was referencing what most of us were saying and feeling. And it was the idea that that was 2023, so three years in. We were saying, okay, the money is now running out for them to have Black stuff. They were like, "We've given you three years. The Black money now is running out." Because at that point, everybody was like, if you didn't have something happening, people were looking at you or they were looking at themselves and being like, "Let's do something quick," and that is a danger.

It's just assessing the moments of can this work, serve the way we've always wanted it to serve? And then the opportunities present themselves. Is this opportunity coming because you really understand the value or you're just trying to do a quick fix? And often, I felt like it was a quick shuffle, and we feel nothing fast like that is ever good. Because you need to think about... not slow, but it must be thoughtful or intentional and applicable. So long story longer, we had requests for folks to do workshops and do different things, and what it was for me was really standing in—you must understand what we are coming here to do, and you can't be saying to me that it's going to be happening just this time in this space in Black History Month, which we don't do. So even in my conversation with folks like the National Theater School, they had reached out after an interview, and it was a bigger conversation around, Why do you want this? Why is this important?

Also recognizing what COVID did was shedding a lot of light on the inequities, the people who lost and then companies who got even more. If we are talking about companies that made billions of dollars in COVID when many other people lost so much, you're like, what is going on? It was looking at all those things, but that commodification, that consumption, that this was like, we recognize that some people were only getting contracts at that time, in this moment. I was saying then, the bigger question to ask these people, what's your five-year plan for this work you want to do? Because after five years, it will fade. I can tell you. I work at the institution. On the heels of George Floyd, COVID stuff, five-year anti-Black racism initiative—Where are the results? Nobody knows. What's the findings? Who knows? What has been done? We hire a few people, start a few initiatives, but you look back now and be like, "Hey." And I think that is what we talked about and read about [with] bell hooks, the rules of representation. To rules, "Come, come. Show me, show me how to do this." Do you really want it? What do you want it for? And I was able to cross-reference that with how folks wanted to work with us to see if it was going to be more long term, but not just long term because they can just say, "Give me this for ten years." But how is it changing your infrastructure?

For teachers who are willing to change your curriculum, great. For teachers who are willing to have different conversations with their students, great. For others who are like, "But no, we just want..." No, sorry, don't have any time. Not available. Because we can't compromise, and it was a real interesting moment because some people were hoping to always get those opportunities, but I don't think those opportunities were good opportunities. Many of them weren't. We often say all money is not good money, or whatever the line we reference, and I think in the same way, these opportunities were not truly opportunities for some. Post that, we saw some folks with a true intention to shift their learning, their education, their pedagogy, their work, and some really did that. I won't sit here and say everybody. No. Because we still work with some institutions and teachers who really took that as a moment to, "I need to unlearn and relearn," and it manifested and shifted. But then we had some that do what always has been done.

RYE: Yeah.

KQ: Let me see if I could use this.

TC: For sure. For sure. And from my perspective, the whole George Floyd, that whole period, the COVID and the crazy of George Floyd around it, it looked to me, and it felt to me, just another time in history that the media gave the Black community a little bit of light. And everything that you can initiate, everything that you can start, everything that you can make really loud, everything that you could whatever within that time was great because the whole world was saying, "Did you see what they did? Did you see what they did to that Black man? Did you see that video about what they did to..." The whole world, and that's the only reason why it had the mileage that it did. That's my perspective, that it was such a long and drawn out, suspenseful account of what it could look like when a police officer just leans on a Black man, not even acknowledging that it's a human. You can't do it to animals.

I think that that was one of those things where everyone is now saying there must be some accountability. Surely there must be some kind of... Black people must be feeling very... Like, "What are we doing for the Black people? The Black people must be feeling a way about all this stuff. Let's do this. Let's do that. Let's initiate that. You're right. You're right. You're right." When you consider the fact that we, Black people, have a history that is so vast, so deep, so rich, so wealthy, that it is more effective for them to keep it on [the] DL like nobody... George Floyd is one of so many, and if we must go back to slavery days, we'll find the heroes of that time. And if we go before that, we'll find the heroes of that time, and the people who are writing the stories only had to write what they wanted to write, and I'm not convinced that that's not the case even now, from my perspective. I do say along with that is anytime and every time we as a community can take the opportunity to really shine as a community at a time when the lenses are on us, we should. We should, but make it purposeful, make it intentional. Build something with longevity, something that we can count on down the line. Something that we can look for down the line. We have no heroes, and that George Floyd in his death had to be that representative of a hero for us for that period and all the time that it was. He was an icon. We have so many.

RYE: It's so interesting because I found after everything happened, I read an article and this guy was talking about—he called it the George Floyd Effect—

KQ: For sure.

RYE: —of how attention is drawn to this one thing, and it's like only when the media draws attention to it, now we all care, and then how it fizzles out. And it was especially interesting to see within the past couple of years how, for the longest time, it was a toss-up between Black folks at the top of the media, and then it was Indigenous folks, and then Black folks and Indigenous folks. It was like this back and forth. And it was so interesting to see how the media's like, "We can't focus on two racialized folks at once." There's lots of space to talk about whiteness and all of this and that over here, but in terms of the injustices that are constantly being forced upon racialized communities, even now, we see the attention for Blackness is out the window because of the attention on Palestine right now.

TC: It doesn't take much. Wherever the lens is, wherever the focus is at any given time, and at the end of the day, who is moving it? The very same engine that destroyed... It's a cycle, and I think that we are evolving through a cycle with different awareness now. Individuals like yourself and individuals like... We're three generations really, three decades. I'm in my fifties and you're in your forties and you're probably in your thirties, yeah?

RYE: Twenties.

TC: Twenties at that, which I knew for sure had to be. But all of us have a different perspective of all these experiences because of our gender group, our age group. And as someone who was born in 1972 and really, as I said, coming from a family where they feared every day that their sons weren't coming home. I was on the road. I was that girl that was unstoppable. I had to be here; I had to be there. I was a baddie stepper. I was out and about. I was doing my thing, and my parents had to worry all the time, but out I was and out I was and out I was. And if I think about it now with two daughters who have a curfew and are home fifteen minutes before the curfew, so I never have to worry. When I think about the things that I dodged and the experiences that I [had] and the things that I saw, and the conversations that I had no business having at that time with people that I probably had no business talking to, it sheds a light really on the power of our community and how effectively they eclipse it. That's all that resonates for me.

It's very real, and I think about George Floyd in situations like that, since because of that murder, our eyes were opened. If we had to be the resistance that we could be, we would be freaking flipping tables, knocking down all the books in the library. If we were as scary and as dangerous as they wish to perpetuate... just because we want to have rights. The cycle would be met. You cannot victimize a group and not expect retribution. It is our goodness that delivers the retribution. That's my perspective.

RYE: I feel like I have chills.

KQ: I don't have the records, but during whatever happened post–George Floyd, our Black communities didn't make any money. Other communities got richer after the tragedy.

RYE: Oh, a hundred percent.

KQ: The points in history always connect. We were in South Africa, right? Hector Pieterson, if that photo was not presented to the world—

TC: Yeah, yeah.

KQ: —the world would not have known the extent of apartheid in South Africa. If Emmett Till's mother didn't say open the casket—

TC: Open the casket.

KQ: —the world wouldn't have known. If the image of the dog attacking a Black man when they were protesting wasn't presented to the media... it's always this cycle. And I feel like they know the cycle. They know.

RYE: There was always someone being killed by policing at any day of the week globally. It's always something. I'm happy to have these conversations to contextualize. It's so disheartening to see the cycle continue to be perpetuated in the way to keep going and the ways in which I can only imagine what it was like at these different pivotal moments in time when all these things were happening. I remember growing up and Sammy Yatim was killed, do you remember that? It was in the GTA [Greater Toronto Area]. He was a young boy who was having a mental health crisis on a streetcar, and he was killed by police—another killing due to the police in Northern Turtle Island. I remember hearing about the shooting and witnessed the way they villainized him in the press. I realized, "Oh, the media just never shifted in his favour." We saw this villainizing with George Floyd, too, right?

KQ: Yeah, yeah.

RYE: The way they villainized him. Alleged that he had counterfeit money—as if that was punishable by immediate death on the street by a cop. That's not how our legal system is supposed to work, even by their terms. The cops said that they were scared. You see the media wavering—some cycles are trying to acknowledge the cops' wrong-doing, at least the more left-leaning ones. But the right prevailed and now we're all saying villainizing things about George Floyd because this is what public perception is now.

TC: That Black lives are still used in American politics. It's disgusting to me that Black lives are still the source of political pandering, it is so ridiculous. Just give the Black people the cotton, make them pick it again. That's the attitude.

RYE: I'm starting to read more about the American and Canadian civil rights movement in the 1960s/70s and am learning about key activists. I am trying to learn more because obviously they didn't teach me any of this in school in Northern Turtle Island in the 2000s.

KQ: They wouldn't. You know they're removing it from the curriculum now—in places where it *was* taught.

RYE: Oh, a hundred percent. They said, "We'll give you MLK [Martin Luther King Jr.]. He had a dream, but we won't play you the whole speech."

KQ: The books are gone.

TC: Because at the root of it, they know they're the ones that have all the power to decide what to teach. Bury the information, bury the pride, bury the wealth, bury the news, bury the history, bury our birthright so that we can continue to flounder, right, in a system built to reduce us so that they can thrive.

RYE: We're talking about "Canada" being on this apology tour, and we're seeing they're starting to apologize, and even to give money to folks that they have wronged. But not to Black people who have been here on Turtle Island! Black reparations, they are never coming.

KQ: Never coming. They'll never give us any money. What they'll give you is a few contracts. They'll say, "Come and perform at a showcase for fifteen minutes, but we are not going to give you any money." We had people leaving the show saying, "I've learned more in this two-hour show than in years of schooling." Our show is full of visual arts by our team members about what is missing from the encyclopedia books. It's our research history about Africville, Charlotte, and Hogan's Alley. And the audience leave saying, "I had no idea."

TC: I love watching Kayin tell the history and getting to watch the engagement of the audiences. They can't help but ask, "How did we never know this stuff before?" Oh girl, there's so much we don't know! He's doing it all with a smile like this. And that's the piece. He says, "Do you realize that there was a time that we would not have even been allowed inside your classroom?" And the kids ask, "Why?"

KQ: Yeah.

RYE: It's fascinating to look at the chronology of our time on Northern Turtle Island. Enslavement, segregation…Hundreds of years of it. This weekend I was at Jazz Fest and there was a performer, Yaya Bey.

One of the things that she said when she was on stage was, "Did my ancestors not do enough work that I should be liberated to this day? I shouldn't be working, but here I am, shucking and jiving for the man for my dollar." Black people should never have to work again. And it's like you're liberated to now work at ten cents a dollar—

TC: If you used our bodies to create wealth to build your businesses…the same businesses that now we must work at in order to have a home, to send our child to school. I must come to work to make you rich every day. Black people need to look at these things and say, "You see this nonsense we've bought into for all these years?"

KQ: Nonsense. That's it. Up the roof we go. Investments in the rum and sugar industry get tax breaks and then say, "Build an institution in my name, please." We are on those properties that our ancestors would have worked to fund.

RYE: And we're fighting to get into these same places too!

KQ: What I do say when students at universities tell me, "I did not know step was going to introduce me to an aspect of my culture and history that I wasn't aware of." One young boy said in one of the workshops, at the end of this school year, I asked, "Hey, how do you feel after learning this first little step," like we do in the class. The little boy said, "I feel like for the first time in my life I'm connected to my ancestors, to my Blackness." Second boy said, "This is the first time I feel like my ancestors are looking down at me very proudly."

TC: When you introduce these types of concepts to children, it changes the world.

KQ: I get to actively think about—although I've never met them, but I've met them, the people before me, that were making the music and stomping and making the noise, knowing that generations later somebody is going to be making the noise and making the music that will carry their history. It's more than I could even imagine. I don't think my head could be wrapped around what it means to embody that in my body, but I'm grateful and present enough to say thank you for it, right? I don't have to understand all of it to be grateful for it, nor am I trying to have to understand all of it to explain it. I don't need to. The people around get it. And even in one of the classes at the National Theatre School, before they did the final sharing at the semester, I said, "I think once they finish, you're going to feel like whoa, you're not even going to know what hit you." They finished doing it, and I said, "But you all feel that, right?" Everybody was like, "Yeah." I said, "But you can't explain it, right?"

Some of the things go beyond the explanation because it's a connectedness to many things that we can't really explain. Culturally, I'm proud of my Blackness. My God, I'm so proud. Being Black is amazing. It's incredible. It's the richness. It's what we have, it's what is feared because of our incredible dynamism and our gifts and our power. One of the things that resonated for us in South Africa was, and my wife watched a little highlight of South Africa today, and she said, "Just the way they spoke," she said, "It was just this assurance of them knowing this is who I am and no second guessing of am I, can I? It was not asking for permission. They were like, here's my story, here's my history." One guy said, "Pantsula is his inheritance. The dance is my ancestral inheritance." So, it's that. That's what it is, it's an inheritance. It's the best way I could, using his words, say that's what it means culturally for me.

TC: And I feel that it's so funny that you would say that because that's what it is, I planted seeds when I was nineteen years old that I'm watching the fruit now, and I had no desire even to remember where I planted, like to hold a tree. Now, I'm moving around in the history, in the performance, in the experience, in the embodiment. Embodiment is like that word that really, really resonates for me with step in general because like you said, when you feel like you are doing something and you're being poured into by something that you cannot explain and that the effect of it is so enormous, but subtle that people are smiling, and they don't even realize they're smiling. For me to watch this happen in Canada, for me to watch this happen where I live is inexplicable. It's not even pride because I was without any desire to hold it. It's not something that I said for the last thirty years, "Oh, I was the one that started step, in my mind, oh, I was the one."

The last thirty years. I was lit. I was the one that started stepping in...I was the one that started stepping in Canada. I started stepping in Canada. Did you know that I started stepping in Canada? I was the one that was responsible for starting stepping in Canada. If that's a narrative that I used for the last thirty years, then I could see why I am living and dancing in the beauty of this experience right now. But I could run into this person randomly in a capacity where I'm doing different art, spoken word... And still see him get on the stage and my heart. It's like the whole falling deep into a love experience again that you could not have imagined. And I watch my life change. I watch my body change. I watch my energy change. I watch as an elder in this group, almost the newest member. I see so many 360s, I see so many alignments. I see so many beautiful messages from the universe saying, "Tashe, you're right where you're supposed to be, right where you're supposed to be. You didn't know. You didn't know. But here it is." I look at the experience. I mean culturally, I think culturally and personally is the same for me. As a Black woman, to know that I was pivotal in bringing a Black art form to a country that is as afraid of Black people as every other country on this planet.

I didn't know I was in the resistance the way I was in the resistance. But looking at it now, I'm so glad that subconsciously I was in the resistance without knowing that I was in the resistance. You all didn't have to call my name then. You didn't have to record, and you didn't have to take my picture, and Montreal doesn't have to acknowledge me. Canada doesn't even have to acknowledge me in what I did because I move with the Montreal Steppers in environments that are celebrated beyond Canada and get fed, fed by Black people. I'm grateful. I'm full. Truly, I'm grateful and full culturally and personally. I am in the greatest time in my life.

RYE: It's so wonderful to hear this richness that you both have with step and the richness that it brings to so many other people and how nourishing Black culture is truly, truly. We are fed. We are full. We are—

KQ: It's the richest.

RYE: I would love to know, what is your dream for Montreal Steppers or for the steps scene in Montreal, or just for this movement art form that is so special?

TC: I think that we are placed in a very specific position to teach a history that we did not even know that we'd be placed to teach. We did not notice, we did not know the significance of our connection right here in Montreal, Plattsburgh, to apartheid and movement around the creation of this art form at that time. I see performances, I see documentaries. I see an awareness of an art form that's essentially missed by many without acknowledging how powerful and monumental we've been here in Canada. If we're talking Black people here, maybe don't think about resistance. Black people here don't think about resistance. Black people here think that they're good. What's happened over in the United States though? Oh, a lot, a lot, a lot. They don't see these actions, they don't know what it means for us to get gigs, to get performances, to talk to people with less than the respect that we deserve for the message that we leave with any audience. But again, they can only know when they're there. They can only know after the experience. And when we're done with it, we get our confirmation and our validation. So really, where do I see? I see a, well, time will say more, but I see an exchange program. I see a mixing of cultures almost to a point that on purpose we're homogenous.

KQ: I mean in five years we've seen what an alignment of heart and history and power can do. That is exponential. I think you can have experts sitting down to say, oh, you start this, it might only go here. It might only go there. But stepping has taken us to places that I can't say we didn't dream of. We put it on paper. I said, in five years we need to be in Africa. I think stepping for me is such a true connection to our history and the story of our people. Not in the art form itself, but what it is raw. It is using what you have. That's it. It is using what you have. If you have hands and feet, a body that you have control over, not everyone does. And that's always been our story. It's always stripped of everything to just what you have. Take your clothes and take your drum, take your shoes, take your hair. Give me everything. Give me your face, give me your nose. They want it all. But I'm going to use it because I know you want this body because this is what's going to build for you, but I'm going to use it back to the resistance. I'm going to make music with it. I appreciate the question of the growth and what you see and all that stuff, and I think what I would say is whatever I think, that I want it to be a hundred times more than that. I could say I want it to be that, but I just want it to be and not for me to have a new recognition. The essence of us is—

TC: Not easy.

KQ: ... we just want to, because we see what it's done for our lives, and we see what it's done for the people who come there. I don't need Montreal to be like, we recognize you, give you this. I also feel those things are distractors.

TC: I'm fifty years old in Montreal. Montreal's as big as a bathtub. Everybody knows everybody in Montreal. But then I say, I was the one and they all go, I know you. I know you have been stepping, but I didn't know that... Come on. If I was motivated by the desire for the recognition, just like Kai was saying, if we were motivated by being on all the television shows and getting all the interviews and whatever, whatever, it would be very, very different for us. It's because our only motivation is to share and to teach. It's because we know how this thing resonates in our body and how it brings health and how it brings joy that we are passing that on, and that people can feel. The recognition will come in another twenty years from my perspective. In another twenty years, Vanier will say, "Did you know our own Natasha Clery..."

KQ: And it's a distraction in that way, I think. People could say, but Kai, look, you have articles in CBC, and you've done it for sure, for sure. That recognition has been there. But I think it's a connection to the community, and at the core of what our community represents is why we have reached so far. I'm using those words loosely, but it's why we've transcended geographical boundaries and borders, when we go to South Africa that somebody around the table says, "This group of people here, this is something." Because I would say a connection to our ancestors enables our ancestors to do work and support us in unseen realms. It takes us beyond what we think. I'm not driven by a desire to say we need to perform at the Bell Centre. If it comes, it's a wonderful opportunity too. But that kind of focus is limiting, because I said to the team at the start of this year, it'll be important for some of you all to come into the schools to see what happens. When they came the first time, they said, "My God, Kai, I see what you mean." Because that's where it is. If you have little kids writing on paper what it meant for them to learn, to wake up their bodies, to make music, that is the stuff that will carry on in generations. You'll have a nice performance at the Bell Centre, but in a month or two, you'll forget. I've had some good times at the Bell Centre, but it moves on. I mean, this is life.

There's something about a deeper planting, a deeper engagement, a deeper connection that speaks louder. I think we say a lot of pots could make a lot of noise, but the empty pots, and in context, please, I'm not referring to any kind of group of artists that I know as empty, but I know that your substance is what will take you. It could make a loud noise, but the sustenance will feed you because an empty pot is an empty pot, but a pot full of chicken and rice and this and that, it sustains you more, so you feel that more. Montreal Steppers will continue to break whatever limitations or boundaries that we even have for it. I mean, there's no doubt. There's no way. To be positioned where I have people around me that are like my family and that invest in this, it's a bigger gift than I could even imagine.

TC: Impossible to describe.

KQ: We have a lot of things right now that are percolating, curating, soaking, people waiting for answers about projects. But yeah, exchange programs, residencies, work performance workshops, feeding back into generations, kids that we're teaching now coming back to teach other generations. I mean, that's the cycle of the work that will happen. It might not be with me, but whoever will take that up, we have to be very mindful of what is trying to be wiped to make sure that we are not falling for the rules. Because of course, they would want me in the big centre, but I don't know if they'll want me as a staple in pedagogy in schools, because now I get to do something with generations of students. But not everybody will see me at a big theatre. That's okay. That's a fun time. I am thinking critically of where we can plant some seeds that will grow, some trees that have roots so deep that they can't uproot them. That's in the capacity of the people who have paved the way for us. That's them. We've woken them up by stomping on the ground, and now they're like, we see you. We see you right here. Keep doing it.

TC: Look at them go, look at them go, look at them go. That's what ancestors are. Look at them go, look at them go.

RYE: We are our ancestors' wildest dreams. Truly.

Notes

1 Benette's nickname.

FROM BOYS TO MEN

by **TonyXTones (Anthony Gebrehiwot)**

TONYXTONES (ANTHONY GEBREHIWOT) SEEKS TO COMMUNICATE without language in an intimate and vulnerable way. Through photography, he portrays the vocabulary of race, masculinity, history, perception, and vulnerability. His latest series titled *From Boys to Men: The Road to Healing* is a visceral display of Black masculinity that exposes the necessary labour of unpacking learned behaviour attached to childhood trauma. Combining contrasting landscapes, Black bodies, and raw human emotion, Gebrehiwot explores the affective power of Black bodies in confronting the viewer's humanity and empathy. The photographs, arranged in a non-linear configuration, aim to destabilize the distinction between past, present, and future. Gebrehiwot's unique visual language extends across temporal sensibilities to trace the thread of trauma to its roots. The metaphors—through the selection of colour, texture, and emotional expression—encourage the viewer to place themselves in the poetry of masculine fragility.

Photographs courtesy of the Artist.

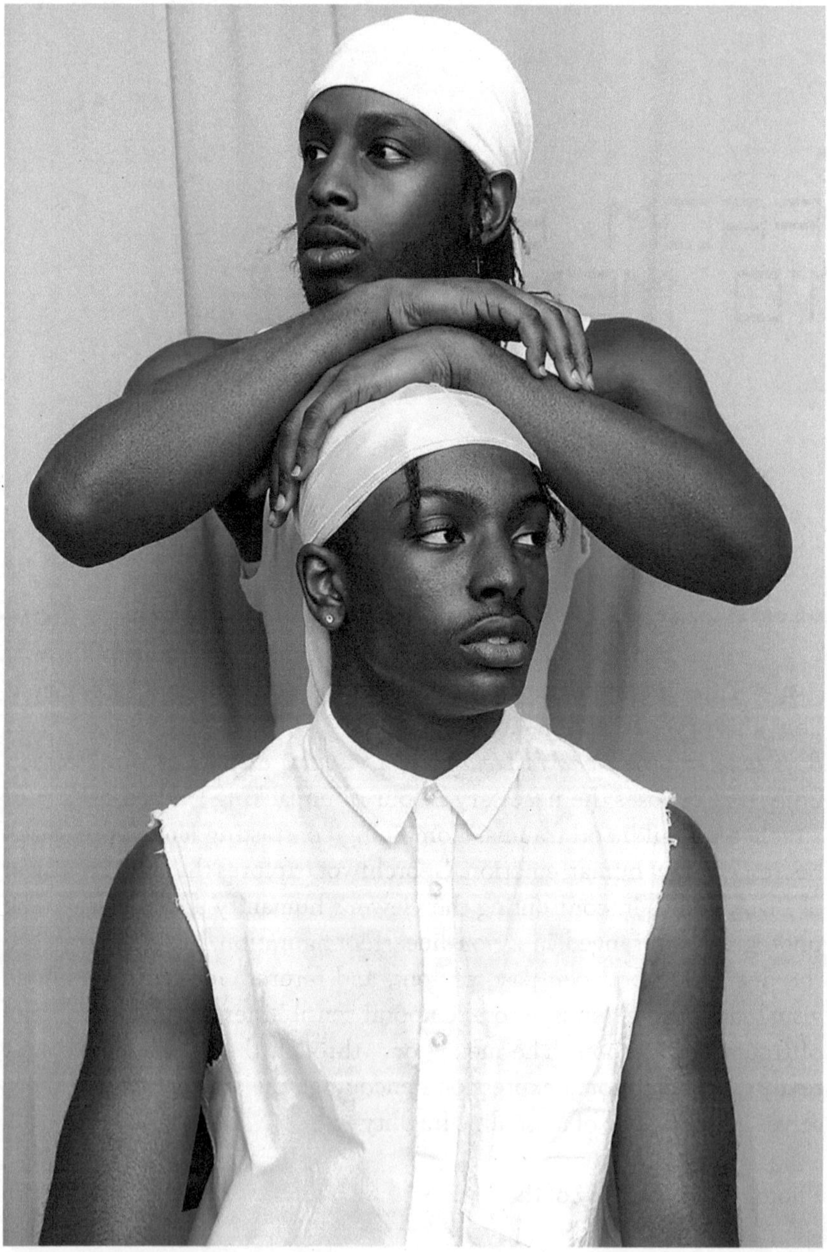

From Boys to Men 1

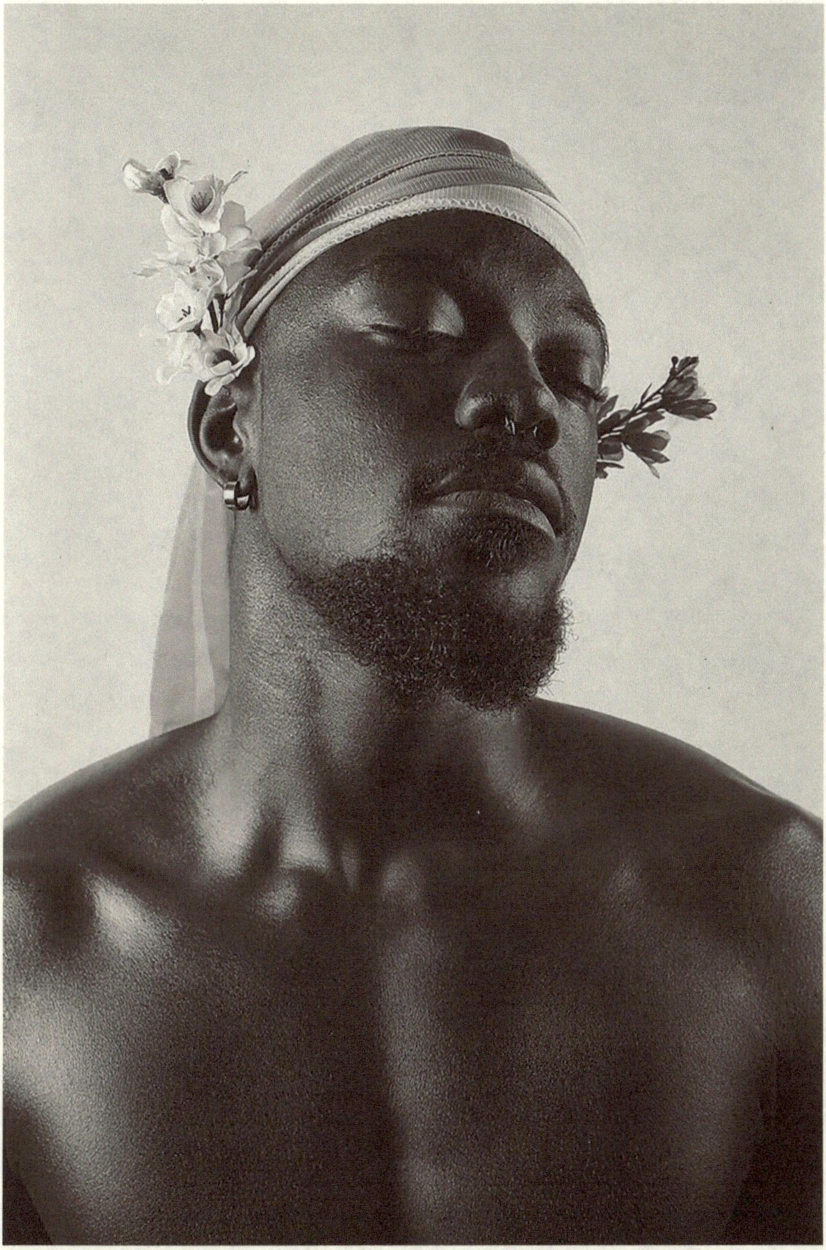

From Boys to Men 2

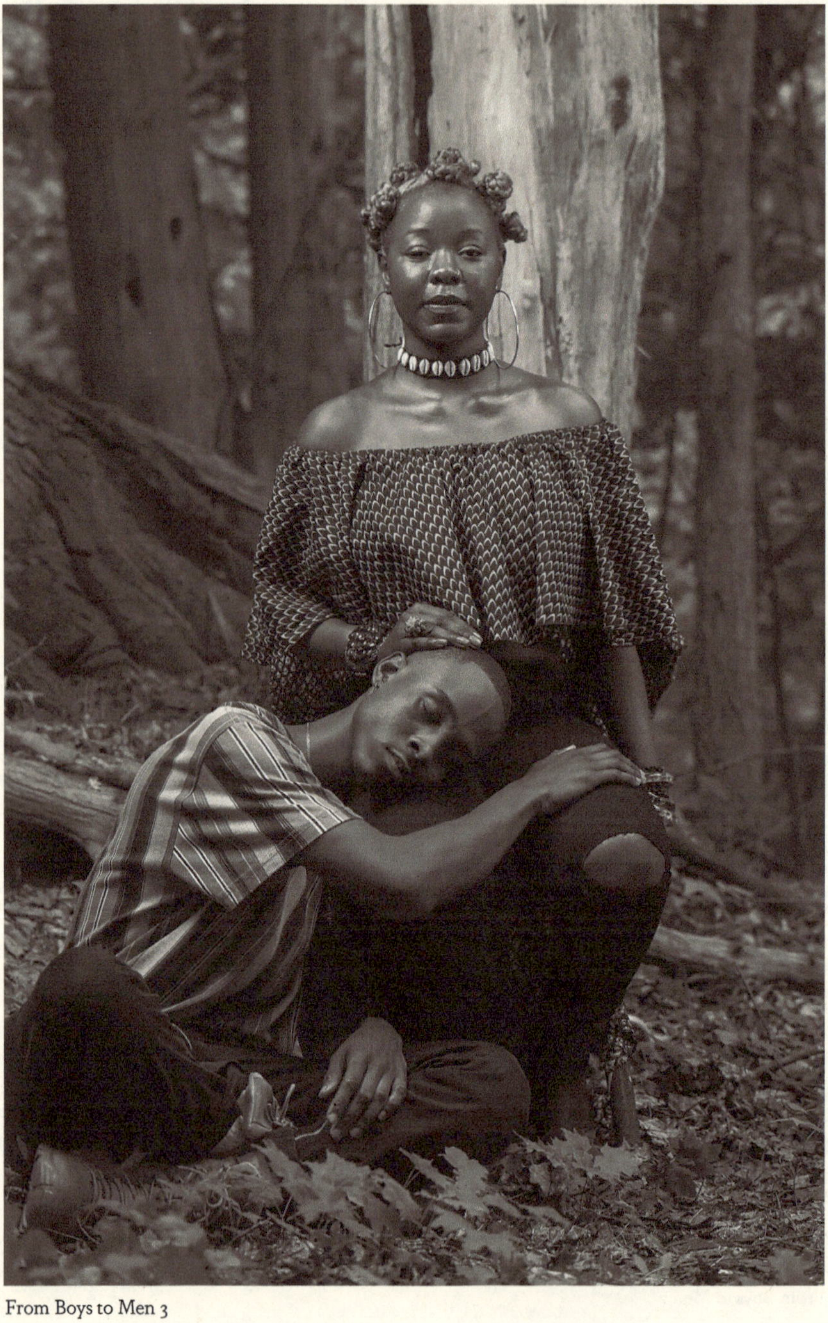

From Boys to Men 3

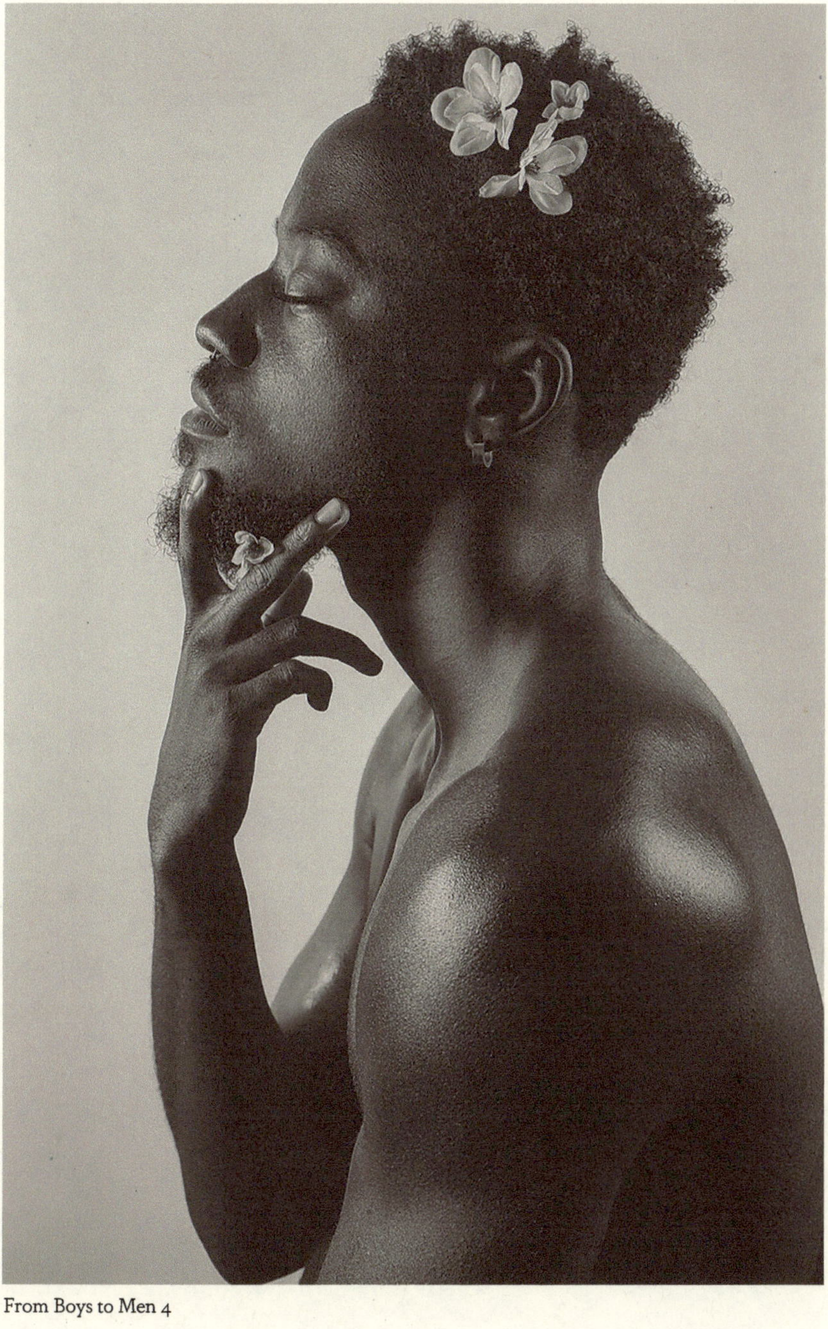

From Boys to Men 4

TAKING [JAMES] MCGILL DOWN

by **Mohammed A. Odusanya**[1]

Introduction

IN THE SUMMER OF 2020, ME AND TWO OTHER MCGILL students, Sarah Ragab and Ayo Ogunremi, co-organized the #TakeJamesDown movement in recognition of, and in response to, the pervasive anti-Black and anti-Indigenous violence that we understood to be constitutive of the origin and continued prominence of McGill University. As evidenced by our movement's name, our demands emphasized the removal of the statue of slave owner and McGill University benefactor, James McGill. We viewed this as a necessary precondition to any gesture of repair that could be offered by the university. Accordingly, we were steadfast in emphasizing that the statue's removal could never be, in and of itself, reparative. Our demands called attention to how "James McGill's wealth, politics, and deprivation of enslaved Black and Indigenous peoples' liberty" haunted the university. Thus, we argued that, "McGill University must be held accountable for the erasure of its colonial history and for the ways they choose to remember its founder."[2] We understood our actions as being directly tied to the broader, transnational movement for Black lives, which, notably, included the toppling of statues of white supremacists in cities across the world.[3]

I was keenly aware that our attempts to transform the site of the university were not without precedent. In my adolescence I had witnessed, through Twitter (now X), hashtags and cellphone-shot videos, as the South African Rhodes Must Fall protests transformed into the anti-austerity Fees Must Fall movement. Moreover, despite the lack of a formal Black Studies program offered by any Quebec university, I had benefited from the diligence of Black scholars in educating young Black people about the histories of Black student activism in Montreal including the Sir George Williams affair, the anti-apartheid activism of the late twentieth century, and the half-century-long struggle to create a Black/Africana Studies program at McGill University.[4] As a consequence, I arrived at our moment of protest with a strong conviction that our demands were not new. This knowledge shaped my perception of what I desired as the outcome of #TakeJamesDown. I perceived our protest as one that could neither triumph nor fail, but rather in our unmasking of the university's origins in transatlantic slavery, serve as an avenue through which Black struggles past and present were being carried forward.

Now, as memories of the summer of 2020 recede into our collective memory, and Black students and scholars grapple with a renewed backlash to Black scholarship and activism in the academy (itself tied to a larger centuries-long backlash to Black people's existence in public space), I look back at our efforts to transform the university's geographies and unveil its attendant imperial visuality (Mirzoeff 2011, 196).[5] In doing so, I seek to situate #TakeJamesDown within a broader genealogy of Black Canadian struggle against racism and settler colonialism that attempts to disrupt hegemonic impositions of space and place.

A Vision of Colonial Violence: The Statue of James McGill

The statue of James McGill was first placed on the downtown McGill campus at the end of the twentieth century, in celebration of the university's 175th anniversary. Sculpted by English aristocrat David Roper-Curzon, the statue was inaugurated with a colonial garden party "intended to recreate the spirit of James McGill's era."[6] Both the setting, theme, and creation of the statue sought to, as scholar rosalind hampton observes, "[create] the sense of transporting the university back in time—or rather, resurrecting and re-establishing the past in the present—with no apparent regard for the presence and perspectives of Indigenous or Black students and faculty."[7] The McGill administration's keenness to promote its coloniality was not limited to this singular commemorative event but would reinforce itself as successive generations of Black students actively avoided being in the presence of the statue,[8] in turn, entrenching McGill's reputation as a white space.[9] In this way, the administration fostered spatial, social, and temporal bounds on *who* James McGill was and, consequently, to whom the public university belonged. Differently phrased, the statue was a geographic feature that bifurcated those who could carelessly revel in their embrace of the slaver's legacy and those who carried the sobering knowledge that their ancestors could have been enslaved by him.

I recall my feelings of disgust as people would pose next to the statue, oblivious—or, perhaps, uncaring—about his enslavement of Black and Indigenous people. As I amassed an ever-growing pile of McGill emblazoned paraphernalia, I began to feel ashamed that I was all too willing to forsake my knowledge of James McGill's violence in exchange for a sense of belonging. For me, and many other Black students, the celebration of James McGill's "legacy" without acknowledgement of his role as an enslaver was not entirely distinct from the engineered whiteness of the student body, the dearth of Black faculty, and the refusal of the university to create a Black Studies department.

Contextualizing the Statue

Contrary to the "spending resurrection," described by university historian Charles Frost,[10] the life-sized figure of James McGill was decidedly unremarkable. The bronze cast statue, standing at five feet, five inches bore little resemblance to the university's founder, reflecting what Nicholas Mirzoeff terms as "loosely indexical" (Mirzoeff 2021).[11] In line with this tradition, the statue's symbolism derives not from its likeness but through its articulation of white supremacist and imperialist signs and symbols. McGill's stance, depicted as walking with a staff in hand as he confronts a blowing wind, suggests his individual tenacity and (ongoing) triumph over the natural world. This visual language references settler-colonial myths of Canada as an underutilized land settled by rugged and entrepreneurial white Europeans who—despite Canada's "inhospitable" climate (and terra nullius, or rather an absented and/or "unproductive"

Indigenous population)—were able to build a wealthy, white-majority society. As the *Reporter*'s description of James McGill reveals, the university's hagiographic commemoration of McGill as a "voyageur, merchant, magistrate, public servant and university founder," readily marries the violence of colonialism with the presumptive benevolence of the university's founding.[12]

Further, McGill University's status as an anglophone university in Quebec is important to understanding James McGill's embodiment of British imperial power. The inscription on the bronze slab at the bottom of the statue reads in part, "Colonel of the Milita, Defender of Montreal, Member of the Legislative Assembly and Executive Councillor of Lower Canada." These accolades reflect James McGill's deep enmeshment in the promotion and maintenance of British colonial dominance in North America—and implicate the university's own history of promoting white anglophone hegemony vis-à-vis declining French imperial power in North America.[13]

The university's commitment to celebrating its colonial origins continued to persist even as discourses of reconciliation became mainstream during the twenty-first century. For example, Hochelaga Rock, a memorial that commemorates a precolonial Iroquois village, was relocated opposite the statue in 2016. While this move was initiated by Michael Loft, a citizen of Kahnawà:ke (Mohawk First Nation),[14] the university's contention that this move supported its fulfillment of the Truth and Reconciliation Commission's (TRC) Call to Action #18,[15] demonstrated its willingness to appropriate decolonial discourses to neutralize the radical visions of change that otherwise threatened its foundations. Indeed, by the time #TakeJamesDown arose, James McGill's statue had, for four years, stood across this so-called tribute to a precolonial Indigenous community.

The incorporation of memorials like Hochelaga Rock into the university's geography served to erase the ongoing violence of settler colonialism, suggesting that these two antithetical markers could co-exist without interrogation. The institution's failure to relinquish the physical and symbolic space that James McGill occupied on campus is demonstrative of a narrow vision of reconciliation wherein Indigeneity could be seamlessly incorporated into a colonial status quo. Yet, the statue's secured place on the grounds of a university that bore only *his* name and celebrated only *his* likeness served as an apt reminder that McGill and his successors remained steadfast in maintaining their monopoly over visuality.

Black Canadian Geography

While not articulated as such at the time, I now recognize the #TakeJamesDown movement as an effort to disrupt the forced erasure of Black Canadian geography within the university. By seeking to transform the university *through* our contestation of its white supremacist geography and visuality, we were contesting how spatialized racial difference manifested through the simultaneous erasure of Black and Indigenous presence, and the valorization of chattel slavery and settler colonialism.

I am drawn to Katherine McKittrick's description of Black Canadian geography. She writes:

> Black Canadian geographies are permanently linked to the Canadian landscape, both historically and presently. This connection between "Black" in/and "Canada" advances two recognizable geographic processes: the domination of Canadian lands and peoples through white and European geo-political meanings, *and the rupture of these geo-political meanings by the longstanding and recent places occupied by Black communities in Canada.* (emphasis added)[16]

As organizers working within this tradition, our call for the statue's removal was not entirely *symbolic* (in the sense of seeking to change the visual field the statue occupied), but a disruption of the epistemes that McGill's status as a prominent university were predicated upon. In contesting the meaning of the statue, and by extension, James McGill's legacy, we were drawing attention to the "blood-presence" of the enslaved Black and Indigenous people whose labour the university's financial origins derived from, and the stolen land upon which his legacy—the university itself—rested.[17]

By urging the university to remove the statue of James McGill, we sought to use his absence to foreground the blood-presence of the enslaved. This impulse to make manifest *through* absence was a way to remap the campus for us, and others, by promoting inquiry about what, and whom, was absented from institutional histories. The sense of haunting, or, as McKittrick may term it, our awareness of the enslaved person's "blood visibility" that I and other Black student felt as we walked by that statue,[18] was not ours alone to carry; it was for all of those who encountered its subsequent absence to become aware of the "geographies that are violently disrupted and/or negated but hauntingly present."[19] Thus, in contesting the forced erasure of the people that James McGill enslaved, we were refusing the whitewashing and enforced ignorance regarding the existence of Black geographies on campus.

An International Black Canadian Struggle

While we were eager to counter dominant discourses that minimized or denied the existence of slavery in Quebec and Canada, I also recall that organizers of #TakeJamesDown were deliberate not to restrict our analysis of the institution's ties to transatlantic slavery to the Canadian nation state. We argued, for example, that just as important to problematize were the Redpath Family (after whom multiple buildings were named) who amassed their wealth through their investments in sugar plantations in the West Indies, and later Cuba and Brazil.[20]

My relationship, and subsequent activism contesting the enforced invisibility of Black geographies was informed, in part, by my own origins as a Yoruba/Nagô Nigerian person who had grown up in Canada. Like many Black people in this country, my connection to a Black Canadian identity was not tied to my family's duration in Canada; instead, it was forged through a sense of collective struggle informed by a political education that had taken pains to draw connections between anti-slavery, anti-colonial, and Black liberation struggles in the diaspora and on the African continent.

Although I do not directly descend from peoples who were enslaved in the Americas, I felt deeply intertwined with this collective history. As scholar Délice Mugabo points out, "Black people from the continent are often said to have no memory of or interest in the history of slavery." However, she counters that, "Black diasporic history manifests in particular ways when, through collective forms of memory, the past reveals itself to still be present...[revealing] how contemporary forms of anti-Black violence...are not confined in space or time."[21] The university's centuries-long exploitation of Black African peoples, be it through James McGill's slaveholding or early university patrons' investments in plantation economies,[22] the university's prolonged refusal to divest itself of its financial interests in apartheid South Africa,[23] or its continued investment in Canadian mining corporations that maintain significant operations in Africa[24] are apt reminders that Black diasporic and continental struggles against anti-Black violence, imperialism, and the exploitation of Indigenous Peoples are indivisible.

On Not Commemorating

Our desire for a proper institutional acknowledgement of the presence of enslavement on the lands on which the university rested was not, in my view, akin to institutional commemoration, nor did I necessarily wish for a monument to this effect. Still, my feelings on the matter were not entirely settled at the time, and as part of our demands, #TakesJamesDown organizers requested that the university create a "a permanent physical memorialization of the people enslaved and oppressed by James McGill and other actors involved in the creation of the institution."[25] The development of this monument, we asserted, must be done with the direct participation, and control, of Black and Indigenous community members.

Similar calls for memorialization have been made by others who challenged the prominence of James McGill's legacy on campus. For instance, art historian Simone Cambridge and scholar Shelley Ruth Butler persuasively argue for it, noting the paucity of monuments dedicated to slavery in Canada. They contend that the memorial must demand of those who encounter it the following:

> What are the implications for such a memorial for the descendants of the Black and Indigenous enslaved? How does a memorial acknowledge socially and politically enabled violence? Can a memorial function as a space of healing and contribute toward reparations?[26]

Nicholas Raffoul also maps, in Dr. Charmaine Nelson's uncertain *Slavery and McGill: Bicentenary Recommendations*, a robust vision of renaming and commemoration that includes, among other things, the renaming of buildings and public spaces, the establishment of an African students' cultural centre, an African Canadian contemporary art gallery, and a public monument.[27]

All these recommendations demonstrate a thoughtfulness and desire to foreground community participation within the memorialization process. Still, what continues to nag at me is whether a monument of any kind is premature, or even worse, an act of ventriloquism that imbues the memories of the enslaved with our own contemporary demands for recognition within the academy.

On Prematureness

My contention that a monument acknowledging McGill University's ties to chattel slavery may be premature is not meant to suggest that it is *undue*. Rather, I am proposing that the permanence of such a monument provides the university a means through which it can enact a narrative closure that, in turn, stifles other radical demands which have the potential to undermine its hegemony. As Christina Sharpe powerfully reminds us,

> if museums and memorials materialize a kind of reparation (repair) and enact their own pedagogies as they position visitors to have a particular experience or set of experiences about an event that is seen to be past, how does one memorialize chattel slavery and its afterlives, which are unfolding still?[28]

Far from being conjecture, the ease with which the University can appropriate marginalized histories to further its own vision was clearly demonstrated in its treatment of Hochelaga Rock. As previously argued, the University's placement of Hochelaga Rock across from the statue of James McGill betrayed its purported efforts at reconciliation.

Evidence of the institution's colonial vision is further supported by the description of the Rock on the website of the Office of Indigenous Initiatives. It states, "The Hochelaga Rock is an enduring historical marker of Indigenous history and settler–Indigenous people's interactions... The Rock marks the historical ties and use of the land by Indigenous peoples."[29] Reading this, one must ask why the university places such emphasis on historicity? One answer, I propose, is that saying so renders the ongoing violence of settler colonialism transformed into a discrete historical event, and land theft, genocide, and exploitation are recast as "settler–Indigenous people's interactions."[30] If such events are firmly past-tense, we cannot begin to conceive of settler colonialism as an ongoing structure.[31] Subsequently, one can, as the university did, congratulate oneself as having "achieved and further expanded" a TRC Call to Action. The effect of this is that we do *not* ask who continues to occupy the lands upon which those memorialized Indigenous Peoples lived, and what the obligations of those current occupiers are to contemporary Indigenous communities and Nations.

In the same vein, I have no expectation that, even with the input of Black and Indigenous community members, our voices would not be cynically subsumed into the university's broader colonial project. It remains inconceivable to me that a university that does not boast a Black Studies department and maintains financial investments in neocolonial mining operations in Africa can create a monument properly acknowledging its ties to chattel slavery and ongoing complicity in anti-Blackness globally. Memorializing, under such institutional circumstances, even if done "correctly," sets up for an encounter with the past that must necessarily seek to construct slavery as a discrete event without an afterlife. The result is that such a monument may be spectacular, in the sense of provoking emotion in those who encounter it, but it does not, it cannot, and will not offer meaningful repair.[32]

Other universities,. namely in the United States, have created monuments acknowledging institutional ties to chattel slavery. One notable example is Brown University's *Slavery Memorial* (2014) designed by African American sculptor Martin Puryear. *Slavery Memorial* was borne out of the recommendations made by the Report of the Brown University Steering Committee, initiated by then-president, Ruth Simmons.[33]

The sculpture, made of ductile cast iron, depicts a partially buried ball and chain. Brown University's website provides the following description of the work:

> The links of the chain are broken at eye level and the surface is mirrored in silver to reflect the sky above. Reminiscent of a ball and chain, the dome also represents the weight of history still half buried, while the reflected sky symbolizes hope for the future... Puryear has transformed a recognizable symbol of enslavement into a statement of recognition and hope.[34]

The artist noted that the material, ductile cast iron, was deliberately chosen for its association with industry, as opposed to bronze which is used for "heroic monuments celebrating respected realities."[35] The work, through its material and form, is meant to convey to those who are in its presence, that the memory of slavery can never be fully evacuated from our collective consciousness.

A decade after its dedication, it remains unclear to me if Black Studies professor B. Anthony Bogues's reminder that a "memorial is not only a marker that creates pause... [it] is also about things to do, recognizing work done but beckoning us forward" has been realized.[36] Brown University professor Emily A. Owens writes that since *Slavery Memorial*'s installation, many students demonstrate a general knowledge about the institution's historical relationship to slavery. She contends that student critiques of the monument often reveal a frustration that the memorial is "hidden in plain sight," having become another feature of the university's landscape. Owens notes that this sentiment is not dissimilar to how community members had felt prior to the *Report*'s commission. Still, Owens is optimistic and proposes new pedagogical initiatives and a research fellowship as potential responses.[37]

I do not disagree with Owens. But I consider, as preface and postscript, Christina Sharpe's note that, "every memorial and museum to atrocity already contains its failure."[38] What Sharpe's note brings forward for me is that a memorial to slavery's attempt to make visible or commemorate what was previously obscured by the very institution upon which it resides is always an impossibility. Indeed, we find ourselves ensnared in a Sisyphean process wherein—as articulated by Sharpe—the climate of anti-Blackness persists, facilitating deliberate forgetting and promoting institutional investment in Black exploitation and suffering.[39] This climate envelops the monument, causing it to recede into the psychic landscape even as some of us strive to bring forward and make visible the ongoing reality of anti-Black violence.

On Location and Captivity

Dr. Nelson reminds us that enslaved Black people in Quebec may have experienced displacement multiple times prior to their arrival in the colony.[40] For example, Marie-Joseph Angélique, in her testimony to a colonial court, stated that she was born in Portugal, was subsequently sold to a Flemish man before arriving in New England, and, finally, New France (Cooper 2011, 20). Nelson further notes that the small population of Africans in the colony coupled with their forced proximity to their enslavers would have meant that enslaved Africans in New France were subject to intense surveillance.[41] Despite this scrutiny, many enslaved persons still resisted their bondage by attempting escape. In fact, Nelson notes that, "the high rate of flight may indicate that Montreal's Black slaves suffered more greatly than their Caribbean Creole counterparts from *isolation, abuse or other factors* which propelled them to risk further violence by escaping" (emphasis added).[42] It is clear, then, that enslaved people in Quebec demonstrated through their resistance that the settler colony was *not* home.

Affixing our collective mourning of the people James McGill enslaved onto the grounds of a university that continues to bear their enslaver's name, in a place where they experienced gratuitous violence and incessant surveillance seems, to me, incongruent with repair. While it remains uncertain whether the individuals enslaved by McGill were born in Quebec, scholarship indicates that they likely lived with him in his home or on his property. But it was not *their* home, nor was it a place where kinship ties were easily formed. For example, Nelson tells us about Charlotte, a woman formerly enslaved by McGill, who married at the age of thirty-nine in 1802. Nelson writes that Charlotte's marriage at an advanced age for an enslaved person may indicate that McGill did not let her get married while she was enslaved by him.[43] Consequently, it was only after her manumission that she would be able to fully embrace self-definition and build her family.

Geographer Délice Mugabo is similarly skeptical about efforts to have a street named after Marie-Joseph Angélique, an enslaved woman executed in eighteenth-century Montreal. Mugabo contends that by inserting Angélique into the origin story of Montreal, a third mode of captivity (the first two being her enslavement and public execution) is enacted. She argues that such projects reflect a "representational politics that uses figures of Black struggle to cleanse the national community of a history and present of anti-Black violence."[44] McKittrick, too, pushes back against poet and scholar George Elliott Clarke's suggestion for a street to be named after Angélique. Instead, McKittrick asks us to consider that Angélique's "streetlessness and geographical absence underscore how Black Canadian geographies are lived, experienced and continually contravened."[45] For both McKittrick and Mugabo, renaming dishonours Angélique's memory by attempting to bolster a nationalist project that she (and other enslaved people) set out to destroy through their resistance.

Similarly, I am unconvinced that commemorating those whom James McGill enslaved will do little more than signal to donors, the broader public, and unknowing students that the university by virtue of memorializing has successfully reckoned with its past. The risk of this—this opening up of new possibilities of re-exploitation of the enslaved in service of the colonial project—is too great.

A Small Note on the Africville Museum

In February 2023, as part of the excursions offered during the Black Law Students Association Conference, I visited the Africville Museum. As I walked around the museum—a reconstruction of the Seaville United

Baptist Church—I was struck by how attentive to Afro Nova Scotian life it was. The museum was filled with objects and images that conveyed what life was like in Africville and demonstrated how joy existed there despite the virulent white supremacy the community was subject to. The museum guide spoke to us about the love residents had for their community, and how that affection persisted, despite their neighbourhood's physical destruction. She noted that former residents had, for instance, maintained a tradition of hosting an annual picnic and supported the education of descendants through a scholarship.

When one of us asked a community elder present why she felt it was important to continue to talk to people about Africville, she replied that she did not want what had happened to her community to happen to others. She talked about the belatedness of the apology offered by the Halifax Regional Municipality and pointed to the empty parkland around us as evidence of the unfinished nature of their redress. She was, in my recollection, keenly aware that the forces that had callously razed her community were still active and that her work of retelling was a small antidote to this ongoing violence.

The Africville Museum, to me, felt less like a memorial and more of a wake: a place where an active and ongoing loss was being identified, mourned, and fellowshipped. It did not offer visitors a facile reconciliatory narrative, nor did it calcify Africville as a community that only existed in the past. They demonstrated how one could, with care and intention, "articulate a method of encountering a past that is not past."[46]

As I revisit my memories of the Africville Museum, the impossibility of such care being enacted at the university feels, in this moment, near impossible. I sense that the desire for the university to enact, through commemoration, a premature narrative closure that renders slavery and its legacies as past rather than prologue, will subsume any radical demands we make upon it.

Conclusion

After a year of sustained pressure (including repeated vandalism), the statue of James McGill was removed from the grounds of the university in the summer of 2021. At the time, the university did not commit to its permanent removal but indicated it was unsure if the statue would be returned after repairs to it were made.[47]

I do not recall any particular emotion I felt about this development. I do know that, in the years since, I have actively attempted to forget about the summer of 2020 and #TakeJamesDown altogether. Remembering felt, and continues to be, painful. My memories of organizing for #TakeJamesDown cannot be disentangled from the incalculable collective loss I witnessed that summer.

However, looking back has also let me consider how remarkable it was that we (students, organizers, staff, and faculty) came together and demanded change. We refused to accept the university's claims to innocence. I am reminded that in our shared struggle we modelled how the "decolonizing university already exists amidst the colonial,"[48] and that if we could do it then, and are doing it again,[49] then we can do it repeatedly until we create something new.

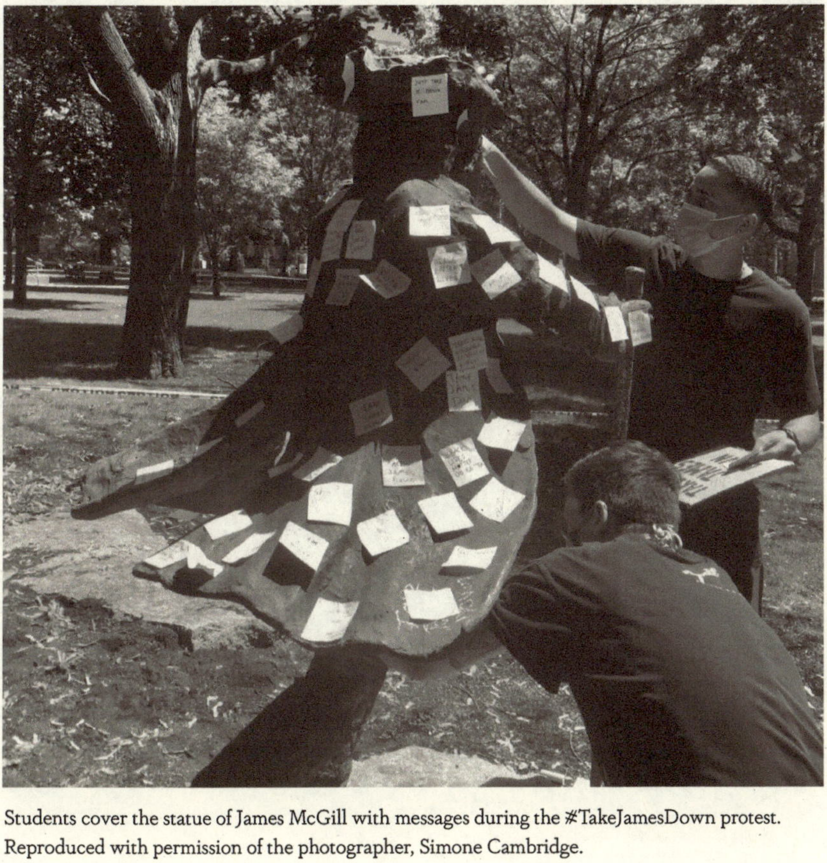

Students cover the statue of James McGill with messages during the #TakeJamesDown protest. Reproduced with permission of the photographer, Simone Cambridge.

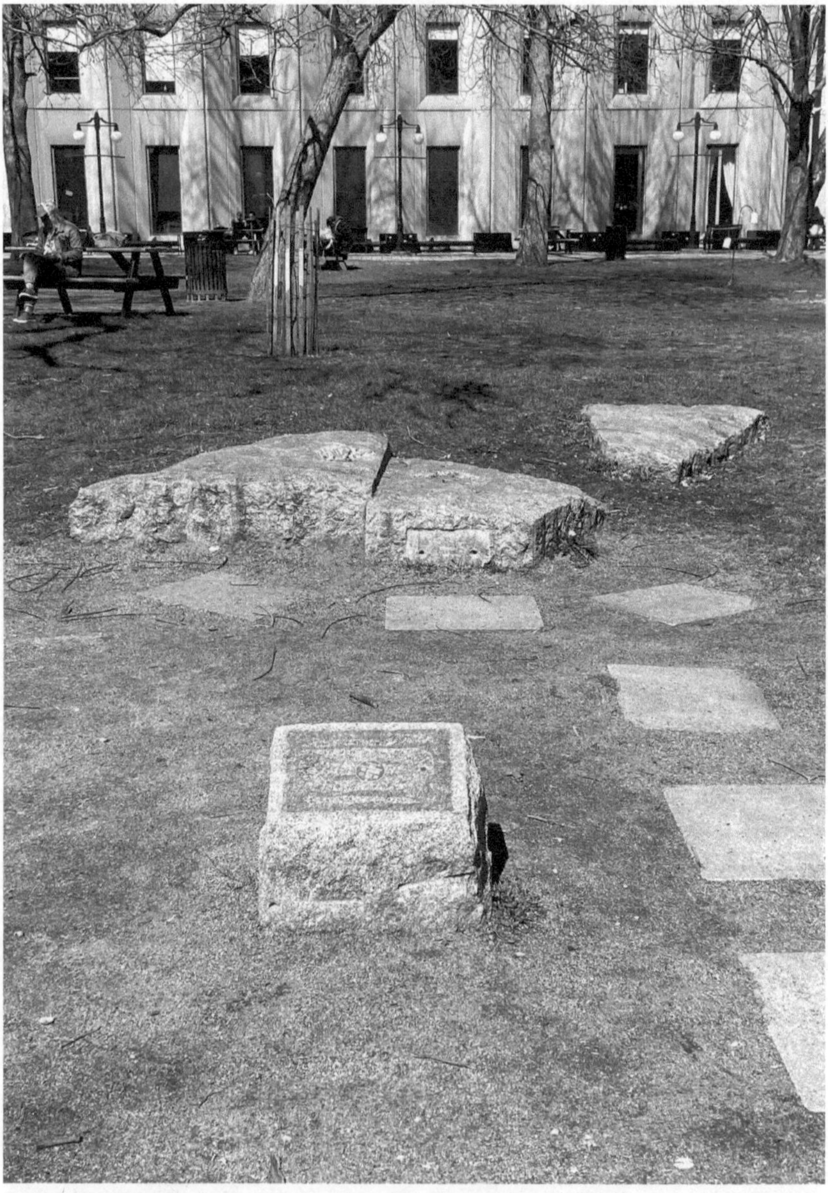

Former location of the statue of James McGill. Photograph by Mohammed A. Odusanya

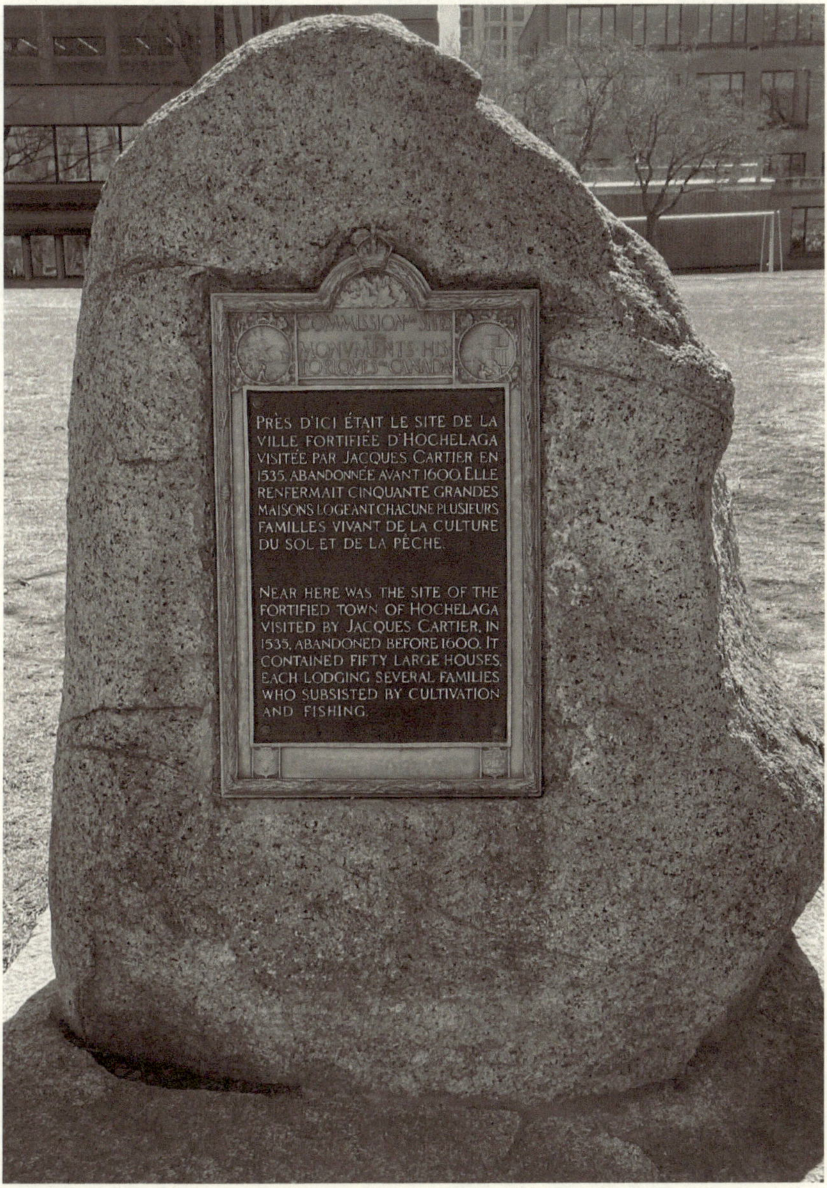

Behind Hochelaga Rock at McGill University's "Lower Field."
Photograph by Mohammed A. Odusanya.

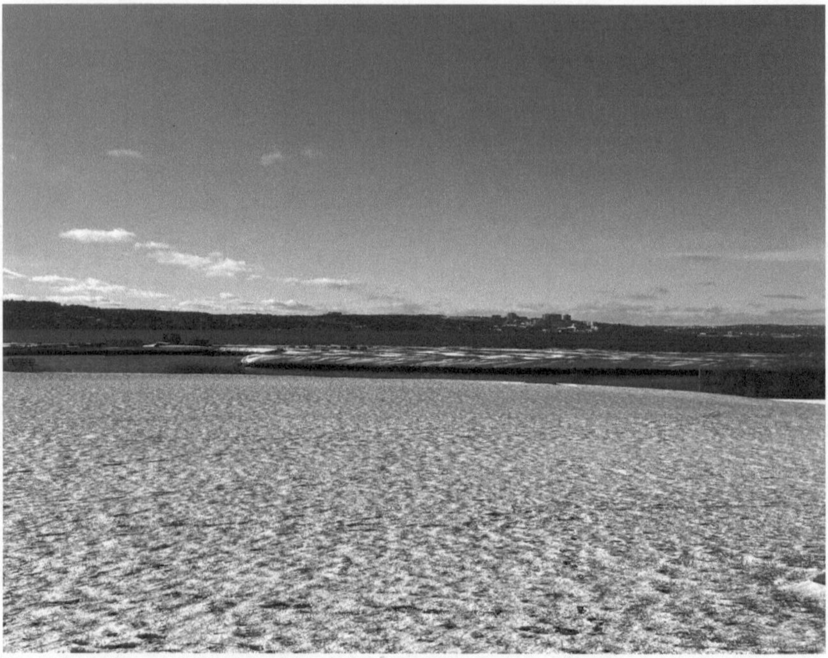

View from Africville Park, Africville. Photograph by Mohammed A. Odusanya.

Selected References

"175th Anniversary Garden Party." *McGill Reporter*. Accessed August 29, 2024. https://www.reporter-archive.mcgill.ca/Rep/r2818/garden.html.

"2. Physical Representation and Symbolic Recognition—Achieved & Further Expanded." McGill University, Office of Indigenous Initiatives. Accessed April 23, 2024. https://www.mcgill.ca/indigenous/calls-action/2-physical-representation-and-symbolic-recognition/achieved-further-expanded.

Bogues, Anthony B. "'A Memorial Is Also about Things to Do,' Transcript of Speech Delivered at Brown University." Brown University, September 27, 2014. https://news.brown.edu/articles/2014/10/bogues.

Brown, Lucy, and Emma Risdale. "Critical Biography of James McGill, Slave Owner and West Indian Merchant." In *Slavery and McGill: Bicentenary Recommendation*, edited by Charmaine Nelson, 55–60. Black Maple Magazine, 2020.

Butler, Paula. *Colonial Extractions: Race and Canadian Mining in Contemporary Africa*. University of Toronto Press, 2015.

Butler, Shelley Ruth, and Simone Cambridge. "It's Time to Commission a Memorial to Slavery at McGill University." *Hyperallergic*, August 21, 2021. https://hyperallergic.com/671979/its-time-to-commission-a-memorial-to-slavery-at-mcgill-university/.

"Canadian Inequities | As of December 31, 2023." The Royal Institution for the Advancement of Learning/McGill University, December 31, 2023. https://www.mcgill.ca/investments/files/investments/us_equities_1.pdf.

Cooper, Afua. *The Hanging of Angelique: The Untold Story of Canadian Slavery and the Burning of Old Montreal*. HarperCollins, 2011.

hampton, rosalind. *Black Racialization and Resistance at an Elite University*. University of Toronto Press, 2020.

hampton, rosalind, and Cora Lee Conway. "(Re)Call and Response: Organizing with Community-University Talks." *Canadian Journal of Higher Education* 52, no. 4 (2022): 86–106. https://doi.org/10.47678/cjhe.v52i4.189801.

High, Steven. "Little Burgundy: The Interwoven Histories of Race, Residence, and Work in Twentieth-Century Montreal." *Urban History Review* 46, no. 1 (2017): 23–44. https://doi.org/10.7202/1059112ar.

"Hochelaga Rock." McGill University, Office of Indigenous Initiatives. Accessed April 26, 2024. https://www.mcgill.ca/indigenous/about/flagship-initiatives-and-projects/hochelega-rock.

la paperson. *A Third University Is Possible*. University of Minnesota Press, 2017.

Magder, Jason. "Vandalized James McGill Statue Removed by University, May Be Relocated." *Montreal Gazette*, July 9, 2021. https://montrealgazette.com/news/local-news/vandalized-james-mcgill-statue-removed-by-university-may-be-relocated.

"Martin Puryear: Slavery Memorial." Brown Arts | Brown University. Accessed April 24, 2024. https://arts.brown.edu/spaces/public-art/collection/commissioned-memorials/martin-puryear-slavery-memorial.

McKittrick, Katherine. "'Their Blood Is There, and They Can't Throw It Out': Honouring Black Canadian Geographies." *TOPIA: Canadian Journal of Cultural Studies* 7 (May 2002): 27–37. https://doi.org/10.3138/topia.7.27.

Mirzoeff, Nicholas. "All the Monuments Must Fall #Charlottesville." *The Funambulist* 37 (2021). https://thefunambulist.net/magazine/against-genocide/all-the-monuments-must-fall-charlottesville.

Mugabo, Délice. "Captivity in Three Acts: Montreal Toponymy and the Politics of Commemorating Marie Angélique." Captivity in Three Acts: Montreal

Toponymy and The Politics of Commemorating Marie Angélique—Events—Geography and Environmental Studies. Accessed April 26, 2024. https://carleton.ca/geography/cu-events/captivity-in-three-acts-montreal-toponymy-and-the-politics-of-commemorating-marie-angelique/.

Nelson, Charmaine A. "Slavery, Geography and Empire in Nineteenth-Century Marine Landscape of Montreal and Jamaica." *Routledge*, 2017. https://doi.org/10.4324/9781315087917.

Odusanya, Mohammed, Sarah Ragab, and Ayo Ogunremi. *Enough Is Enough: Take James McGill Down (#TakeJamesDown)*, 2020. https://docs.google.com/document/d/19ZaM7OsTYMihUaH7Zq7y_Fw64gz22ZmuY316tSjehLQ/edit.

Owens, Emily A. "Teaching Slavery after the Slavery and Justice Report." *Brown University's Slavery and Justice Report*, 2021. https://doi.org/https://doi.org/10.26300/bdp.sj.owens.

Puryear, Martin. "Something in the Nature of an Industrial Artifact." Brown University, September 27, 2014. https://news.brown.edu/articles/2014/10/slavery. Transcript of speech delivered at Brown University.

Raffoul, Nicholas. "Redressing McGill's Colonial Legacy: Renaming and Commemoration." Edited by Charmaine Nelson. *Slavery and McGill: Bicentenary Recommendations*, 2020, 91–95.

Rowe, Daniel J. "Hochelaga Rock Honoured in Prominent Spot." The Eastern Door, September 26, 2016. https://easterndoor.com/2016/09/26/hochelaga-rock-honoured-in-prominent-spot/.

Sharpe, Christina Elizabeth. *In the Wake: On Blackness and Being*. Duke University Press, 2016.

Sharpe, Christina Elizabeth. *Ordinary Notes*. Macmillan Audio, 2023.

"Steering Committee on Slavery and Justice." Brown University, 2006. https://slaveryandjustice.brown.edu/sites/default/files/reports/SlaveryAndJustice2006.pdf.

Wolfe, Patrick. "Settler Colonialism and the Elimination of the Native." *Journal of Genocide Research* 8, no. 4 (December 2006): 387–409. https://doi.org/10.1080/14623520601056240.

Notes

1 I am grateful to Simone Cambridge, MA, Doctoral student (Northwestern University), for encouraging me to begin writing, once more, about the things closest to my heart: Black people and art.

2 hampton, *Black Racialization and Resistance*

3 Odusanya et al., *Enough Is Enough*.

4 There are many Black people who, through symposiums, lectures, and conversation, contributed to this knowledge. In no particular order, I recall Professor Rachel Zellars, Shanice Yarde, the Black Students' Network of McGill University archives, and the Living Black Studies conference that took place at Concordia University in 2019, as key contributors to this knowledge during my time as an undergraduate student. See also, hampton, *Black Racialization and Resistance*; Robyn Maynard, *Policing Black Lives: State Violence in Canada from Slavery to the Present* (Fernwood Publishing, 2017). One example of the tradition of fostering dialogue between Black scholars and community members in Montreal is discussed in hampton and Conway, "(Re)Call and Response."

5 Here, the use of the term "visuality" draws upon Nicholas Mirzoeff's description of imperial visuality. He writes:

> Imperial visuality was an abstracted and intensified means of ordering biopower... [and] ordered space and set boundaries to the limits of the possible, intending to make commerce the prime activity of humans within a sphere organized by Christianity and under the authority of civilization. Imperial visuality imagined a transhistorical genealogy of authority marked by a caesura of incommensurability between the "indigenous" and the "civilized."

6 *McGill Reporter* 1996, found online at https://www.reporter-archive.mcgill.ca/Rep/r2818/garden.htm on October 3, 2025

7 hampton, *Black Racialization and Resistance*, 60.

8 hampton, *Black Racialization and Resistance*, 61.

9 Montreal's broader history of segregation also contributed to the sense of isolation from local Black communities that other Black students and I felt on campus. For more on this history, see, for example, Steven High, "Little Burgundy: The Interwoven Histories... of Race, Residence, and Work in Twentieth-Century Montreal," *Urban History Review* 46, no. 1 (2017): 23–44.

10 "175th Anniversary Garden Party."

11 Mirzoeff uses Charles Sanders Pierce's theory of semiotics to describe this concept.

12 "175th Anniversary Garden Party."

13 hampton, *Black Racialization and Resistance*. rosalind hampton's discussion of McGill's position as a wealthy anglophone university in a francophone province, and the resulting tensions stemming from competing settler nationalisms, is instructive.

14 Rowe, "Hochelaga Rock Honoured in Prominent Spot."

15 (McGill University 2024)

16 McKittrick. "'Their Blood Is There'," 27–37.

17 McKittrick, "'Their Blood is There'," 27, 34.

18 While I borrow the terms blood-presence and blood-visibility to contest hegemonic geographies, the use of the term blood, both in McKittrick's original formulation and in my own understanding, does not signal a genealogical impulse. It is a method of re-marking place that emphasizes the struggle and suffering of Black people on lands that have attempted to do away with their presence.

19 McKittrick, "'Their Blood is There'," 31.

20 hampton, *Black Racialization and Resistance*, 42.

21 Mugabo. "Captivity in Three Acts."

22 hampton, *Black Racialization and Resistance*, 42–3; Brown and Risdale, "Critical Biography of James McGil," 55–60.
23 hampton, *Black Racialization and Resistance*, 126–128.
24 See: "Canadian Inequities | As of December 31, 2023"; Butler, *Colonial Extractions*. Of the corporations listed, Barrick Gold Corporation, Ivanhoe Mines, and Wheaton Precious Metals Corp, all maintain operations on the African continent. Canadian Natural Resource Limited, which is involved in oil production, has operations in South Africa and Côte d'Ivoire. For more on the relationship between race and Canadian mining operations in Africa.
25 Odusanya et al., *Enough Is Enough*.
26 Butler and Cambridge, "It's Time to Commission."
27 Raffoul, "Redressing McGill's Colonial Legacy," 91-95.
28 Sharpe, *In the Wake*, 20.
29 "2. Physical Representation and Symbolic Recognition."
30 In critiquing the university's placement of Hochelaga Rock, I do not discount the thoughtful participation of Indigenous community members within the process of relocation. As noted earlier in this essay, the decision to move Hochelaga Rock to a more prominent position on campus was prompted by Michael Loft, a former McGill professor and citizen of Kahnawà:ke. What I am trying to emphasize is McGill's commitment to coloniality means that community intentions can be subverted to promote a vision of history (and the present) that is counter to a community's vision.
31 Wolfe, "Settler Colonialism and the Elimination of the Native."
32 Sharpe, *Ordinary Notes*, 36.
33 "Steering Committee on Slavery and Justice."
34 "Martin Puryear: Slavery Memorial."
35 Puryear, "Something in the Nature."
36 Bogues, "A Memorial Is Also about Things to Do."
37 Owens, "Teaching Slavery after the Slavery."
38 Sharpe, *Ordinary Notes*, 38.
39 Sharpe, Ordinary Notes, 102–134.
40 Nelson, "Slavery, Geography and Empire," 79.
41 Nelson, "Slavery, Geography and Empire," 80.
42 Nelson, "Slavery, Geography and Empire," 77.
43 Nelson, "Slavery, Geography and Empire," 92.
44 Mugabo, "Captivity in Three Acts."
45 McKittrick, "Their Blood Is There," 35.
46 Sharpe, *In the Wake*, 13.
47 Magder, "Vandalized James McGill Statue."
48 la paperson, *A Third University Is Possible*, 52.
49 Here, I am referring to the diverse coalition of students, staff, faculty, and other community members that continue to protest the university's complicity in the oppression of the peoples of the Global South.

FRAMING THE NORTH

Black Arts Beyond the Metropolis

by **Isak Vaillancourt**

in conversation with

Dr. Ra'anaa Yaminah Ekundayo (ABD)

THE FOLLOWING IS A CONVERSATION-BASED INTERVIEW on arts and activism by comrades and cofounders of Black Lives Matter–Sudbury. Frequent artistic collaborators Isak Vaillancourt and Ra'anaa Yaminah Ekundayo delve into the importance of centring Black experiences beyond urban centres and the critical emergence of conversations of anti-Blackness through an artistic lens in Northern Ontario. With a particular emphasis on N'Swakamok (Sudbury, ON), the pair reminisce on life, community care, and organizing across the region since their arrival to activist organizing in 2020.

Ra'anaa Yaminah Ekundayo (RYE): Isak, thank you so much for chatting with me today. I'm super stoked to talk about your practice, Afrofuturism, and the experience of Black artists in Northern Ontario. Let's dive right into it. How would you describe your creative practice?

Isak Vaillancourt (IV): I like to describe my creative practice as multidisciplinary. So that mostly includes photography, a lot of portrait work, editorial work, and filmmaking. More specifically, short documentaries and video installations. I've also been doing more artistic programming, such as a series of workshops for Black, Indigenous, and racialized youth, and hosting community gatherings that bring people together. Through this programming, community members can share their lived experiences and join in creating new work regardless of whether they consider themselves artists. And I would say, my art practice is very much rooted in social justice movements, love, and care. So, I like to describe my creative practice as coming from a lens of Black healing. I am always considering Black aesthetics, queer aesthetics, and my Somali ancestry throughout my work.

I'm also interested in exploring this theme of decolonization within my work and processes. This can take many forms; for example, by embracing collaborative storytelling practices, I can actively engage with my communities throughout the filmmaking process, to ensure authentic representation and avoid mischaracterization. Also, ethical and informed consent principles are very important to my work. At each stage of the creative process, I check in with whom I'm working to ensure their agency and autonomy are central to the project. When I photograph people, I'm thinking about their aesthetics, their stories, their personalities, and their identities, especially how people dress or how people create themselves through their wardrobe. It's a collaborative and fun process. My work is a love letter to Black folks, to queer folk, to Indigenous folk. It's a love letter to my communities and other racialized kin.

RYE: I love that sentiment so much, and I think it truly is very evident in your work. The way your work has continued to progress over the past couple of years, you can see the trajectory, which is so fabulous. I'm thankful to be talking today because a lot of my work is connected to and inspired by yours, and, I mean, we work a lot in tandem, in collaboration with each other. Speaking of this, thinking back to 2020 when I was the guest curator for *Up Here 6*, I invited you to direct and produce your first short documentary *amplify*. This project was so significant, and it really did kickstart aspects of Black activist art narratives that are happening now in Northern Ontario. Can you talk about what the significance was of developing a project of this magnitude at this time?

IV: Yes, well first, throwback! 2020 feels like it was a lifetime ago, but I feel like my sense of time and how I reflect on time has changed greatly since the start of the COVID-19 pandemic. Going back to 2020, it was a really difficult time for a lot of Black folk. Especially living within Sudbury, Ontario. I vividly remember reconnecting with you at a protest in support of Black lives at the courthouse in Sudbury on May 31, 2020, and it was an incredibly transformative day for me. I remember I saw you and you were writing on a protest sign, and I thought to myself, I don't really know this person, but they have nice calligraphy, so I'm going to take a candid photo. It wasn't until later in the day that I realized we were mutuals online, so I sent the photo to you, and that sparked a wonderful creative relationship that we have nurtured ever since, which has been special to me!

Both of us were living in Sudbury at the time. Sudbury is a predominantly white town, and you being named the guest curator for *Up Here*, the largest arts and music festival in the region, was really fricking cool. It was something that Sudbury had never really seen or experienced before [i.e., putting a Black person in a leadership position for an arts festival]. *Up Here* obviously had a lot of white guilt, so they really wanted to try to appear more "diverse"—and I'm very grateful that they did because we created and produced a series of meaningful and radical projects using that little foot-out-the-door that we got during that tumultuous time in our lives.

Essentially, the idea for the documentary, titled *amplify*, was to highlight this discourse of the Black Lives Matter movement within a smaller town because, at the time, especially within mainstream news cycles, there were conversations in Toronto, there were conversations in bigger cities, in the United States. However, no one was really talking about systemic racism and its many forms within a Northern Ontario context, even though it's very real. With this documentary, we really wanted to centre the lived experiences of Black folks living specifically in Sudbury. And that's something that rarely takes place.

We were able to work on this documentary so quickly, like we honestly—from preproduction to production, to postproduction, to circulation, it was probably less than six months, which in the documentary/filmmaking world is a really short time. And honestly, this documentary was very much the catalyst for my future film-based work. After this documentary, I was truly empowered and realized that I could be a successful filmmaker and that I could produce and distribute meaningful work. This first project wouldn't have been possible without the wonderful interviewees who shared their knowledge on camera—Shana Calixte Pitawanakwat, Josephine Suorinen, and Nia Ekiyor-Katimi—so I just wanted to thank them for their kindness and willingness to be vulnerable, which isn't always easy.

RYE: It's so wild to see how far we've come from those days because I remember writing on that sign. I remember you taking the picture, and I remember at the time I was like, "I don't know if I should send him a DM [direct message] and if we should connect." I was so nervous, because I was already so enamoured with your photography. And I was like, "He's just so cool." And I was just this kid trying to figure it out. The ways in which people build these phenomenal friendships and like BLM and our artistic practices, it's all so magical. I'm just so thankful to be here in this space. And this really...I mean, this, all these questions come into each other when we start to talk about...cause they're really, I think like connecting. You and Shana Calixte Pitawanakwat, TiCarra Paquet, ER Simbagoye, and the Black Lives Matter–Sudbury folk, really have brought to the forefront this idea of community to me and like chosen family and this is the importance of that, and I know this is so evident in your practice and your life, you're always talking about it, which I love so much. What would you say community means to you and what is the relationship between community and your artistic practice?

IV: I didn't really have a lot of people who saw the world the same way that I did, and it wasn't until my early twenties where I really found other folks who were radical in their thinking and really wanted to imagine new futures, free of oppressive systems, rooted in love, care, and kinship. Over the past few years, I've been able to meet great activists and community leaders, photographers, filmmakers, and creatives, who also hold their community near to their heart. Community for me is also just being a part of a larger support system, based in mutual aid and shared values. We're all here for each other, and I truly feel that. In terms of the relationship between my community and my artistic practice, I mean it's very closely connected. My artistic practice reflects my community, and my community reflects my artistic practice. Like it's a very…a symbiotic and reciprocal relationship. For me, mostly because my artistic work is so heavily driven by my identity, which is inherently political, being Black and queer, my artistic expressions represent that and those are also the communities that I'm a part of. So, it's a very strong connection, to say the least!

RYE: Your work speaks in detail about themes surrounding Blackness, Indigeneity, and the relationship between communities through radical kinship. How do you integrate these cultural values, such as prioritizing care, community involvement, and relationships with land and ancestors into your artistic process to authentically reflect the themes explored in your work? Can you share some examples?

IV: Let's get into it! I first started really thinking about my community and my identity through the organizing work of Black Lives Matter, and it was really through that work where I was able to start unpacking systemic racism, discrimination, and the importance of culturally responsive care and incorporating culture in my life. I've learned a lot about abolition and world-building in this work as well, and that has been transformative and provided me with hope. Over the past few years, I've also had the opportunity to support the work of First Nations- and Indigenous-led organizations, and it was through this work where I noticed significant parallels between the conversations Black communities were having and the conversations Indigenous communities were also having. Topics such as lack of infrastructure, lack of culturally responsive care, overpolicing in public spaces, state violence, exclusion from fair housing and equitable housing opportunities, and I could go on for much longer. It was really through this work where I realized that there was very little discourse between these two communities, which for me is strange since I view Black liberation as being inherently tied to sovereignty for Indigenous folk on Turtle Island. Once I made these connections, I started to really understand the importance of coalition and solidarity work.

Sometime after, I started my Master of Arts in Media Production at Toronto Metropolitan University (TMU), and I had the opportunity to further explore this idea of Black and Indigenous solidarity, commonalities in injustices, and shared futures of liberation. My supervisor was Dr. Lila Pine, a new media artist and scholar of Mi'kmaq descent, and I was also supported by Dr. Rai Reece, an interdisciplinary scholar-activist and Black feminist. It was an honour being able to work alongside these two powerful community-driven researchers and practitioners. And it was through this extensive research-creation work, that I began to embody and deeply understand the connection between Black and Indigenous communities. Our connections are rooted in shared struggle against white supremacy, settler colonialism, and capitalism on Turtle Island. These systemic factors all influence our communities in very distinct ways.

Through my work, I explored this at a deeper level and learned that precolonization Indigenous Peoples in Africa, and here on Turtle Island, engaged in similar structures and practices. This included systems of mutual aid, social support networks, bartering systems, and land-based practices. Both African and Indigenous communities had strong roles and responsibilities that contributed to the well-being and unity of their societies, but of course, colonization done had to mess it up for all of us and eroded the foundation of these traditional practices. Fast forward to contemporary times, largely due to the influence of the colonial state, these shared histories and common struggles of racialized communities are overshadowed or forgotten. When advocating for priority issues, especially in dialogue with the Canadian government, these interconnected histories and solidarity efforts are truly lost. The divisive approach fostered by colonial frameworks creates a zero-attitude, making it seem that there is only one seat at the table. It's either you care about Black issues, or you care about Indigenous issues, or you care about another racialized group's issues in isolation. And oftentimes it creates an environment where it feels like our communities are pitted against each other, which is a deliberate strategy to keep us apart and prevent us from seeing the strength in unity and solidarity. We know that our struggles are interconnected and that our liberation is tied to one another, so we need to reject these imposed divisions and remove ourselves from these colonial structures. We need to create spaces and systems that truly understand and honour the diverse needs and nuances of our communities.

Ultimately, all this work led to the production of a short documentary based in research-creation, titled *Collective Resistance*. The project included a written component highlighting the historical and contemporary implications of injustice on Turtle Island, and strategies to build solidarity among Black and Indigenous communities, and the documentary built on these themes through visual storytelling. The film featured Ravyn Wngz, Afro Indigenous activist, dancer, abolitionist, and co-founder of Black Lives Matter Canada. It also featured Shanese Indoowaaboo Steele, Afro Indigenous activist, writer, educator, and founder of the Aazhganan Project, which aims to bridge the gap between Indigenous and other racialized communities. Oftentimes, Afro Indigenous folk see themselves as a bridge between their two communities, so it was special to have these two icons share their unique perspectives on the theme of solidarity work. The documentary premiered at Inside Out Film Festival last summer, and we had an opportunity to watch it at the TIFF [Toronto International Film Festival] Lightbox,[1] which was really amazing, and since then it's been screened at many film festivals across the world, including a very special hometown community screening.

With my artistic practice, I intentionally incorporate principles of respect and care into each step of the process. Ultimately, I'm here to honour and prioritize the well-being of participants and challenge colonial narratives and exploitative practices, which have become the norm in the media production world. What does that look like in practice? Well to start, it's as simple as providing equitable honorariums for folks who are sharing their knowledge on camera—I am so tired of Black and Indigenous people being expected to provide free labour—I'm over it.

RYE: You talked about *Collective Resistance*, and the work that you did at TMU. I just wanted to take a moment and celebrate this work because, I know as artists and academics: sometimes we forget to just sit in the moment. These are two award-winning documentaries: *amplify*, *Collective Resistance*, and there are likely more on the horizon. These future works will continue to transcend so many conversations and make such important space. I'm not a crier, but the first time I watched *Collective Resistance*, I sobbed, I cried. It was magical, not just like listening to what Shanese and Ravyn were saying but thinking about the process we went through to create it and how healing the process was, how community-oriented the process was. And for me, that was my first experience ever on a film set. I can never go out there and work on a "traditional Eurocentric patriarchal" set because it's never going to be the same. I'm going to be like "Where's the snacks? Where's the love, the care, and the community connection?" I'm so thankful for that perspective shift. I'd like to touch on what you were saying about this idea of the table and the ways in which dominant society suggests that "there's only one seat at the table," and it's for the one Black person or the one Indigenous person or the one racialized person with one queer person. They really pit us against each other. But the way that you talk about coalition work and being stronger away from this table is fascinating. There is space for all of us, and we just got to lean into that. I think that's magical.

IV: These systems were designed to keep us apart, right? These systems were not designed to empower us at all. I think it's important for us to look at it from a systemic lens and to really understand the larger operation at hand; the façade really fades away.

RYE: Your work often features queer persons and themes surrounding queer identity. I was wondering if you could speak to the centring of the unique experiences of queer persons of colour because there are so many layered nuances and all that.

IV: I think all my work is through a lens of intersectionality, understanding race, gender, class, sexuality, and different identity markers and how they create unique experiences. I think for myself in my film work, my artistic work is empowered by my community as a Black queer person. I'm friends with a lot of Black queer people. It's not always intentionally radical. It's just leaning on people that I surround myself with on a day-to-day basis. And it's not only until I do public speaking opportunities or when I show my work in a public context that I'm reminded that it's a political statement. And let's be real, multidimensional representation is so much more dynamic and entertaining than relying on tired-ass stereotypes and single-issue depictions [laughs]. Of course, it's always important to showcase light-hearted and hopeful stories as well. During my undergrad, I read an article titled "Suspending Damage: A Letter to Communities" by Eve Tuck, and it really reinforced my thinking around desire-based frameworks. Of course, it's important to understand and highlight the historical and contemporary trauma and violence experienced by Black folk, and queer folk, but I also want to consume and create art that answers the question: Where do we go from here? How can we empower these communities moving forward? So that's a bit of the nuance on that.

RYE: You've been talking a lot about your experiences. Ours are so different, as I grew up in the GTA and you grew up in Northern Ontario. As a Black person living in Northern Ontario, can you talk about some of the unique challenges from the radical expressions in rural communities in Northern Ontario? But how does this differ from larger cities? What's your Sudbury experience been like?

IV: I think something different in Northern Ontario, that's often forgotten by GTA folks, is that geographically we are all far apart. If you look at a map, there are a lot of vast areas in Northern Ontario and often towns are spaced out. It's harder to find your community because you're just physically so far apart. And if you don't have access to a vehicle, good luck! The public transportation systems are not ideal in the North, so without a car, you really don't have a way to easily go from one place to another. So that makes it difficult, on top of the nuances of being Black and queer in predominantly white, heteronormative spaces and institutions. Also, a big challenge is culturally responsive care—like finding a Black mental health practitioner in Sudbury is nearly impossible. But, I also think, yeah, we're often left out of conservations and narratives as well, as we know, when there's a larger discussion about race or cultural barriers at the provincial level, it's often from the perspective of folks in Toronto or Ottawa. And we're often grouped in with people that don't live in Northern Ontario and/or don't understand the realities, so it can be very frustrating.

Urban areas or metropolitans are often more progressive than rural and northern communities, so it's important to consider the politics of living in Northern Ontario and how it differs. For people like us who are trying to do this radical work, it can create a lot of additional barriers since we have less support at all levels. When I discuss social justice movements and organizing work, I'm interested in place, in the Northern Ontario aspect. I'm also interested in the history of those who have come before us in this region and have engaged in this work; however, it's hard to find those documents and traces because most of the time it's not documented in Northern Turtle Island. It's mostly

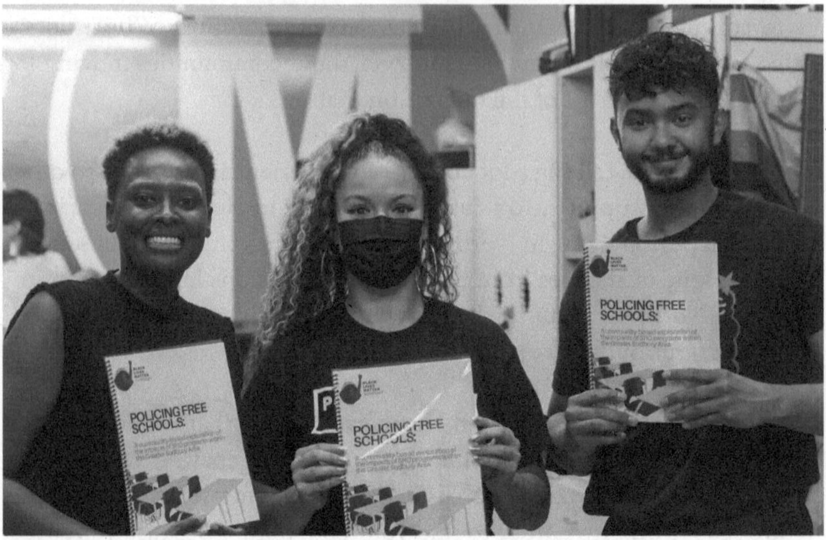

Policing Free Schools Art-Making & Social. Photograph courtesy of Isak Vaillancourt.

on-the-ground or ad hoc work, and it can be hard to find those histories. I'm very interested in building that archive and ensuring that Sudbury and folks in more northern regions have access to it as well. Sudbury is the largest city in Northern Ontario, and I also want to acknowledge that for those comrades even farther north, in Timmins, Thunder Bay, and Kenora, it can be even more taxing and difficult.

RYE: My research would not exist without you, so... There's me writing about Black people doing the work here.

IV: It's so undocumented, right? And there's some erasure as well. This is really upsetting and sad to think about, but I'm happy to know people like you and organizers from Black Lives Matter–Sudbury that are actively doing that work and building connections and ensuring that this history can be passed down to future generations to come.

RYE: The Northern Ontario perspective is so unique. We have reduced access to resources and reduced access to knowledge and documentation. People don't document things the same in Northern Ontario and rural communities, so we don't even know what exists and what doesn't exist. Black Lives Matter–Sudbury and the work that we do, a lot of it's doing the research and getting the statistics and the numbers when we think about like, the *Policing Free Schools* report and the years of work you put into that and how it took so long to even get there because the stats and the knowledge—no one was documenting it. We must be the researchers as well as the people conducting all the educational-based work as well. So, thank you for that.

IV: Yeah. It's like we're very much starting from the ground up most of the time. And that takes a lot more capacity and that takes a lot more time and a lot more energy than building onto something that already exists. And I think that's something that's important to highlight as well.

RYE: We've been talking about temporality and time, and you're talking about how time is moving differently since you've entered the activist sphere. I'm really intrigued by how your practice talks about these issues in the here and now, but it's also looking forward to the speculative tomorrow, like Afrofuturism, and this looking back, looking forward work. Your work contemplates the temporality of social justice movements, and so I am wondering how this implied atemporality has influenced your work. I'm curious about time and space and work and activism, and how it permeates in your practice.

IV: I think it's important to know your history and where your ancestors have come from. Once you have that understanding, that historical knowledge and sociopolitical context, it becomes a foundation for envisioning a stronger future. For me, I like to look ahead, dream ahead, and envision possibilities beyond the barriers we have inherited. There are so many incredible Afrofuturists, who are dreaming of new worlds free from the barriers that colonization and white supremacy have imposed on us. And honestly, that's exhilarating. It's liberating to dream of new systems and structures that are built for us and by us. Lately, I've been particularly fascinated by sci-fi and speculative futures. When you look at the sci-fi genre, Black folk are rarely represented in those visions of the future, which is a missed opportunity. My next project delves into these themes and is tentatively titled *Can You Feel It Now?* This film will explore speculative futures, Afrofuturism, and Indigenous futurism. It stars a Black woman and Indigenous man who use poetry to centralize ancestral teachings and knowledge. This project feels like a culmination of everything I've been working on in the past few years. It blends film work, research, aesthetics, solidarity efforts, and poetry into one beautiful project, and I am so excited to bring this vision to life. It's going to be an experimental way to highlight the deep connection between Black and Indigenous communities, shining a light on both Indigenous teachings and Afrodiasporic wisdom. It's about showing how these communities can find common ground and solidarity through a futuristic lens. My hope is that this project will reach folk who may not have considered the intersections and solidarities before!

RYE: I think your work is so powerful because a lot of people aren't talking about solidarity work beyond the performative land acknowledgement and ancestral acknowledgement, which, don't get me wrong, they're so important, but I think a lot of people are doing them out of this performance but aren't really talking about how we can further integrate in our practice and in our lives, and I think that's something that's so special about your work. As a Black person who is speaking about Blackness and Indigeneity, but outside of these colonial binaries but also just embodying these practices and who you are as an individual.

IV: When we talk about world-building, abolition, futurism, it can get theory-heavy, which is great. It's important to have that theoretical backing, but I think for myself, I'm really interested in how these elements and these values can be lived on the day-to-day like through the decision-making at an individual level. Because I think it's also important to practice what you've been preaching to.

RYE: Conversation done. Book closed. Finished. That's a wrap. [both laugh]

Notes

1 The flagship theatre of the Toronto International Film Festival.

ACTIVIST WALLPAPER SERIES

by **Dr. Syrus Marcus Ware**

I'M A TWIN—AND I'M CURIOUS ABOUT REPETITION. AS AN activist I've also been interested in experimenting with subtle interventions in daily life to bring about change making, such as lining residential walls with activist wallpaper. Instead of traditional toile wallpaper with its depictions of white elite frolicking in bucolic scenes, these experimental wallworks offered images of George Jackson, Ravyn Wngz, Kim Ninkuru, and OmiSoore Dryden—activists and organizers building community across the country. It is my hope that these wallworks do something when they are shown—they offer an alternative spatial landscape for the Black folks depicted within—a space where perhaps we are free, and where we can meet others fighting for justice across space and time.

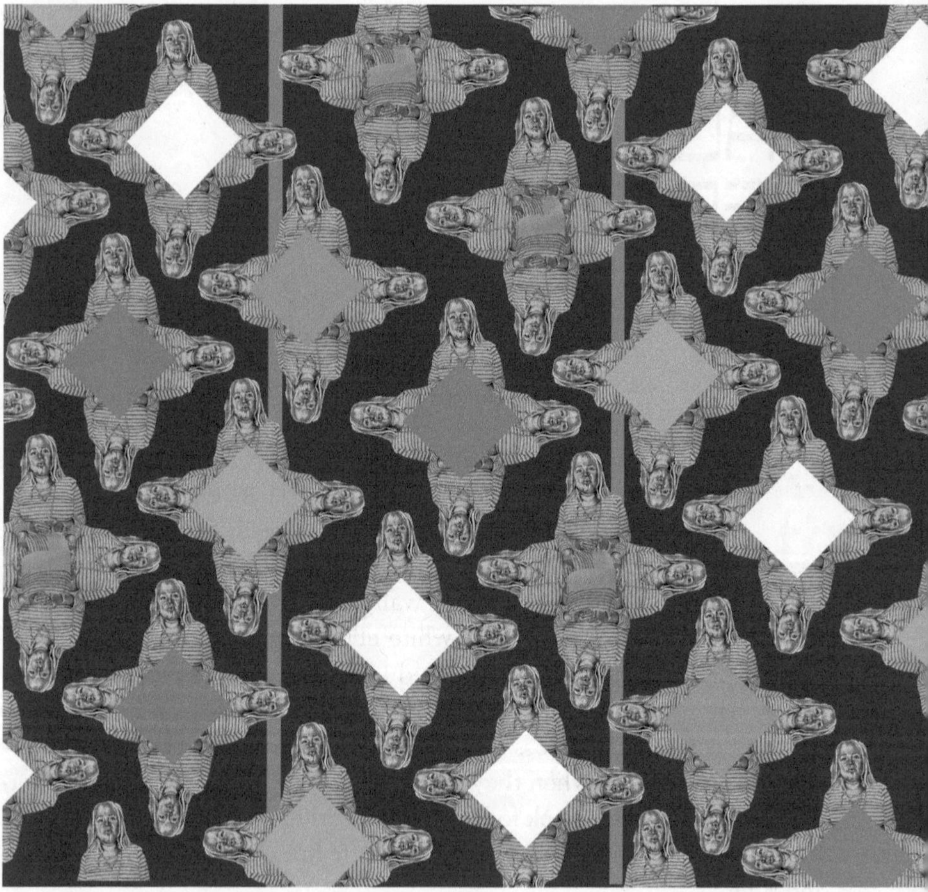

Syrus Marcus Ware. *Activist Wallpaper Series: Portrait of Dr. OmiSoore Dryden*, Zimmerli Art Museum, 2024.

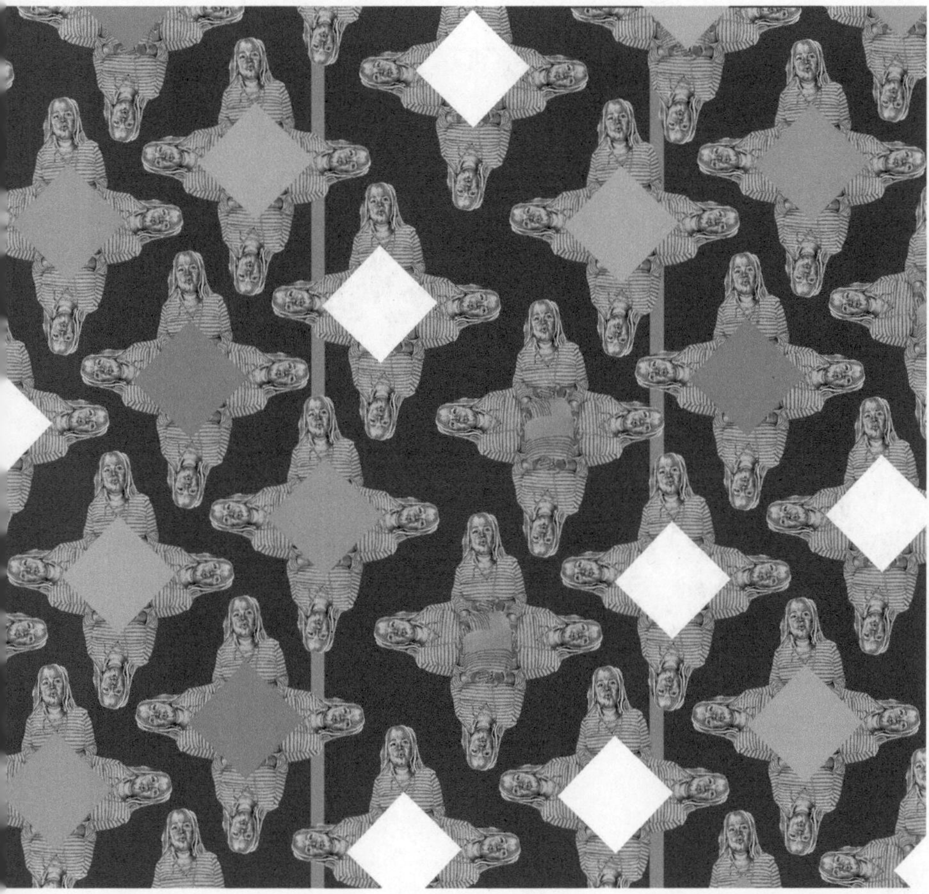

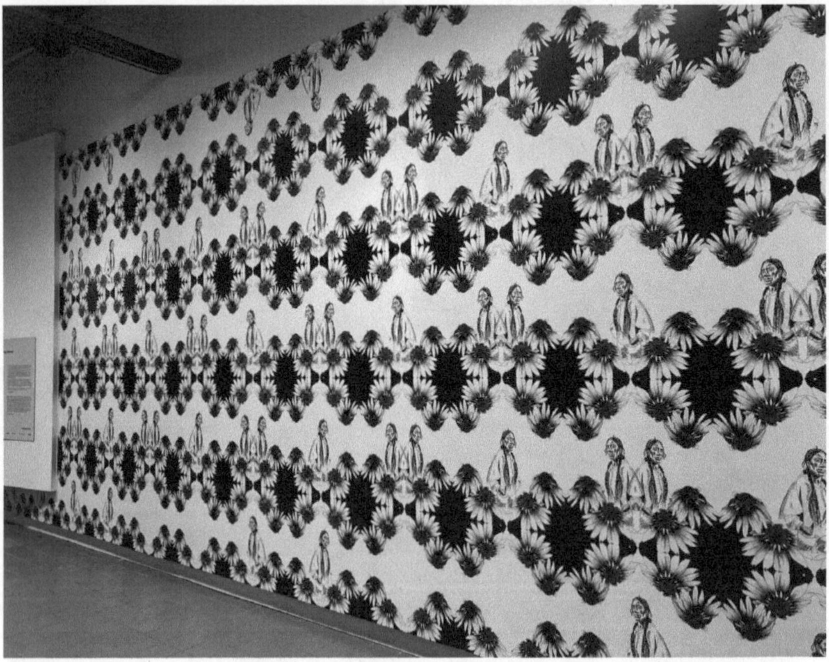

Syrus Marcus Ware. *Activist Wallpaper Series: Courage Bacchus*, 2022. Courtesy of the Artist.

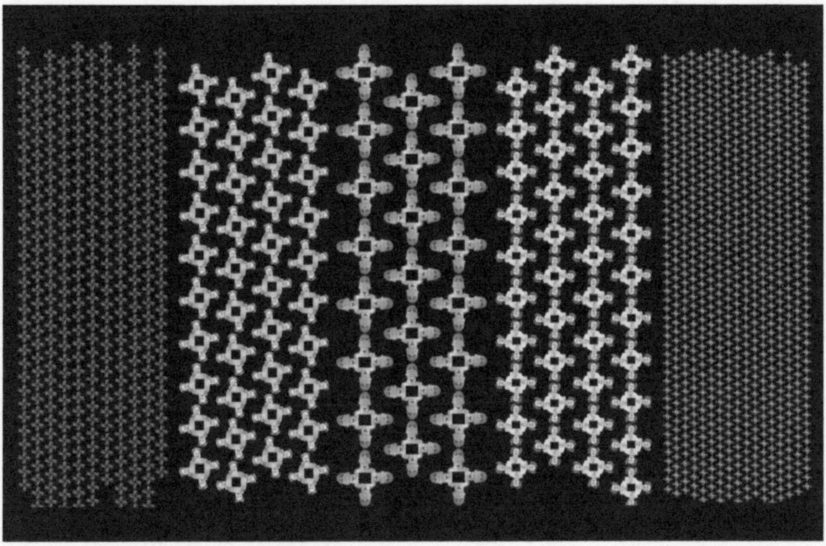

Syrus Marcus Ware. *Activist Wallpaper Series #1: Black August*, 2014. Courtesy of the Artist.

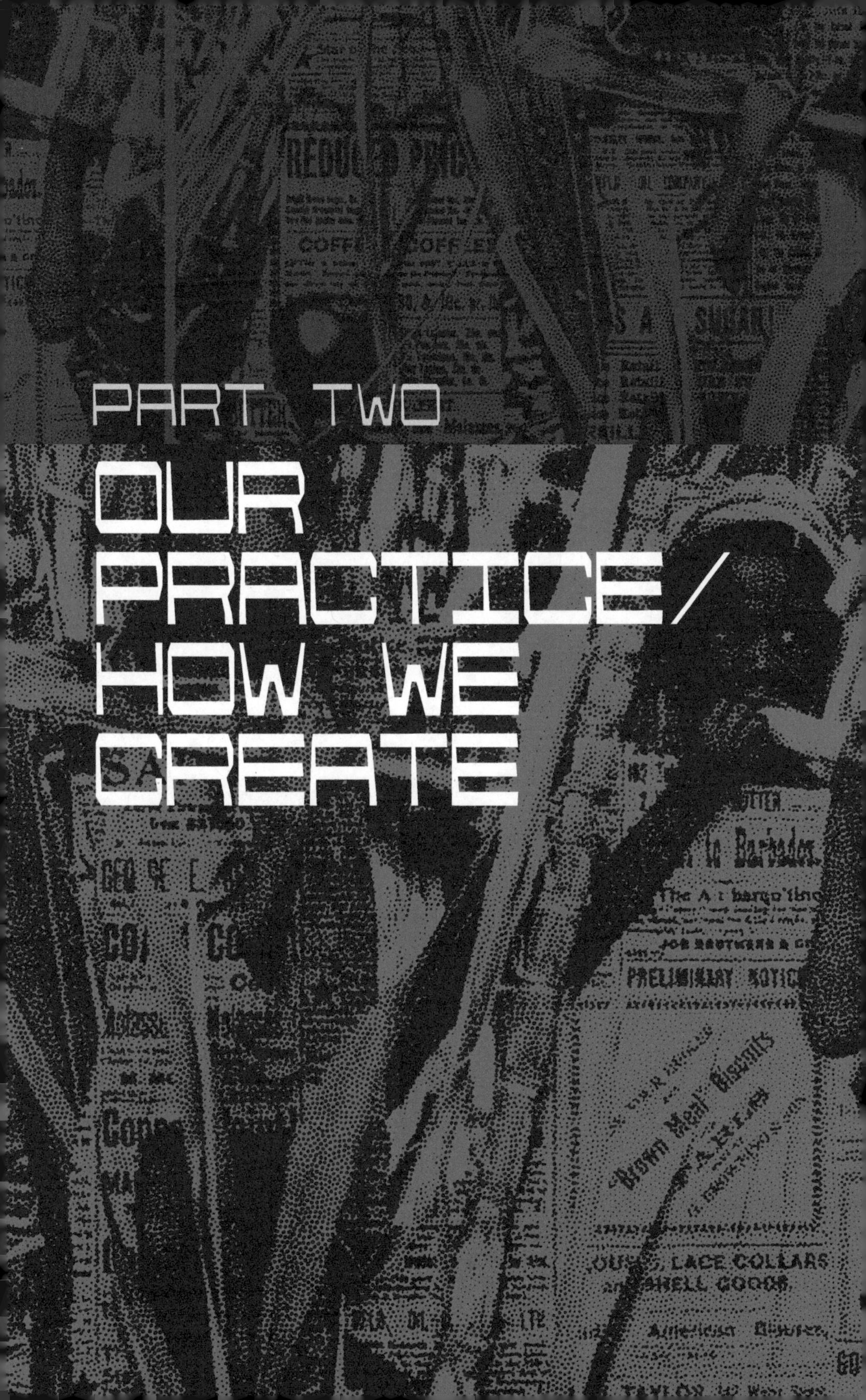

PART TWO

OUR PRACTICE/ HOW WE CREATE

THE SPIRITUAL ARTIST

by **Dr. Winsom Winsom**

in Conversation with

Dr. d'bi.young anitafrika

THIS IS AN INTERVIEW WITH DR. WINSOM WINSOM ON HER life and practice as a multidisciplinary visual artist, conducted by d'bi.young anitafrika. In this conversation, the artists consider a lifetime of work across continents and borders and relish the incredible work of a Black arts Elder.

> It was spring '92 when an anti-racism protest turned into an uprising along Toronto's Yonge Street. The protest, first in large response to the acquittals of the LAPD [Los Angeles Police Department] officers who brutalized Rodney King, later intensified when news broke that Peel Regional Police had killed a young Black man named Raymond Lawrence. This uprising, described by some as a riot, served as the catalyst for the creation of a groundbreaking, Black artist-led youth mentorship called Fresh Arts, whose visual arts section was led by Winsom Winsom, the Ashanti Maroon multimedia artist, educator and activist. Fresh Arts gave many marginalized and disenfranchised youth in the city a much-needed outlet to channel their frustrations and lived experiences into art.[1]

d'bi.young anitafrika (d'bi): Welcome, Dr. Winsom Winsom. Thank you for making the time to talk with me. I have been learning at your feet, Auntie Winsom, since I was fourteen when I visited Toronto for the first time [in the] summer [of] 1992. You were leading the Fresh Arts Visual Arts program. This moment was my introduction to Northern Turtle Island and to visual arts, and having you be the one to mentor me into the beginning of my arts practice on this land was a special rite of passage for me. Since that time, you have auntied me repeatedly, provided space for me to grow my practice as an artist, to share my work here and abroad, and to have an Elder to turn to in moments of disillusionment. It is beyond my honour to talk with you today about your life and practice.

To begin, how do you identify as an artist?

Winsom Winsom (WW): I am considered or thought of as a multimedia installation artist. I think of myself as a painter, sculptor, writer, surface textile designer, and set designer. I do a lot of set designs for theatre groups. I do everything except music, but I include music in my work by using other people's music or asking others to write music for my projects. That's who I am.

d'bi: What did your emergence as a multidisciplinary arts practitioner look like?

WW: I started doing art as far back as I can remember. At three years old I told my father that I was an artist. I did my first show at ten years old. I set up a show on the veranda of my parents' house and invited someone visiting from the States to see my work. The person looked at it and asked if I was selling them. I said yes. She saw one painting with coconut trees and the ocean and asked how much it was. I said $20, thinking $20 was like a million dollars in those days for a child. She said she didn't have the money with her but would bring it. It turned out it was my aunt. I told her she didn't have to pay, but she insisted. She went to her room and brought back twenty USD. I sold my first painting at the age of ten for $20. Years later, I realized she wanted me to know that my work was worth money. I framed the $20, but it got lost over time. That's how I started doing art.

I also started doing theatre and performing with shadow puppets. I'd put up a lamp and make puppet shows, inviting people to watch after supper. That was my theatre work at the beginning. I eventually went into making puppets and had a puppet troupe.

d'bi: What pulled you toward storytelling?

WW: It was that nobody listened to me as a child. I was a middle child, and nobody listened to me. By doing puppetry, people would see what I was saying. Sometimes, I would put what I wanted to tell them in the puppet show. If I was mad, it would come out in the show. I realized I needed to do art; it was a necessity. I made my own dyes from fruits to paint on paper. If I didn't do that, I think I would've gone crazy. I had so much in my head and so many questions. I would ask questions, but they would tell me not to worry about it. I often wondered why we were living in Jamaica and not in Africa. That was my main question. Africa seemed nicer than where we were. They would tell me I didn't know anything about Africa, but I felt like I knew a lot.

Years later, I realized people referred to me as a "throwback," meaning I was from the ancestral world, receiving messages. I would remember seeing things and knowing they were in Africa, not here. I did things without knowing why, like turning chairs upside down on the porch. My mother would get mad, but my father mentioned that his grandmother used to do that. It wasn't until I was in my fifties, when I went to Africa, that I saw it being done and learned it was to prevent spirits from sitting on the porch at night. I had been doing it since I was a child without knowing why.

A lot of things I did, I turned into games or plays because if I said I had spirit guides with me, I would be told I was strange or mentally ill. Now I know I wasn't, but back then, it was a survival mechanism to turn what I needed to do into something acceptable in my household.

d'bi: As you developed in your artistry, how did your approach to your work support your sense of personhood and beingness? Is there any connection with your self-identification as a spiritual artist?

WW: For me, being a spiritual artist means seeing all of life through a spiritual lens. Nothing happens by chance. The universe is rotating, I'm rotating, and I can be in this world at this moment and be in other worlds. So, tomorrow and today are all mixed together for me. Most of my work comes through dreams. A lot of my work comes from dreams, and I may not know what it means at the time when I dream it. I dream everything I do. Almost every night at three o'clock, I wake up with images and ideas. Some of them seem bizarre, but I feel compelled to follow them. People thought I was mentally unwell, but I knew if I didn't put these ideas out there, I would lose my mind. During the day, when I'm awake and working, it's like a constant dialogue between the spirit world and me.

The spirit world shows me things and teaches me how to do them. I just do it because I must. If I don't, I get sick—sick. Doctors couldn't figure out why, but I knew it was because I wasn't doing what I was supposed to. Once I committed to doing it, I would get better. The spirit world heals me.

d'bi: There's a deep intrinsic relationship between your personhood and the spirit world.

WW: I put out what I'm told by the spirit world. Sometimes, I look at my work and feel the need to connect it differently to the Western world because they see things differently. I balance both worlds. For example, I once dreamed of using fans in my work, and after researching, I found that fans were used in Ancient Egypt. This allowed me to connect the Western world with Africanism in a way that viewers with a Western lens would understand.

d'bi: One of those critical moments I remember was when you invited me to work with young arts practitioners in Belize. I had the opportunity to work in multiple spaces because of your community connections in the country. Could you talk about what led you there and some of the experiences you had?

WW: I spent 2000 in Belize. Funny enough, when I was getting ready to go, I was at a show opening at a photography gallery. A man was talking to me. We were discussing Belize, and I mentioned I was thinking of going there. He asked if I had been before, and I said no. He looked me up and down and said he had a place in Belize on the ocean and offered it to me. That's how I ended up in Punta Gorda. He gave me a name and said I should rent a place in town for one night and then see this person at the gas station the next morning. I followed his advice, and it turned out he had a house right on the ocean. I ended up staying there for a year, and it was the most amazing time. I swam with dolphins, not even knowing they were there until I saw them. I even wrote letters about it and am thinking of putting them together in a book.

After that year, I learned how to connect with nature in ways like what I learned in Africa. I spent time with the Dogon people in Mali, learning sacred rites and how to read the ground for signs of animals. For the year in Belize, I was by myself, facing the ocean. Marlene and Tara came down for two weeks at Christmas, but the rest of the time, I was alone. I learned to predict the weather by watching the leaves and ants. I had intense spiritual experiences.

After that year, I decided to move to Belize permanently to honour what a native shaman had told me. I wanted to live in the mountains instead of by the water. I was told in a dream and others told me too. Marlene and I were looking for a place to buy, but we couldn't find anything in town or the mountains. Then my mother got sick, and I had to return to Canada. Before she died, she told me in a dream where to find the right property. When I got back to Belize, I found the land, just as she had described it—where the hill runs backward.

I lived in Belize for nearly twenty years. During that time, I set up the Winsom Foundation, which is still going, though we haven't done much due to lack of funds. We ran art programs for kids, helping about sixty kids through school, from primary to high school. We also brought in artists from abroad because they didn't have that opportunity there. The kids who got scholarships were asked to teach others what they learned. One of the young men is now the chairman of the village. A lot of the kids have gone on to do amazing things.

After twenty years, I decided to move back to Canada because I wasn't getting much of my own personal art done, and Marlene wanted to be closer to her family. It hasn't been easy coming back. I feel isolated, especially as an older artist. I've been to events, but people don't want to hang around. Most of the people there are younger, and I often end up going back home alone. I wish galleries would have meetings where artists could gather and talk about their work. We don't have that sense of community anymore.

d'bi: Do you experience ageism as an older artist?

WW: I think ageism is alive and well in the art world. Sometimes I feel that younger artists don't think we have anything to offer because we're older, but I have so much experience and knowledge to share. Some young artists do see that and want to learn from me, but many don't. I also think about how artists get marginalized as they age. Galleries and institutions focus on younger artists because they're seen as fresh and innovative, but older artists have wisdom and depth.

d'bi: And that ageism further compounds the already existing capitalist undervaluing of your work as a Black womxn?

WW: Yes. I recently did a solo show. I was paid for the show and they also covered the expenses. But later, I found out that another artist with the same amount of space was paid ten times more. That doesn't make me feel good. Shortly after, they rented my piece to two prominent galleries.

Art should be accessible to everyone. Every student should have art in all forms. When I teach art, I try to make it fun because art should be fun. It's your joy, your spirit, that makes you alive. I used art and spirituality to reach young people. Art is a way to engage all the senses. When I do shows, I use incense, smells, and lights to create an immersive experience. I've worked with youth in prison, helping them see their worth and potential. Many of them went on to mentor others. I believe artists need a community, and we should set up community arts centres where we can live and work together.

When I was in Toronto, A Space Gallery had a program where artists could show their work and get constructive criticism. We would have social gatherings afterward, but now, I feel there's a lack of community. Teaching art to kids, I showed them the old methods and new methods, so they had every form of expression available to them. One man recently told me I influenced him so much that he decided to become an artist. He was in theatre but wanted to do something with his hands. I told him not to give up acting but to use art as a release from the pressures of being a Black actor.

d'bi: When you think of the political grassroots movements of the 1990s and compare them to now, what are your thoughts on our creative and political growth as a community?

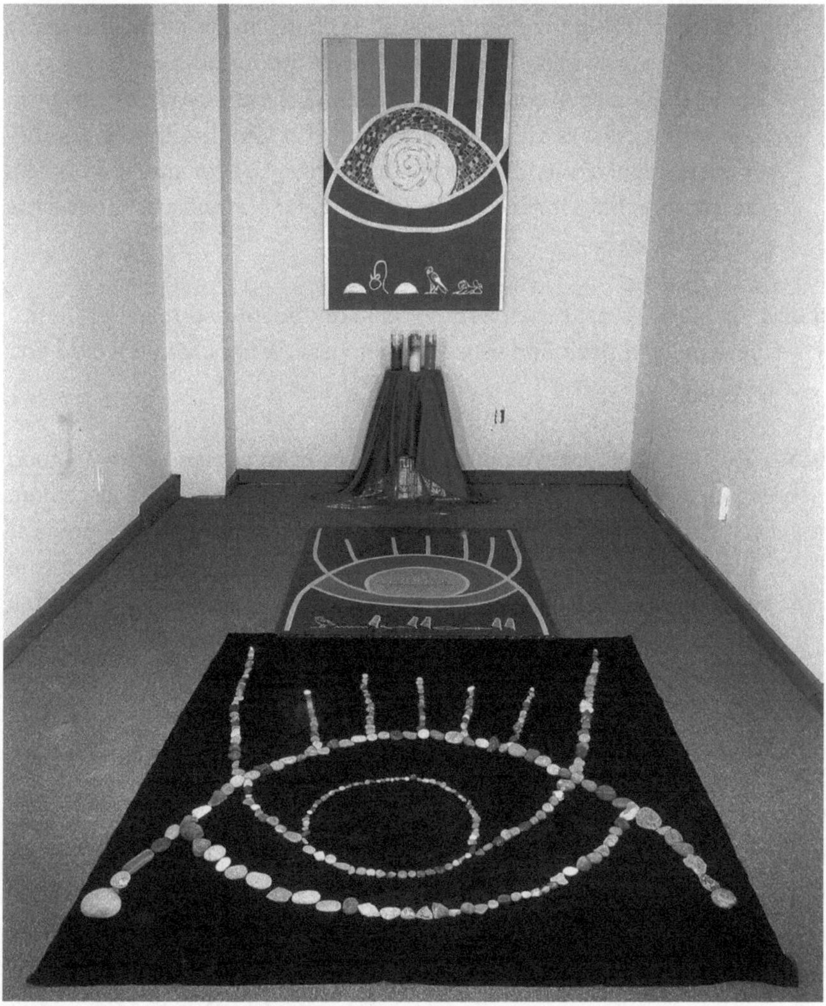

Winsom Winsom, installation view. Courtesy of the Artist.

WW: I think we've gone backwards, even beyond 1992. I know 1992 very well; the police broke my hand during a protest. I see a lot of violence today, similar to what happened back then. In Canada, I feel things are boiling over, the whole world is boiling over. Canada has money to support mental health, social programs, and arts education, but it would rather invest in wars abroad.

I remember the Fresh Arts program after the uprisings in the early nineties. I was a part of a group of activists who rallied the government to provide funding for that program. It changed the lives of so many young people including Jully Black, Trey Anthony, and even you, d'bi. We need that sense of community. In Belize, there was a stronger sense of community. I was talking to a cousin who said his circle is family—they meet regularly and support each other. But for me, it feels like there's no one here for me. I don't have anyone in the arts around me, and it feels lonely.

d'bi: I am sorry to hear that, auntie. So many people, so many of us, are experiencing a profound sense of aloneness. What change would you like to see?

WW: My ideal situation would be to be a part of an artist co-op with good people—people who are loving and communicative. A place where we can have small studios, and maybe a larger space for big projects. I'd like to see a mix of ages, not just seniors or young artists, but a true community. And I believe that senior artists should receive a living wage and have an assistant to help with their work, just like in some European countries.

d'bi: That is a beautiful vision.

WW: It is. And I hope that someday it can become a reality.

d'bi: Thank you for sharing your time, reflections, and wisdom with me today, Auntie Winsom. I appreciate you from this universe to the next. Walk good.

WW: You are welcome, d'bi. You are welcome.

References

Matharu, Pamila. "Where Were You in '92?" *AGOinsider*, September 14, 2022. https://ago.ca/agoinsider/where-were-you-92.

Notes

1 Matharu, "Where Were You in '92?"

ESU CROSSING THE MIDDLE PASSAGE

by **Dr. d'bi.young anitafrika**

synopsis

ESU CROSSING THE MIDDLE PASSAGE IS THE FIRST PLAY in d'bi.young anitafrika's Orisha Trilogy, which also features *shx mami wata* and *lukumi dub opera*. Each play experiments with formulations of biomyth, panto dub opera, Afrofuturism, and social justice activism through the lens of Yoruba Ifa spiritual tradition. In *esu crossing the middle passage*, anitafrika confronts the impact of the transatlantic enslavement system on the Black body through the character of Esu, the trickster Orisha within Yoruba cosmology. Set aboard an enslavement vessel, the play shifts between the past and the present, embodying the complexities of the Black experience through incarnations of Esu across time and space. Esu's journey sits at the crossroads between material and ethereal worlds and mirrors the intersections of gender, sexuality, race, class, and culture in a world versed in practices of harm toward Black people. esu crossing the middle passage celebrates the continued surthrival and Sankofa of Black people.

production hxrstory

esu crossing the middle passage was first presented at the storefront theatre, in partnership with the watah theatre, in april 2016, with the following company:

playwright/performer	d'bi.young anitafrika
musicians/vocalists	amina alfred and tuku
choreographer/director	bakari i. lindsay
co-choreographer/co-director	charmaine headley
musical director	tuku
set designer	rachel forbes
lighting designer	melissa joakim
sound designer	waleed abdulhamid
costume designer	holly lloyd
stage manager	kathleen jones
assistant stage manager	sashoya simpson
producer	brett haynes
associate producer	matthew hines
videography	lucius dechausay

characters/cast

ancestor 1/esu/elegua	d'bi.young anitafrika
ancestor 2/yemoja/yemaya	tuku
ancestor 3/osun/ochun	amina alfred

props

large calabash bowl
bottle of water/rum
ritual broomstick
wooden box

costume

egungun masquerade
printed bodysuit
2 abstract dresses made of fabric strips (similar to pitchy patchy)

music
2 large kpanlogo drums
musical anklelet
shekere
frikywa

■ ■ ■

prologue

egungun

the story begins in the lobby of the theatre. ancestor 2 and ancestor 3 provide instrumental accompaniment to the dance that ancestor 1 dances in egungun costume to members of the audience, representing the community masquerade.

capture

ancestor 1 stumbles (1 min) and falls to the floor as they are captured by enslavers.

as they stumble, ancestor 2 and ancestor 3 remove instruments and begin painful grunting. ancestor 2 and ancestor 3 become quiet when ancestor 1 falls to the ground fully.

while on the ground, ancestor 1 removes the egungun costume from off their head and leaves it hanging off their left shoulder.

the long walk

ancestor 1 stands and begins the long walk into the theatre space with ancestor 2 and ancestor 3 providing vocal accompaniment. ancestor 1 is following ancestor 2 and ancestor 3, being led through the audience in the corridor. everyone stops at the door. ancestor 1 is the first to go through; takes 2–3 steps and stands still inside the doorway of no return.

the doorway of no return

ancestor 2 and ancestor 3 wait two beats and then usher the audience in. ancestor 2 stands stage right, ancestor 3 on stage left, with their vocals getting louder as the audience comes in.

once the audience is in, they fade and do quiet "oohs" under the following text.

movement one

crossroads

beyond the door of no return the ancestors transition into esu, osun, and yemoja (osun and yemoja continue "oohs" quietly).

esu: esu owner of the crossroads. esu keeper of the crossway. esu protector of the crosswalk crossing corners confronting catastrophe climax contingency change change change choice esu concrete constraint convulsions compulsions. esu called by many names.

esu bypass byroad byway backstreet back-alley, esu big-trouble, esu bridge bond break the binds, esu break the bonds, esu bisection bisexual bewilderment bind.

esu disaster dilemma deadlock difficulty distress depression duress deadline direction departure detachment divergence division. esu disentanglement esu death esu deadline deadlock death death

esu extreme extremity entanglement emergency expressway eventuality. emergency, emergency exit

esu freeway fix firm fortuity farewell.

esu gathering farewell going farewell gone. esu farewell farewell

esu happening highway of hardship ahead. esu ships ahead ships ahead

esu impasse interchange intersection impact instant imperativeness irreversible incident interface imperfect.

esu juncture joining juxtaposition.

esu line lane link.

esu in this mythic mystic marketplace of messy moments melting down down down to the misadventure meeting point.

esu necessity. through attention

esu expressway tension roadway status tension esu passing throughway urgency probability pride puzzle perplexity plight predicament pressure passage passage passage

esu point of no return. doorway of no return. no return. esu *(esu glances back at the doorway of no return).*

osun and yemoja do one more big swell of "oohs," then are silent for the rest of the section.

movement two

survey

esu begins three circles around the broom and bowl. each time esu passes by the upstage side, they stop, and a different sentence or image is projected onto the floor then travels up onto their body.

movement three

libation

osun, yemoja, and esu chant together while esu is performing a libation ritual.

at the end, esu stops on the upstage side of the bowl, slowly looks up at the audience, crouches, and knocks the ground three times with the end of a ritual broomstick, then touches the broomstick to their chest once.

esu stands, sweeps a circle (starting and ending downstage), raises the broom above their head, then places it on the ground.

knocks the ground 3 times, then picks up the rum.

lifts the bottle into the air, pours 1 drop on the ground, then raises the bottle again while standing.

cross upstage right, offers the bottle, pours 3 drops, lunges backward.

cross downstage left, offers the bottle, pours 3 drops, lunges backward.

cross downstage right, does a circle in the corner, offers the bottle, pours 3 drops, lunges backward.

cross upstage left, offers the bottle, pours 3 drops, lunges backward.

cross back to centre stage, sits on their shins.

takes a sip of rum, which they spit out.

places the rum bottle in the bowl.

places hands on the ground, shoulder-width apart.

esu: call dem... call dem... call dem... call dem.

esu & osun & yemoja: call them... call them *(repeatedly)*

esu: maferefun eguni, call dem maferefun.

yemoja: olorun.

esu: mo juba olorun call them... call them *(repeatedly)*

osun: egun

esu: mo juba egun call them... call them *(repeatedly)*

osun & yemoja: *(layered on top of each other)* esu.

esu: maferefun ochun.

osun: obatala.

esu: maferefun obatala.

yemoja: ogun.

esu: maferefun ogun.

osun: shango.

esu: maferefun shango.

yemoja: ochosi.

esu: maferefun ochosi.

osun: orunla.

esu: maferefun orunla. call dem…call dem *(repeatedly)*

yemoja: yemoja.

esu: maferefun yemoja call dem…call dem…call dem…call dem.

osun: oya.

esu: maferefun oya maferefun oya maferefun.

yemoja: ochun.

esu: maferefun maferefun ochun call dem…call dem…call dem… call dem.

yemoja & osun: *(layered on top of each other)* esu…esu…esu *(repeat)*

osun & yemoja stand and cross to esu at upstage centre.

esu: esu close *(repeat)*

yemoja picks up the bowl, and osun takes up the broom, then they both press on esu's back. esu pushes them off by sitting up; osun & yemoja cross stage left and stage right.

yemoja & osun: esu close.

movement four

possession

yemoja & osun in background whispering "maferefun" repeatedly, some whispers are spoken with melody (sitting on the ground, doing a swimming scoop arms movement).

esu: mo juba olodumare, olorun, olofi.
mo juba egun mi. mo juba ancestors.
maferefun esu. maferenfun ogun.
maferefun ochosi. maferefun osun.
maferefun obatala. maferefun shango, kabio sile!
maferefun orunla. maferefun aganju.
maferefun yemoja. maferefun oya.
maferefun ochun. maferefun yewa.
maferefun dada. maferefun nana bukuu.
maferefun orishaoko. maferefun gbogbo orisha!

a large arm scoop brings esu up onto their feet.

esu: omi tutu

esu's left leg crosses toward downstage right, arms spread, right arm forward.

yemoja and osun vocals, back to centre stage, arms slowly fall.

esu: esu . . . ona tutu.

esu's right leg crosses toward downstage left, arms spread, left arm forward.

yemoja and osun vocals, back to centre stage, arms slowly fall.

esu: esu . . . ile tutu.

esu's left leg crosses toward downstage right, arms spread, right arm forward. clench fists, turn upstage.

esu: laroye tutu.

esu spreads arms again on upstage right—downstage left diagonal, open to the sides instead of front and back.

movement five

esu open the pathway

yemoja and osun create vocal sounds of hurt and pain and despair.

esu slowly drags one leg in and drops arms.

yemoja and osun do three circles around the beams and walk downstage for borderlines.

esu: esu what is dis? what is dis esu? what is dis captivity? esu who are dese ofe? I am esu open the pathway. I am esu open the pathway. how is dis journey now? how is dis journey esu? esu esu esu open the pathway. open the pathway esu. captivity clear away! esu open the pathway. come come come mek wi fly away. who can't run away jump overboard. who can't jump overboard fly away. olokun will make room for wi. dive into the sea. esu open. esu open. I say esu open the pathway. open the pathway. open the pathway!

right elbow up; left arm up; right arm up. pivots on left while turning to face downstage, legs shoulder-width apart facing downstage, arms up and crossed.

movement six

whose law—the auction block

arrival in the new world.

esu, osun, and yemoja transition to becoming elegua, ochun, and yemaya.

elegua: here we have a negro wench. 1 pound 1 pound 1 pound, 2 pound 2 pound 2 pound, 3 pound 3 pound, 4 pound 4 pound, this negro wench comes all the way from africa *(continues to auction in a speedy, unclear speech pattern)*

ochun picks up a wooden box and brings it to centre stage. yemaya moves down to centre stage. ochun slams the box down and elegua stops. yemaya and ochun zigzag across the stage like their knees are shackled, heading to stage right, while vocalizing.

elegua slowly moves their legs together then moves onto the wooden box and repeats each of the laws spoken out loud.

elegua: 1655—the law says africans are chattel and infidels.

1662—the law says any child born to an enslaved african womxn will also be enslaved. *(elegua turns and face downstage right)*

1667—the law says baptism does not bring freedom to africans. *(elegua turns and faces centre stage right)*

1668—the law says that african womxn are taxable property. *(elegua turns and faces upstage right)*

1669—the law says a white oppressor is within their rights to kill an enslaved african. *(elegua turns and faces upstage centre)*

1672—the law says anyone can kill an enslaved african. *(elegua turns to face upstage left)*

1680–1705—the law says the police are responsible for policing enslaved africans. *(elegua turns to face centre stage left)*

1680—the law says enslaved africans are forbidden to gather including at funerals.

ochun and yemaya have their left hands in front of their mouths and right hands behind their heads.

elegua turns to face downstage left. ochun and yemaya bring their hands back to their sides with palms facing forward.

elegua: 1691—the law says any white person married to an african is banished. *(elegua turns to face downtage centre, ochun and yemaya clasp hands)*

1692—the law says enslaved africans are to be denied the right to a juried trial. *(elegua places right hand on mouth, left on back of head)*

1705—the law says that free and enslaved africans do not have the right to testify as witnesses in court cases. *(elegua steps down off wooden box, takes a few steps forward while speaking)*

1787—the law says enslaved africans count as three-fifths of whites. *(elegua stops at down centre stage)*

enslaved africans are forbidden to arm themselves for either offensive or defensive purposes. punishment: twenty lashes on one's bare back. *(punishment—elegua turns upstage, head bowed, hands clenched)*

enslaved africans are forbidden to leave the plantation without the written permission of the white oppressor. punishment: twenty lashes on one's bare back. *(ochun puts hands down and turns upstage with head bowed)*

enslaved africans are forbidden to lift up their hand against any christian. punishment: thirty lashes on one's bare back. *(yemaya puts hands down and turns upstage with head bowed)*

2016—african canadians account for 2 percent of the population yet make up 6 percent of people incarcerated in federal correctional facilities and 7 percent of those serving time in the community. *(elegua stands up, walks to centre stage, and moves the auction block offstage then walks downstage left)*

2016—african americans constitute nearly 1 million of the total 2.3 million people incarcerated.

ochun moves to stage right, yemaya moves to stage left. they both walk down to the audience, then cross each other by walking across the front of the stage and landing in the downstage position.

elegua: 2016—african americans are incarcerated at nearly six times the rate of whites.

2016—together, african americans and hispanics comprise 60 percent of all prisoners.

2016—one in three african american males born today will spend time in prison during their lifetime.

ochun moves to centre stage left, then to centre stage right, then walks a couple steps upstage then goes on diagonal. yemaya follows suit.

elegua: 2016—1 in 100 african american womyn are in prison.

movement seven

border lines

elegua: seaports airports crossroads four-ways ship docks auction blocks black bodies bound

mothxr country colony imperial capital slavocracy black bodies bound

imf. world bank. un. unicef. black bodies bound.

farmworkers. domestic workers. sex workers. import. export. export. import. black bodies bound.

passports. no-ports. visas. illegals. deportation. stealing nations. stealing nations. deportations. black bodies bound.

imf. world bank. un. unicef. black bodies bound.

portugal. england. spain. france. netherlands. america. kanata. black bodies bound.

genocide. homicide. penitentiary. schools to prisons pipeline. free trade factory. black bodies bound.

genetically engineered diseases. health crisis. racial experimentation. biological warfare. black bodies bound.

seaports. airports. crossroads. four-ways. ship docks. auction blocks. black bodies bound.

elegua moves into a forward lunge with their right leg and right arm forward; then they use their left leg and left arm in a forward lunge, then they lunge forward with their right leg and both arms lunge.

yemaya and ochun take one step forward, pivot, then take one step back. repeat.

elegua: white up *(stands, arms straight up)* black down! *(gets back on the ground, crouching with arms and head down)*... no one's passing...

millions passing! millions millions passing… middle passaging… triangular trading… white mxn profiting…

yemaya and ochun cross the stage, together they do another pivot when they hit the wall.

elegua moves back into lunge movements for the rest of their lines.

elegua: esu, open the pathway… esu, esu, esu open the pathway… esu open the pathway *(in a forward lunge)* now! *(stands and spreads arms)*

elegua stands centre stage. yemaya & ochun begin 'ooooh' sounds reminiscent of the waves of the ocean. elegua gently rocks back and forth, then closes their eyes and begins to touch themself slowly all over their body; feeling their blackness, their beauty, their uniqueness, their divinity.

elegua slowly pulls their hands in to rest at their side.

movement eight

the solitary dance

with water songline

elegua slowly folds to the ground in a fetal position on right side, head toward stage left (back to audience).

one (top) leg slowly reaches out, then is quickly pulled back in.

slowly rolls one shoulder over, looks up to the ceiling, reaches up with their left hand, pushes off the ground with their right hand.

elegua slowly looks down at the ground.

turns in a circle using their arms (butt/legs still planted on ground), until they are facing stage left again.

elegua lies back down on the ground with their head down.

movement nine

yemoja

yemaya and ochun begin chanting. elegua is curled up on the floor.

voiceover: I'm a traveller. I have been my whole life.

elegua: yemoja… yemoja… yemoja

voiceover: I'm a traveller. I have been my whole life.

elegua: mothxr yemoja… yemoja… yemoja

voiceover: I'm a traveller. I have been my whole life.

elegua: yemoja. yemoja, see what they do to your children? mothxr, you see what they do to your children? yemoja, fish at your feet, shell in your hand. liberation, liberation, liberation, liberation, liberation for all womxn and mxn. mothxr, see what they do to your children?

elegua sits up on the "shell," holding on to the right side of their body on the word "liberation."

their legs are open with knees up.

elegua starts flipping side to side on each hand doing closed-fist chin-up hand movements.

elegua: umbilical cord get cut.

on the line "umbilical cord," their right arm moves across their neck to their left shoulder and they cut their right elbow out.

elegua: umbilical cord get stretch.

elegua stretches their arms out as they turn to face stage right.

elegua: umbilical cord get wrap up, wrap up, tie up, tie up.

arms making wrapping/tying motion.

elegua: umbilical cord to bury nowhere.

hands straight out to their sides. on the ground—elegua bends over to reach as far out as possible. on "bury," elegua's hands come in as if moving dirt into a pile and then come to a standstill, elegua sitting on their knees.

elegua: no tree to grow roots / no tree to plant roots.

movement ten

traveller olunike

olunike's story

voice over: I got to the border of fort erie, and as we were checking in with homeland security, they asked me if I could take a seat, until they come back and deal with me.

elegua slowly sits up, dragging their hands back to their side. d'bi is fully upright by the line "take a seat."

yemaya and ochun start walking in, circling elegua.

voice over: after waiting for two hours, they brought me to a back room and a lady came in and put on some latex gloves.

Yemaya and ochun mime putting latex gloves on, then move to the sides.

ochun on stage right, yemaya on stage left.

voice over: shx asked me to remove my clothing *(elegua waves their arms like they are being pushed from side to side)* and said that i'm going to have to undergo a full body search *(elegua moves into a plank)*, and I asked hxr "why? why does—why do I have to do that?" shx replied, "ma'am, please ref-refrain from asking questions, this is a check and you have to remove your clothing to get a full body search." this terrified me *(elegua dips down on left hip)* because I had no idea what was going on and to go with the rules of the border, because they have all the authority. I did so, and I felt very degraded because I had to bend over.

elegua moves into downward dog with legs spread wide.

voice over: then shx searched my vagina to make sure, I don't know, to make sure of what because I don't know what they were looking for, but to make sure that I didn't have something up there, *(elegua slowly turns over with right leg raised high in the air, coming down to rest on their butt, with legs spread facing us and hands raised straight up in the air)* and ah, you know they checked around my body and my mouth, and then I was asked to put my clothes back on *(elegua places their hands on their breasts)* and to wait in the room. *(elegua closes their legs, sitting on the floor)*

elegua turns over on their right side, turning to face stage left.

voice over: I waited in the room, it took another couple of hours before an investigator, *(elegua comes up onto their knees, left leg moves up)* of some sort, came into the room and started asking me questions about a female that was imprisoned, and that they believe that I knew hxr. and, so they proceeded, hx proceeded to show me a picture *(on right knee with right hand in the air, elegua does a slow turn while seeing the photo)* of this female and shx was a young, in hxr teens, white female and supposedly shx was travelling over the border with a bag of ecstasy pills. and hx proceeded to say that the gxrl said that shx knew me and that I was a part of it, and I had no idea who this gxrl was.

elegua stops and touches their arm and runs their left hand up their right arm and across their chest while slowly dropping their right arm.

voice over: at this point, i'm terrified, because i don't know what these people could possibly pin on me and lie about, to destroy my character and my future, *(elegua stands and stares at the audience, laughs with recording, then serious face)* and what are my parents gonna think, because they didn't even want me to go on this trip by myself to new york in the first place.

they did not believe me. they kept asking me those questions. they kept asking me questions, and to the point where six hours had gone by. *(elegua flops from left to right like a sleepy ragdoll: flop sideways, stand, flop the other way)* it was really early in the morning at this point, and i was falling asleep at the table; they kept banging on the table using sleep deprivation to wear me out. eventually, the investigator said to me, "you're free to go." *(elegua moves down on one knee, then opens crossroads arms when the audio says, "you're free to go.")*

movement eleven

protest! esu laroye

elegua: esu laroye!

yemaya & ochun: wah gahn gah. *(repeat. on third repetition, yemaya and ochun place their right fists in air, elegua has both arms in air)*

yemaya and elegua then move downstage to the audience, and get the main audience to join in the "wah gahn gah." they then move to side stage, and get the audience along the side(s) to join in the "wah gahn gah."

elegua has both fists in air, then arms to sides, then up again on each round; body is bobbing.

ochun starts chanting "esu laroye!" while drumming with yemaya continuing on "wah gahn gah."

elegua faces centre stage. they begin a movement sequence.

movement twelve

police

elegua: why, how, where, when, how you policing we, me police?

yemaya and ochun cross to elegua. yemaya and ochun stand and stare at elegua, reaching the upstage side of the points of the crossroads on "when."

elegua: you still policing me, police?

still refusing to protect and serve we, police?

your occupation get its inception from lurking on the outskirts of the hinterlands of the moddah land trying to enslave the nation.

your occupation get mass curation when you was policing me pon di plantation.

your occupation get further expansion when you use we for target practice in your province-created ghetto nations.

we say we don't want no blow-wow, police.

no beasts of burden pon di streets.

to beat we down and knock we to the ground.

on "ground," yemaya and ochun bend out from torso, falling to the ground on their sides.

elegua: is annodah tent city inna disya shitty. *(repeated a lot with yemaya and ochun)*

yemaya and ochun raise their right hands in fists, they both turn and walk straight to stage left and stage right, then walk down stage to end of audience.

elegua: inna disya shitty is annodah tent city, police. we're going to dance; we tenting out pon your headquarters, police. we're going to dance pon your headquarters. we're going to skank and boogie on your headquarters. we're not going anywhere, police. we're going to stay right here, through the hail and through the storm, we're going to stay right here. we camping out pon yuh headquarters. we dance and sing and shout pon yuh headquarters 'til you learn to change your dutty, dirty, stinking, racist, classist, homophobic, transphobic, ableist, misogynist, anti-indigenous, anti-people, anti-life, anti-planet. your dutty stinking behaviour right here pon ya headquarters, police!

movement thirteen

in whose name

elegua stands as projections on info regarding police killings of black people are shown on the ground or on their body. yemaya and ochun are downstage saying "asé" with each name elegua calls out (see below), a cross between acknowledgement and spiritual sound.

the projections begin on elegua's back; they are standing up centre stage.

elegua very slowly turns, with their face in profile, looking to stage left.

then, elegua slowly looks to audience.

elegua slowly walks downstage while saying the names below.

elegua: andrew loku, buddy evans, albert johnson, anthony griffins, lester donaldson, michael wade lawson, leslie presley, marcellus françois, richard moore, justin sipp, dante price, melvin lawhorne, jonathon howell, rayon rayon rayon bagnaut, raymond lawrence, bo morrison, trevor kelly, clifford coley, albert moses, arnold minors, junior manon, alwy al-nadir, reyal jensen, jardine-douglas, michael eligon, sammy sammy sammy sammy yatim, tommy anthony barnett, andrew bramwell, wayne rick williams, hugh dawson, henry musaka, eric osawe, frank anthony berry, jermaine carby, donald johnson, dwayne brown, duane christian, angelo angelo angelo clarke, nehemiah dillard, wendell allen, michael limbhard, marquez smart, jersey green, robert dumas junior, kendrech kendrech kendrech lavelle mcdade, tendai nhekairo, ervin jefferson, sharon jackson, stephen rodriguez, christopher christopher christopher kissane, atwain white, stephon watts, cameron tillman, laquan mcdonald, jeffrey holden, miguel benton, dillon mcgee, levi weaver, sergio ramos, roshad mcintosh, vonderrit myers jr, eric eric garner, michael brown, andrew loku, alex wetlauffer, sandra bland.

elegua is down centre stage by the end of the list.

movement fourteen

we cannot live without our lives

yemaya & ochun: *(singing)* we cannot live without our lives *(repeatedly, slowly moving upstage)*

elegua joins in on the third repetition.

elegua: we cannot live without our children
we rebirth ancestors as children, we rebirth ancestors as children

their arms move upward overhead, scoop downward to their front, then up again.

elegua: we, our children dying alone in concrete cages cold, erased, and alone

elegua turns to the left, in a squat with their hands on their lap. alone, elegua hugs themself in a squat on "concrete," and turns left. on "cold," elegua turns left.

elegua: we cannot live without our lives

elegua turns to the front, right arm to the right of their face.

elegua: we bludgeoned and betrayed

on "bludgeoned," elegua moves their right arm across their body, hand flat. on "betrayed," elegua moves their right arm back to the right side of their face.

elegua: by wounds and knives

on "wounds," their right hand turns in toward their face.

elegua: barbed wire and bombs

on "barbed," their left arm wiggles out.

elegua: that explode our heart

on "explode," their hands open and close,
continuing through the next two lines.

elegua: our homes, our streets
we caught in the crossfire of property and potential

on "caught," elegua's left arm slashes across their body and lands on their right thigh. their right arm is on their left thigh. on "property," both hands are on their thighs, with their arms up to the sides.

elegua: the trophies of war

on "trophies," they move both hands above their head. on "war," they move both hands in front.

elegua: silence, ownership, violence

on "silence," they move their right hand in front of their mouth; on "violence," their left hand covers their right. then, arms open.

elegua: we cannot live without our lives

elegua's body pulses inward, then out again.

elegua: we stitched lips shut

on "stitched," elegua's right hand waves across their face, then the hand is thrown away.

elegua: necks noosed broken

neck and head fall to stage left.

elegua: hands bent backward

right arm falls to sit behind their back.

elegua: cunts carved open

elegua squats, their right arm moves straight down between their legs toward the ground, then their right arm swings out to the right.

elegua: we are no feeding ground for hungry monsters of humanity

bends over, scooping the ground. repeat three times.

elegua: who eat ourselves

brings hands up, claws in front of their stomach for the next eight lines.

elegua: who eat our children who eat our water who eat out our hxrstory who eat our culture who eat our music who eat our womxn our mxn our seeds
our forests
our animals
our air
and eat our music
and eat our culture
who eat and eat and eat and eat and eat and eat and eat and eat and eat and eat
when will we have enough?

on "when," elegua crosses their left leg behind their right leg, squats and turns upstage, stands, and brings their hands down at their sides.

elegua: ancestors when is enough, enough? *(elegua asks audience repeatedly)*

on "when," elegua crosses their right leg behind their left leg, squats and turn downstage, stands, and brings their hands down at their sides.

yemaya and ochun move upstage.

elegua: who amongst us carries the sage secrets of loving? our elders? our children? who walks with the all-time knowledge of a healing love, an unapologetic love, an uncompromising love, a nonracialized love, a non-gendered love, a nondiscriminatory love?

who amongst us carries the sage secrets of loving? where are our elders? where are our children? where are the ones who walk with that knowledge? if you tell me I will sit studently by the rivers of their feet, washing away all the unknowing I have come to know relearning a language of honesty, forgiveness, compassion, empathy, integrity. who amongst us carries the sage secrets of loving?

forgive me for not loving you. how can I love you when there is fear all around me? how can I love fearlessly when there is fear all around me? how do we love, mama, when there's fear all around me? courageously, courageously? you and me?

let us begin to know, let us begin to know

elegua's right leg turns in, their flat right hand curves in toward chest.

elegua: to deeply know

elegua's left leg turns in, their body moves, their flat left hand curves in toward their chest to make a heart shape. they end in a forward lunge with their left leg out, facing downstage right.

elegua: that we indeed make this world go round

on "we," elegua breathes in. on "indeed," they breathe out, then open their body and open arms wide.

elegua: that this 365 days of r/evolution around the sun

their right arm does full revolution, which ends on second "revolution."

elegua: is a r/evolution brewing in the witch's cauldron

their right arm and left arm mime a stirring motion.

elegua: because the times of whippings, lynchings, stakes, and burnings must end

on "whippings," elegua's right arm goes up; on "lynchings," their right arm down; on "stakes," their left arm goes up; on "burnings," their left arm down.

elegua: shootings must end
shootings must end
shootings must end
hate, hate, hate must end
hate must end
hate must end
hate must end
love, love love, love

on "must," they bring their arms out, moving toward each other.

on "end," they clap their hands together.

elegua gets down on their shins and opens their hands to eat. they rest their hands on their heart and breathe, calming down. they put their right arm up and left arm down, then both hands go up and cross in the air.

movement fifteen

gogo

elegua is still standing down centre stage. yemaya and ochun are standing upstage in the curve. ochun is on stage right and yemaya is on stage left.

yemaya: I am the daughtxr of a mothxr.

elegua giggles.

yemaya: tra la la la la la
who is the daughtxr of a womxn, tra la la la la la

elegua chimes in singing "tra la la la la la" then does a circle around the crossroads.

ochun: I am the child of a mothxr, tra la la la la la
who is the child of a womxn, tra la la la la la

elegua chimes in singing "tra la la la la la" then does a circle around the crossroads.

elegua then sits down at centre stage, just upstage of the crossroads.

yemaya and ochun: and we cannot live without our lives! *(repeat five times)*

everyone starts to move to centre stage.

elegua sings the "esu laroye" song as a child and skips around.

yemaya and ochun move in toward elegua.

yemaya kneels behind elegua, ochun stands behind elegua.

elegua: granny look at what I've planted. granny thank you for raising mommy. thank you for raising me. every day you comb my hair, feed me, prepare mi food, and take me to school. tell me stories about esu and yemoja and oya and ochun. granny I love it when you hug me tight and I wrap your arms all across my body and hold me tight tight tight granny. my arms all around your body. my arms are too short but yours bundle me up, and I remember way back to when I was a baby. granny, your arms make me feel so good and safe. granny, I love it when you look into my eyes like this because then I know I'm a very special somebody. granny, I wish that all the grandchildren in the world had grannies like you to love them, granny. when I grow up, I want to be a grandmothxr just like you. they make the whole world feel like sunshine, and I know when I look into your eyes that I am a very special somebody.

yemaya and ochun nod.

elegua: if people treated each other the way that you treat me granny, oh the world would be full of joy and full of so many happy children. when I grow up, I want to be a grandmothxr just like you. the whole entire world should have grandmothxrs like you to love grandchildren like me.

granny, what is me? what is at the centre of me? the burning core of me, like, the burning core of the earth. what makes my body work? my cells, my organs, my muscles, my limbs? wrapped up in my skin. what does this skin mean? this brown chocolatey skin that I am wrapped in.

yemaya puts their arms on elegua's shoulders.

elegua: is it the same as other skins? is it different, granny? what sits at the centre of me?

yemaya and ochun sing "love," then place one hand on each of elegua's shoulders in front. yemaya moves head to elegua's left side, and ochun moves head to elegua's right side.

elegua: love?

yemaya and ochun sing "love."

elegua: love sits at the centre of me, granny? is that why you love me so much? because I am made of love? is everybody made of love, granny? are the little gxrls who sleep on the streets who have nowhere to live, nothing to eat, no shoes on their feet, are they made of love?

yemaya and ochun slightly shake their heads.

elegua: the little gxrls who look just like me? the little black gxrls who look just like me? is everybody made of love?

if you love somebody, how do you treat them?

and if you don't love them, do you get to hurt them? why don't some people love other people, granny? and why, when someone says they love you, do they still get to hurt you too? why do some people hurt other people, granny?

ochun: *(sings)* fear

yemaya sits stage right of elegua, ochun sits stage left; they sit with their legs out toward centre stage.

elegua: fear? fear, granny? fear of what?

yemaya: *(sings)* fear

elegua: you know what I'm most afraid of? if you go away like daddy to that never never place and never come back, then I will be alone, all alone in this big place. I don't want you to go to that never never place like daddy; are you afraid of that too? why did they send daddy to that never never place?

granny, what are you most afraid of? granny, you know how sometimes you send me to bed and I am not ready to go but you make me? are you made to do things that you don't want to do, granny? how does it feel on the inside of you? does that make you afraid? I don't like the feeling of doing things I don't want to do.

granny, why are we here alive together now? what are we meant to do with our time? how will we feel about each other tomorrow? how will we feel about each other today?

you know, yesterday I was over by suzy's house, and I was telling hxr about all the stories you tell me about oshun and obatala, and, and, shx brought out hxr dollies, granny, and I asked hxr if I could play with hxr dollies, and shx said no. how will we protect ourselves from harm? how will we decide who else to protect? what is the value of our lives? granny, why don't some people like to share with other people?

yemaya & ochun: *(sing)* greed

yemaya and ochun start slowly standing up, and stand just behind elegua while they speak.

elegua: greed granny? does that mean suzy's greedy? granny you know yesterday suzy was telling me about hxr axntie who went across the the the border, and I ask suzy what is the border and shx brought out a big piece of paper with lots and lots and lots of lines and I asked hxr what are those lines and shx said those were the borders. but who decides those lines granny? who decides where those lines are drawn on that piece of paper granny what is fairness? who decides what is fair and what is not fair? granny what binds our lives together with all the people in the village, in the country, in the world?

yemaya and ochun are standing upright looking down at elegua.

yemaya & ochun: *(sing)* power

elegua: power, granny? what binds us all together in the world. is it the type of hair that I have?

yemaya and ochun lift elegua.

elegua: is it the colour of my skin, granny? is it the amount of money that we have, granny? or, whether or not we have a bank account? suzy said shx had a bank account. do we have a bank account? or, is it whether or not we have a passport, granny? suzy said shx had a passport, do we have a passport? what binds us together?

is it the type of hair that we have, or the colour of our eyes, or the blood that flows in our veins, or the blood that spills from our bodies, or is it the amount of money we have, or whether or not we have a bank account or a passport?

granny, what are borders and who decides where they are drawn?

granny, how did the world come to be this way? can we change it, granny? do we want to change it? granny, I am tired. is that how you feel when you get old? you feel tired like me right now? will I get old granny, like you? will I die? will I be killed?

yemaya and ochun rest their hand on elegua's shoulder.

elegua: granny, I don't want to die. granny, I don't want to be killed.

ochun: *(sings)* everything is born and everything dies.

yemaya: *(sings)* even the sun shining above will die someday.

yemaya crosses down stage left to pick up egungun costume; ochun is washing elegua centre stage.

ochun: *(sings)* it is the moments in between that matter.

yemaya crosses to stage left side of elegua.

ochun: *(sings)* the choices that we make in those moments that matter.

yemaya: *(sings)* there are always choices to make at the crossroads.

ochun: *(sings)* remember what esu teaches us? iwapele: be of good character.

elegua: yes, granny.

yemaya: *(sings while holding egungun costume up)* choose wisely, choose carefully, choose with a good head and a good heart.

ochun: *(sings)* choose wisely, choose carefully, choose with a good head and a good heart.

yemaya & ochun: *(sing)* you ready?

elegua: yes, granny.

yemaya places the egungun costume on elegua's head.

yemaya: *(sings)* dance for the ancestors, child. dance egungun for your ancestors.

yemaya and ochun begin to sing the esu barak bo song. elegua, as the child, dances the egungun dance for the ancestors, moving into the audience with yemaya and ochun following.

elegua spins in a circle, bent over, does four circles, then stops. elegua's arms continue, then they drop and swing their arms around to the other side, and a third time. then elegua drops and circles upstage left. elegua pushes forward on their right leg, then back. they put their arms together and spin to face downstage; pushing forward on their left leg three times, then turning to face stage right. elegua then steps forward (left, right, and left), then walks backward (right, left, and right) all the way down to centre stage. elegua does two turns, then exits through the doorway of no return with yemaya and ochun following!

end

. . .

Excerpt from *esu crossing the middle passage*, reprinted with permission of the author.

WE GATHER

On the Work *We Gather* by Sandra Brewster

by **Erica N. Cardwell**

I VISITED SANDRA BREWSTER'S HOME STUDIO DURING A moment of protest writ large. It was late March 2024, and for nearly six months, the world had been watching the state of Israel ruthlessly brutalize innocent Palestinians. Outside, a biting late winter chill swirled under the grey afternoon sky.

Inside, Brewster's home was warm and inviting. Brewster was playing music for a concert she hoped to attend with friends later that evening. Her house had a circular framing—several rooms that open onto others. Her kitchen was filled with jars of spices and teas. She doesn't have coffee, she told me. I didn't want coffee. She makes turmeric tea. The music didn't quite match the vibe, so Brewster quickly changed it to *The Omnichord Real Book*, the most recent album by Meshell Ndegeocello, which lent a soothing, unintrusive rhythm to the foreground. That day, the art workers at the Art Gallery of Ontario were on strike for better compensation. This context was top of mind, so we quickly open Instagram, the twenty-first-century town square, seeking updates from friends.

Protest signs declare: "Show Me the Monet" and "Modern Art/Medieval Wages"

We shared a laugh about how artists and curators make some of the best protest signs. This was an intimacy that I craved in the pandemic days.

This is a reflective association on how the zeitgeist has truly reshaped our methods of gathering. A casualty of the pandemic as described by Brewster was "the importance of gathering," an element of life we were each required to avoid, now compartmentalized as we reflect on that experience of shared isolation. It is a time that feels both near and far, its nearness counted by fewer documented cases of COVID now, the lone presence of a masked person on the subway, or even the sound of a lingering cough in the distance. Certain pinnacles of life have disappeared or have been replaced, be it a loved one or a complete occupation, altogether.

Cutting down the centre of 2020 were the racial uprisings in the wake of the murder of George Floyd. In 2024, it will be four years since Floyd was killed. In the video taken by the then seventeen-year-old, the world watched as Floyd died underneath the knee of law enforcement, Chauvin's eyes ablaze. Despite the horror of this moment, I have always believed that this wasn't the primary rallying cry to hit the streets for certain members of the collective. Grief, certainly, but there was something else crawling under the surface. "The importance of gathering" might have been the emphatic reasoning, a disposition that measured risk with relationship.

Elements from Brewster's signature exhibition, *Blur*, appear throughout her home. Several of these large-scale works featuring Brewster's notable approach to Black figuration languished in a friendly, easeful manner throughout her house. Before tilting each image to observe the next, I asked if I could look more closely. Brewster replied, "Sure, you can pull them out too." Her openness mimicked the tone of her home, inviting and in conversation. Brewster and I had met, having been introduced to each other by a mutual friend, before this studio visit. Once, we even marched alongside each other at a pro-Palestine protest in Downtown Toronto. Each time, we skipped the small talk and immediately spoke with frank, emotional detail about the helpless casualties, eventually divulging business typically saved for close relations. Her energy invites such comfortable disclosure. Much like her artistic practice, Brewster is always inside of thought and quick to bring you along.

While studying at the University of Toronto, Brewster focused on gel transfer, noticeable in the *Blur* series. It is her painting background that piqued my interest, the intentional pixelation and additions of colour enhancing or obscuring recognizable shapes: "[I use] colour to emphasize the person who is in the piece, their soul." Humanity is the theme, and opacity the method. Each pixelation is like a fingerprint, her

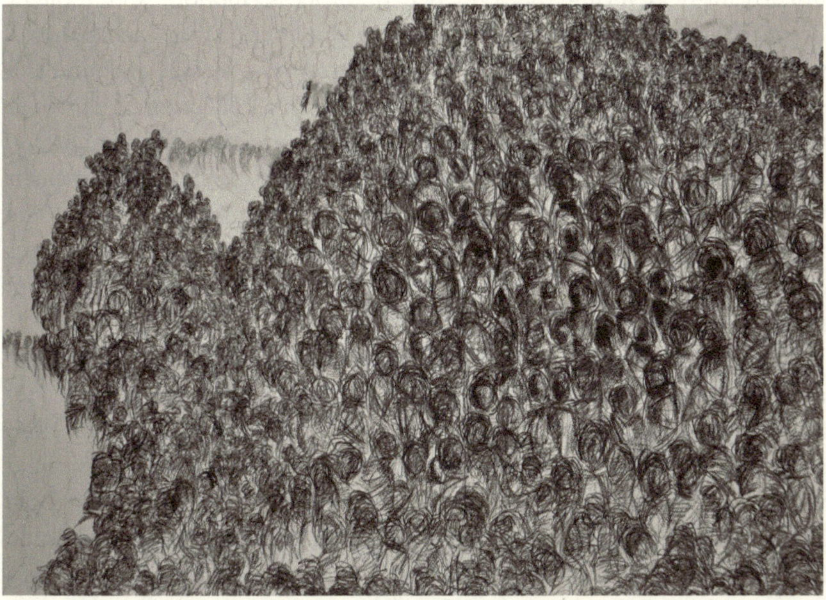

Sandra Brewster, *We Gather* (animation still 115), 2016–2017, charcoal on paper.

Sandra Brewster, *We Gather* (animation still 183), 2016–2017, charcoal on paper.

fingerprint—delivering the evidence of process, motion, and thought. Brewster considers this "precious but not precious." With each film still from Sandra Brewster's short video *We Gather*, the viewer encounters a sketch of faint figures, sparse in one corner with a collection of figures in the far-right corner. Most recently, the still appeared in a short animation at Kenderdine Art Gallery in Saskatoon, the figures become more concentrated with each still. To create this aesthetic, Brewster placed figures side by side or, quite poignantly, overlapping. The small heads of the figures are continuously reinforced circle after circle. The increase is gradual, but the tone shifts drastically from still to still.

The "importance of gathering" is a central theme of *We Gather*. The artist recalls attending Caribana with her family as a young girl. Her mother would wake her and her sister with breakfast and lace up their shoes before heading out to the festival. In our follow-up studio visit held via Zoom a few months later, Brewster describes being "lifted by people in the crowd," an organism all its own. Gathering as relent—the gratitude in knowing one could rely on the other. Brewster considers, "Carnival is a movement; an action of presence."

Multimedia artist Kenturah Davis manages a similar opacity in her depiction of the Black figure in her large-scale wall drawings. Davis will often construct figures that utilize oil paint with rubber stamps, a dimensional practice meant to both convey humanity but also consciousness. Motion, the performance and the reality of it, are useful in each steady marking, like the effect of a brushstroke. I am thinking of Davis's "The Bodily Effect of a Color (2021)" in which the layered form is both figure and shadow, arresting interiority obtained through careful abstraction. A similar, if also parallel, tone is contained within Brewster's *We Gather*, alongside her *Blur* series. This processional entity, a pulsing crescendo famously deployed by South African artist William Kentridge. His projected drawings work with a similar crescendo style aesthetic, highlighting the process of shifted imagery with subtle lines introduced, certainly inspiring Brewster and Davis for that matter, though with slight revision. Brewster's work fascinates, the "trace of a person moving." Neither artist requires animation; abstraction is both a method and a tool. This distortion allows precious distance while drawing the viewer closer, even making us feel involved.

I began drafting this essay while in Buffalo, New York. I was accompanying my partner on a work trip. This gave me about a day and a half in the small city, to walk around and explore. Our timing happened to coincide with the second anniversary of the horrific killing spree at the TOPS grocery store in Buffalo, where ten mostly elderly Black people were targeted and senselessly murdered for being Black. The local news was ablaze with updates on the court case. The killer had the audacity to claim insanity for his murderous premeditated act of terror. The incident occurred on the east side of town. We parked our car across the street from TOPS the afternoon we arrived. We were staying on the west side, with little context for the division of the city. The next day, as I wandered the neighbourhood, looking for lunch, a Black man ambled down the street in my direction wearing tattered garments that appeared to be stained by smoke. In his hand, he carried a filthy paper container, the kind that would hold a greasy order of fries. Briefly, he lifted his hands in front of his body, like he was holding a gun, then drops them softly, a fleeting and imagined retaliation. "That man just shot all of them people," he murmurs, more audible now as he made his way past me. His eyes are wet and glossy, hovering above a thirsty mouth. He is walking east, perhaps hoping to gather.

THE ZOO

Abolition, Filmmaking, Art, and Uprisings from 2016–2024

by Kyisha Williams
Dr. Syrus Marcus Ware

SYRUS MARCUS WARE SAT DOWN WITH ACTOR AND FILMmaker Kyisha Williams to discuss their work and practice, tying abolition into research-creation and creative practice. During the pandemic lockdown, Williams created two new films, *The Zoo* and *Mothering in Quarantine*, both focusing on Black queer parenting in key moments. *The Zoo* is an abolitionist film that takes folks through a narrative story about a young queer family navigating life just after a probationary period ends post incarceration.

Syrus Marcus Ware (SMW): I've been watching your creations for years. You're a filmmaker, you have an artistic practice, and you have woven this into your scientific work. You have a Master of Public Health degree and are a health activist in your community. Could you tell us just a bit about who you are as an artist?

Kyisha Williams (KW): I am a Black, queer, nonbinary femme, I live with various invisible disabilities, and I make art in any way that I can. I would say that my art started from a place of survival, really needing to explain and express the things that I was experiencing and that my communities were experiencing in the world in a way that I felt was more palatable than me ranting or yelling or even writing an essay. I have been paying attention to the power of moving images and entertainment in quotations. They spoke to me as tools that I could use to create change and build understanding and empathy for myself and my communities—to be able to humanize us and how we experience the world and what we go through.

SMW: Having done that and moved in this way through your practice, what was the impact of 2020 on…So many things happened, right? It was a global pandemic. We were in lockdown for a long period of time, but then there were the uprisings that happened all through the summer. What was the impact of 2020, if anything, on your practice?

KW: Lots of different impacts…

SMW: I know you made a film about mothering at that time.

KW: *Mothering in Quarantine*. Lockdown was intense for all of us, and I think it was particularly intense for Black people, trans people, Black trans, all the intersections of those identities. And a lot of things happened. One was that I felt like non-Black people were, for the first time, realizing what anti-Black racism was, and how it was permeating everything in our society. I did get some more eyes on my work, I would say, and some financial donations sent my way, and that was an interesting experience. My Patreon went from five people to ten people or fifteen people, and I was like, "Whoa." Still a rather humble number, but the exposure I felt was a bit different, people were checking in a different way. It gave us a little bit of permission to speak out more.

I think also for me, it was interesting because it was maybe the first time people were seeing who I was. The exposure increased, but my work was already there, so I didn't really have to do much. More people took in my work and engaged with my work, which was cool. I guess one thing that happened was the arts-based project that I was about to do in some of our women's prisons this year got squashed because of the pandemic and because of lockdowns and restrictions. I feel like our community's access to prisoners changed a lot, and prisoners' access to community changed a lot at that time, and I don't know that anything has really changed back since then.

I made *Mothering in Quarantine*, which was a doc about how some Black moms were navigating and experiencing the lockdown and the pandemic, and [the] racism and misogyny they were experiencing. 2020 was a very strange time. People were watching and listening a little bit more, and so many terrible things were happening. It was a very complicated time to be an artist, but I just kept on keeping on, if that makes sense.

SMW: *Red Lips: Cages for Black Girls*, your film made in 2010, became essential watching for so many in 2020. It always was essential viewing, of course, but I think with the politicization of so many people around issues of abolition during the lockdown period, more got turned on to abolitionist films. When the uprisings broke out in the streets, people were hungry for abolitionist and radical content and for information about justice. And you gave us this offering of *The Zoo*, which tells this decidedly abolitionist story that is precise in its depiction of Black experiences and parent experiences in the system. Maybe you could tell us a little bit about making *The Zoo* and about the story.

KW: *The Zoo* follows a person who is recently incarcerated and still navigating the carceral system in the form of probation and parole. The story is about this person reintegrating into their family, they're a mom-slash-parent, and they're navigating time that has passed, moments that have been missed, and just trying to, I was going to say, get back to normal. But there is no getting back to anything. It's more moving forward and finding a new normal perhaps. And with the film, I really wanted to talk about the impact of prisons on not only the person who's experiencing that, but also their family, their community, their support systems, and how they're also impacted by the experience, be it emotionally or even financially—having to send money in, having to pay for really expensive phone calls, having to drive in to visit perhaps, if that's even possible. So, there's real impacts on the family during incarceration and afterward as well.

I really wanted to talk about that process because I think that a lot of the time we think of prisoners as in prison, but we really don't think about when folks come out, which is the majority of folks. I wanted to pay attention to that and to try and push us to create more resources and have more support for folk who are reintegrating, and to have more compassion and understanding for how difficult and layered and challenging and beautiful it is.

SMW: There's this opening moment in the film at a parole office where it's the last day and this person is about to be "freed" from the system and the hooks remain. So, there's this thing that gets written down on a Post-it note that gets followed up with at the end of the film in a moment that is depicted, I think so brilliantly in silence... Or not in silence, but in the absence of dialogue with atmospheric music, and just about how much the state interferes with any possibility of moving forward in your life or attempts to.

What you showed was the crushing weight of that reality, but also our resistance to it because we have the statement, "Nothing can break us." This dance between the harsh reality and some hope or possibility for something different is present for me in this film. And I'm wondering, if you could just talk a bit about your own relationship to hope or possibility or maybe pessimism and apocalypse.

KW: Thank you for those beautiful words about the film. I'm very glad it has resonated. In terms of hope, I try my best to have it. I think it's a practice of cultivating hope. I engage in that when I create my work because I think it is important for us to know what the terrible, horrible, hard things are that we're experiencing, but also to hope for what we need and want. I think that that is super integral to change because we must be able to visualize it and dream it to bring it into reality. I wanted to make sure that I was truthful and honouring the situation and what would likely happen, and what has happened: tons of accounts of folks that people have shared that these types of things have happened time and time again. I wanted to make sure that I showed that and that resilience was focused on our power and ability to survive and hopefully move toward thriving or cultivate thriving.

I feel like there's a place in my work for hope. I don't always feel it or feel connected to it, but I try my best to do that because I think without hope and without love, we're just in a bad space and place. I hope that we won't be here for much longer. And I also see the changes that have come to pass in just my lifetime. I go to my kid's school and see trans positive posters and just beautiful things that a hundred percent were not present when I went to school. But in just one generation, things have shifted in a positive direction. And I also think that children, our children, are intensely connected to hope and our ability to hope and dream and see the future and plan. That was also an important piece of *The Zoo*, to include children and family and that parent–child relationship.

SMW: In *The Zoo*, we have this intergenerational experience of the prison industrial complex, and then it's multilayered, as you say, it's this story: there's francophone components, people speaking French. It feels so wonderful to have gotten to a time where we get to have real stories that are about all our lives, not just one or two characteristic characters who have two things that are focused on, that feels hopeful. I'm wondering what it is that you are hoping and dreaming forward into in your dream abolitionist future. What are you making art for?

KW: Yeah, first and foremost, I'm making art for myself and my community. That's just what it is. It must be in my dream world. I think the first thing is decarceration for all nonviolent crimes, everything related to poverty and drugs and things like this. Everybody just gets let out of prison. But also have the support to reintegrate back into the world. I think that in terms of "violent crimes,"[1] we need to look at the context and assess folk's... I want to say risk, but I feel like that word is loaded. I feel like we need to look at what people need and work on providing that. I think that there may be a place where people need to go and chill and be by themselves if they're harmful to the community, but it doesn't need to be a prison. It doesn't need to be punitive. It doesn't need to harm more than it does good. It doesn't need to make money. We need to take all of that out of the equation.

SMW: I was talking to Giselle Dias about in Cree communities, about when there was real harm or damage that happened in the community, that there would be a practice of inviting the person to go out and live on the land until they came back into harmony with creation. And then, they were back into the community so that it wasn't a banishment. And I think of that a lot now in relation to prison and carceral systems, this idea that if you've caused harm, you must be disappeared. She is saying, "We have to remember that there are old ways that worked, where we would go live with the land, go live on a stream, go to eat berries every day and come back more healed because of that."

KW: Yeah, a hundred percent. I think that we would either not have money or not have to pay for food, water, and shelter. We would have communities of support that would check in on each other. Our community with disabilities would be tended to, and able-bodied folks would be in support systems to help people. And not even help people, that's a weird way to put it, but just to be in community and take care of each other. That's part of my dream. Anyway, there's lots more, but I think those are the basics: free health care. Non-stigmatized health care.

SMW: I was watching a video earlier today of Fred Hampton from 1968, and he was talking on video about how what was needed at that time was action and not just talking about it or writing about it. And he said, "we didn't talk about a free breakfast program. We started a free breakfast program. And I'm not sitting here counting how many breakfasts we're feeding to be able to fill out a report, but I know that we've fed 4,000 kids this month. We're just... just doing it." And then he was like, and I'm paraphrasing, "We have photos and video that are proof that we're doing this, and you can see that we're doing this and so we don't have to worry."

And I was thinking about how in some ways that's true. It's a record. But who has access to the record? The archives around the Black Panthers really got lost for a little period, and in the nineties when I was coming up, it was hard to find accurate information that wasn't going to help stuff that they had put out. So, it was hard in the nineties to get accurate data, and as a result, we didn't get to learn as much directly from some of those lessons in the way that we are learning about them now. So, I'm wondering for you, if you wanted to make sure that something survived forty years from now, from this time, from this moment of art and uprising, what would you want to make sure is in the archive? And it might be an artwork, it might be a story, it might be a document of something, but what would you want to make sure remains remembered from this moment of art and uprising?

KW: Octavia Butler books. She is a legend, and her texts contain magical and pertinent information for us here, I would say. And I would also say just accurate telling of the Black Lives Matter movement, and what we have been able to accomplish and why our movement is necessary and continues. I've heard a lot of people refer to 2020 as the Black Lives Matter era. It's not done. It's not a fad; it's not something that blipped up. Obviously, the things that we've been struggling against are decades and centuries old, and we are always going to be here despite their desire that we are not. Our movement needs to be properly represented, properly celebrated, and properly grown to create change, meaningful, long-lasting, futuristic change.

SMW: Beautiful. Thank you, Kyisha. That's a great place to end.

Notes

1 Crime is a relative concept, rooted in white supremacy. Actions are criminalized differently depending on the perceived race or community connection of the person doing the action. The state criminalizes Black communities for things that they don't criminalize for non-Black communities.

DECOLONIZE LOVE

by **King Kxndi**

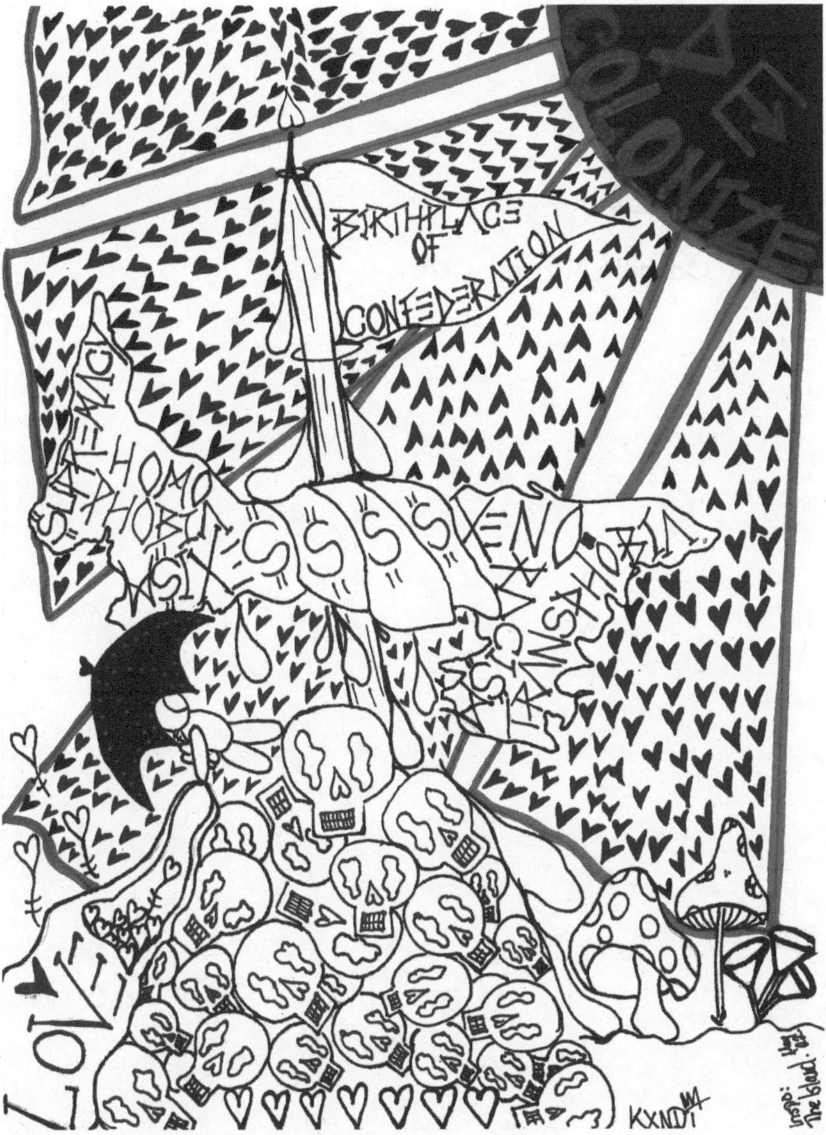

tr. King Kxndi. *Decolonize Love*. Courtesy of the Artist.

NAVE

by **Camille Turner**

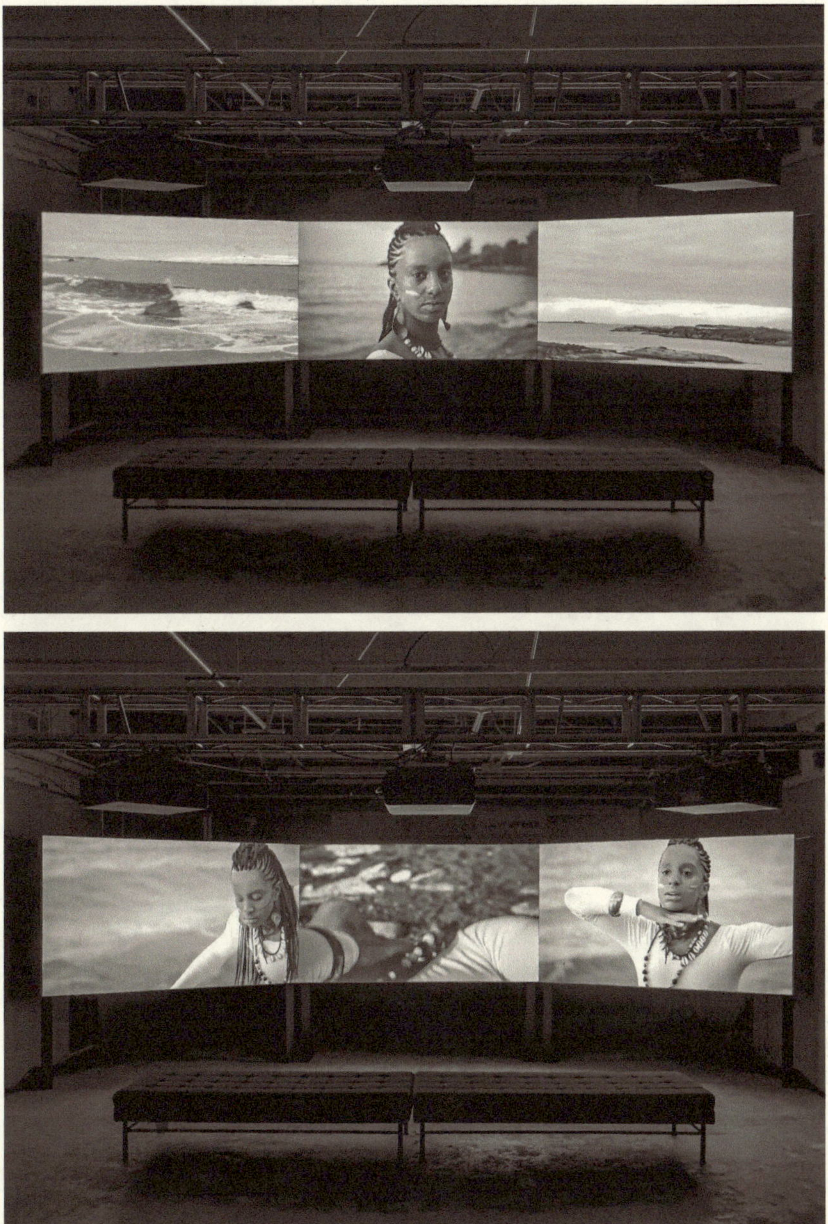

Camille Turner, *Nave*, 2022, 3-channel video installation (12:32). Filmed by Esery Mondésir and Cody Westman, edited by Chris Wiseman, composed by Ravi Naimpally, performed by Camille Turner and Emilie Jabouin (Zila). Commissioned by the Toronto Biennial of Art. Photo by toni hafkenscheid. Courtesy of the Artist.

FUGITIVE SOUND ART

Sound as Refusal, Sound as Refuge

by **jamilah malika abu-bakare**

SOUND ART IS UNDERREPRESENTED IN A HYPER VISUAL art world, but this practice may provide respite from burnout plaguing Othered artists by refusing spectacle and shifting the artist's relationship with the audience. This essay expands on a previous piece published in *Canadian Art* magazine in 2021, with a new focus on fugitvity as a conceptual framework developed by people who freed themselves. Thinking alongside the fugitive and the artists and scholars inspired by them, this essay explores how sound can tune us into art as abolition.

. . .

The abolitionist movement today grows from deep roots. Individuals resisted, organizers mobilized, crowds gathered to hear leaders speak, and critical publications circulated to end enslavement across Turtle Island. Reading fugitive or captive writers from that time period can help us think about abolition and art now, especially in relation to sound and sound art. Too much discourse focuses on Black sound and sound art (by Black and non-Black writers alike) as music or musicality like singing, hip hop, electronica, dub, or DJing. While radical thought can emerge, the continuous framing of Blackness through spectacle or performance grows tiresome. Stereotypes, like the singing and dancing sort, grew popular as the abolitionist movement grew. Art historian Lisa Farrington explains that "through such visual conventions fears concerned the perceived threat of large numbers of recently freed blacks to the social and economic status of whites were allayed."[1]

An alternate approach to theorizing sound and sound art dates to the same era but focuses on the fugitives who continue to inspire thinkers today. Writers like Katherine McKittrick, Dionne Brand, Christina Sharpe, Saidiya Hartman, Joy James, and Hortense Spillers think alongside fellow Black woman writer Harriet Jacobs, who freed herself from her enslaver by hiding in her grandmother's crawlspace for seven years. Artists like Simone Leigh and Torkwase Dyson resurrect fugitives like Jacobs, Henry "Box" Brown, and Anthony Burns (and others unnamed) in their sculptures and paintings in and outside the gallery. Amid these fugitives, scholars, and artists exists a nuanced articulation of sound as freedom (even quiet sounds or silence). Following their cues, we can hear a new field of abolition and art growing: fugitive sound art. Using this term, we can describe sound artists Jeneen Frei Njootl and Soledad Fatima Muñoz as honouring the spirits who have always resisted genocide and terror (like Leigh and Dyson). Fugitivity can move with and beyond race, history, and reality and build solidarity across difference. Many of us "shared dreams of freedom, linked in flight from coloniality," and connecting these struggles is how we get free.[2]

Fugitive

The Latin root of "fugitive" is *fugere*, meaning runaway. Synonyms include refugee and renegade. Sometimes this shadowy figure flees persecution, other times incarceration. They are people running from capture because capture means captivity, danger, and/or death.

In Black Studies, fugitivity recalls a specific historical context across Turtle Island: the *Fugitive Slave Acts* of 1793, 1850, and 1862. Enslavers lobbied Congress to make running away from the plantation (or helping hostages run away) a crime. The laws were buttressed by the circulation of public notices, ads, and rewards encouraging everyone to surveil any Black person as pathological, criminal, or certifiably insane (enslaved Africans who wanted freedom were diagnosed with a made-up mental illness). Mobs of unemployed white men were granted the authority to patrol, meaning absolutely terrorize, free and enslaved Africans.[3] The people today who police (and call police like some personal concierge service) are shaped by these laws.

In 1835, at the height of the *Fugitive Slave Acts,* Jacobs fled. When it came time to write her memoir for the abolitionist cause, she authored each word with both strategy and generosity. In a chapter entitled "The Flight," she described her escape from her enslavers house: "At half past twelve I stole softly down the stairs."[4] The word "stole" refers to both escape and the illegal theft of herself as property. The title references flying decades before the airplane; before Toni Morrison's 1977 novel *Song of Solomon,* or Faith Ringgold's 1988 story quilt *Tar Beach,* Jacobs makes allusion to the Myth of Flying Africans. In *Listening to Images,* scholar Tina Campt defines fugitivity in connection to flight: "the concept of fugitivity highlights the tension between the acts or flights of escape and creative practices of refusal, nimble and strategic practices that undermine the category of the dominant." In "Belly of the World: Black Women's Labour" writer Saidiya Hartman articulates this complex, even contradictory, range of liberation strategies to include running, plotting, dreaming, poison, abortion, suicide, infanticide, giving birth, and living.[5] Jacobs's book *Incidents in the Life of a Slave Girl* records her diabolical enslaver's relentlessness. Jacobs dedicates a chapter to the garret where she spent seven years hiding from him entitled "The Loophole of Retreat." She opens with a description of the dimensions:

> The garret was only nine feet long and seven wide. The highest part was three feet high and sloped down abruptly to the loose floorboard. There was no admission for either light or air.[6]

■ ■ ■

Consider pausing this reading to measure those dimensions wherever you are, imagine the slope and seven years of your lifetime.

■ ■ ■

Like "stole down the steps," "The Loophole of Retreat" is a laden turn of phrase. A loophole is an ambiguity you can use to get away (with something—in this case, getting away is the something). Jacobs hid in shocking proximity to her enslaver, who she secretly saw regularly from above. In *Demonic Grounds,* Katherine McKittrick explains, "Brent's position in the garret—above ground level, unseen while being able to see within and across the plantation—quietly critiques and undoes traditional geographies."[7] She infers that fugitives like Jacobs could sense freedom beyond the plantation. Leigh abstracted this posture in a magnanimous sixteen-foot bronze sculpture, *Brick House* (2019–2021). The braided, black bust sat high above a busy intersection, with no eyes, refusing to return your gaze. Writer Kevin Quashie theorizing around silence as resistance imbues Leigh's imposing sculpture with power.

Jacobs finds a way to be free in an unfree state (a practice we need now badly). Her 1861 book is exceptional in an archive where masculine authors dominate. Jacobs's nuanced writing, its mere existence in that time and this place, contradicted common knowledge and the law in many cases. Texts were published by enslaved people while reading and writing was illegal for enslaved people in many states. Fugitive William Henry Heard wrote,

> We did not learn to read nor to write, as it was against the law for any person to teach any slave to read; and any slave caught writing suffered the penalty of having his forefinger cut from his right hand; yet there were some who could read and write.[8]

Hundreds of autobiographies by fugitives and their amanuenses were sold and circulated in support of the abolitionist movement. Jacobs wrote explicitly in her preface that her story was a call to action to free women to act on behalf of the over two million women "still in bondage."[9] Fugitive or captive writing, insofar as a literary category, can contain autobiographies like Jacobs's from the nineteenth century, Assata Shakur's 1973 letter "To My People," and *any text* authored by a political prisoner today. Jacobs called her small space a cell throughout her book, relating herself to anyone who is incarcerated. In this condition, she describes sound as a kind of solace:

> Morning came. I knew it only by the noises I heard; for in my small den day and night were all the same. I suffered for air even more than for light. But I was not comfortless. I heard the voices of my children. There was joy and there was sadness in the sound.[10]

For a fugitive, refuge is safety or respite from capture. This can be wherever or however we resist oppression and move toward freedom in real, felt ways. Both the garret and sound helped Jacobs feel connection and move toward freedom. She even heard her son talk back to her enslaver in defiance. In *Listening*, Campt explains that sound is a vibration we feel, meaning sound touches us.[11] Jacobs's son made contact with his mother in her cell through sound. How did the sound reach her? I imagine the sound as a wave of protection that helped Jacobs attune to her freedom alone inside a crawlspace. Some nights, her grandmother would come and whisper with her, but this tender care posed a horrific risk—if these free and fugitive Black women were heard, they could be punished, imprisoned, killed along with their family. Seven years is roughly eighty-five months or 2,550 days and nights. Jacobs fled north in 1842 and was emancipated in 1853.

The Fugitive's Progeny

In 2022, ceramicist Simone Leigh represented Turtle Island at the Venice Biennale. Leigh turned the "US" pavilion into an homage to Black women's labour with Jacobs as an inspiration. At the same time, sound artist Sonia Boyce filled the "UK" pavilion with Black women's voices. Never have either of those nations named Black women to represent them at this international, elitist spectacle. Leigh used her platform to hold "The Loophole of Retreat," a three-day gathering of Black women to celebrate the power of our labour. The entrance to her pavilion read "Sovereignty," a term most often associated with nation states to mean freedom, power, and authority. We can attach these qualities to Leigh who got a proverbial seat at the table and said "Yes, here I am and I brought all my friends and ancestors." Hundreds of international guests and dozens of acclaimed speakers thrummed together holding Jacobs as a model and teacher. By citing Jacobs's title and experience, Leigh braids Black women's past, present, and future together.

Leigh invokes Jacobs and her chapter title often. In a 2019 installation by the same name, Leigh collaborated with Black Quantum Futurism co-creator Moor Mother on a sound component. Leigh read an article about Debbie Africa and the birth of her son while Africa was wrongly incarcerated after the 1978 attack by the police on MOVE members' rowhouse residence. They were targeted as a revolutionary Black power movement. Africa was in her third trimester when she was imprisoned, and her baby was born weeks later. The women in the cells nearby organized to make noise and muffle the sounds of the newborn so that mother and baby would not be separated by the guards.[12] Their soundings gave her three days with her baby. Leigh described their care as "sonic protection."[13] She sculpted a closed, conical vessel with three braids partially enclosed in breeze block walls. Moor Mother composed an audioscape to emanate from inside the vessel (inside the walls), weaving together popular songs from 1978 with reports of the 1985 MOVE Bombing and recordings from a 2019 riot at the Metropolitan Detention Center in Brooklyn when the heat went out during the polar vortex. They used sound to demand care. Transporting their protest into the gallery and collapsing timelines of state violence and carceral systems through sound is fugitive sound art. Leigh and Moor Mother put listeners in physical touch with the urgent need for abolition then and now. The sound hides in the sculpture and calls for freedom.

In *Wayward Lives, Beautiful Experiments*, Hartman re-imagines a prison riot in 1919 described in a *New York Times* article, "Girls on 'Noise' Strike":

> Three of the girls started it. They began to rattle the gates of Rebecca Hall. Others joined, and when the guards shooed them away, other prisoners began to jangle their cell doors, throw furniture against the walls, scream, sing, and use profanity. In the opinion of one of the noise-makers, the medley of sounds, "the Reformatory Blues," may yet make a hit on Broadway, even if the officials appear to disdain jazz.[14]

One participant felt music and the reporter joked about performance. Incarcerated people in 1919 and 2019 across the same state in different facilities deployed sound to protest poor conditions. The Bedford Hills Correctional Facility for Women remains open and is one of the few prisons across Turtle Island where incarcerated people can give birth inside then the two live together inside for up to one year. Some are freed with their toddler. Giving birth inside a prison like them or Debbie Africa offers a literal understanding of what scholar Joy James describes as the captive maternal. More broadly, the captive maternal is any caregiver who must protect and defend their children's freedom from a state that wishes to enslave and imprison those children. James, like writer Hortense Spillers, notes how the condition of slavery was passed on, by law, through the mother.[15] Both James and Spillers theorize with Jacobs. Presently enslavement, or involuntary servitude, is only legal on Turtle Island today if you are incarcerated. If Harriet Jacobs were alive today, she would not be enslaved, but if she were a pregnant, Black, teenage single mom (as she arguably was) would respectability politics give her a moment of freedom? Would she have a chance to raise a child who wouldn't likely be snatched up by patrols, I mean police?

In truth, Harriet Jacobs was an alias. Her name was Linda Brent. An underrecognized historian, Jean Fagan Yellin, dug around in North Carolina archives to reveal Brent's true identity in the late 1980s.[16] Brent understood what most men in her position did not: opacity is of the highest order for the fugitive. Fugitive or captive writing published in this era shared many traits: they were autobiographies of enslavement, escape, and freedom often published under similar titles that included the fugitive's name: *The Narrative of*... or *Adventures of*... or *Life of*... In one of his three autobiographies, *My Bondage and My Freedom*, Frederick Douglass specifically admonished Henry "Box" Brown and other fugitives for so explicitly naming their methods of escape.[17] Brent did describe hers before enslavement was abolished so she was reasonably afraid of her family suffering as a result of the *Fugitive Slave Acts*. She likely chose her title for anonymity and safety for her and her loved ones but also to impress upon her reader that her story is representative of any and every "Slave Girl."

There is more and more scholarship unearthing the anonymous Black women who resisted enslavement—by Tamika Nunley, Karen Cook Bell, Simone Brown, Kellie Carter Jackson, Alexis Pauline Gumbs, and others. Their poems, writing, and research reframe the dominant body of knowledge which asserts "women" were more tied to the plantation than "men." In her book, Brent describes dressing as a sailor when she finally walked on her own two legs somehow out of her grandmother's house, headed for a boat. While we know people like she and Ellen Craft existed, we have yet to reckon with how the gender binary, transphobia, patriarchy, and misogynoir obscure our assumptions assigning gender to fugitives or the fact that birthing people ran pregnant and even with child(ren) in tow. Instead, we are more familiar with a fugitive like "Box" Brown as a result of his sensational feat of escape from enslavement in a wooden crate via the postal system.

"Box" Brown's life after escape is completely unlike Jacobs's. She struggles to gain custody of her children and commits her life to teaching and abolition. "Box" Brown does not return to Virginia to look for the family he laments losing in his autobiography. Instead, he finds fame in England.

A ticket to his stage show in the archive promises magic and prizes. One could easily criticize "Box" Brown for making a spectacle of his trauma, but he is most generously theorized by scholar Daphne Brooks in *Bodies in Dissent*. She describes performing with his panorama as an innovative way to tell his own story after "Box" Brown's amanuensis inserted himself in the first publication. "Box" Brown did republish his autobiography, but he also used theatre strategically to tell his own story. His relationship to sound before escape is pained: he cannot speak up when his family is sold by his deceptive enslaver, and he must be silent in the "Box" (even when he is dropped on his head). He wrote that after twenty-seven hours in the box, he waited some more, finally emerged, fainted, regained consciousness as if resurrected, and broke into a spiritual. He would go on to re-enact his escape complete with song (sans fainting) for audiences for years to come.

Curator Anisa Olufemi's lecture "Watching Me" connects the current surveillance of Black gender-marginalized people to enslavement and explains that the violence of the plantation as spectacle has paved the way for today's trauma porn and viral lynching videos. They observe,

> That kind of paranoid relationship to looking and being seen has seeded our predisposition to operate in responsive, performative ways tailored to the observer or the environment of observation. I'm wondering what it might look like for Black gender marginalized folks to resist and transcend that vicious circle.[18]

How would "Box" Brown have spent his remaining years had he not felt compelled to parody, refute and trouble misperceptions about himself and enslavement?[19] "Box" Brown travelled across the Atlantic to perform with a panorama: a giant, unravelling, landscape painting (like a scroll on its side) that depicted the suffering of enslavement across Turtle Island. Some research suggests "Box" Brown lifted imagery from another fugitive, artist, and poet, Charles C. Green.[20] British critics were more concerned his presentation was exaggerated and gross.[21] But imagine you were denied speech all that time? Not to excuse plagiarism, but instead to consider the ways in which BIPOC artists respond to fetishists in the art world and to consider Brown's performance in relation to Kobena Mercer's question in "Black Art and the Burden of Representation":

> If, after many years of struggle, you arrive at the threshold of enunciation and are "given" the right-to-speak and a limited space in which to tell your story, is it not the case that there will be an overwhelming pressure to try and tell the whole story all at once?[22]

Artist Torkwase Dyson's works of abstraction elegantly neutralize this tension. Her monumental black structures are installed from the gallery to the desert. Dyson developed the term Hypershape to describe the three geometric forms that repeat in her enormous black sculptures, paintings, and drawings: triangle, square, and curve.[23] Her massive works like *Liquid a Place* (2021) or the 2022 *Beloved Stillness (Hypershape)* are developed from drawings she's made for years repeating the three shapes, like the 2018 piece *Tuning (Hypershape, 200–410)*. A 2017 series in wood or 2018 installation in pale beams and black string show Dyson's devotion to experimenting with Hypershapes in various materials, mediums, and sites. She lovingly refers to a pile of black-and-white works on paper as "drawings for my ancestors."[24] Each shape honours a fugitive: the triangle represents the garret for Jacobs, the square symbolizes the crate for "Box" Brown, and the curve connotes Anthony Burns's escape in the hull of a ship. Fugitive Anthony Burns was twenty-eight when he died in 1828 on Anishinaabeg and Haudenosaunee lands from "health problems related to his post-trial confinement" after spending his life as a free man studying religion and becoming a pastor.[25] Prior to his formal studies, he was self-taught and cited his deep faith to advocate for abolition. In response to a letter excommunicating him from his former church for his crime of liberation, Burns wrote,

> You charge me that, in escaping, I disobeyed God's law. No, indeed! That law which God wrote on the table of my heart, inspiring the love of freedom, and impelling me to seek it at every hazard, I obeyed, and, by the good hand of my God upon me, I walked out of the house of bondage.[26]

His complete letter reads as a touching predecessor to Dr. Martin Luther King Jr.'s 1963 writing as a political prisoner. Maria Stewart and Sojourner Truth gave language to intersectionality and misogynoir before contemporary Black feminists coined terms we cite. Part of our work as artists, scholars, and organizers is to look to fugitives like Jacobs, "Box" Brown, and Burns because abolition exists on a continuum that begins with them. If we understand fugitivity as a condition of capture and theft of one's labour, then the *Fugitive Slave Acts* bring us to the present prison industrial complex. Through her installations, Dyson recreates "The collective spatial intelligence of Black refusal provided a foundation for transformation."[27] Like Leigh, Dyson mobilizes repetition to centre or focus their purpose: to create art that helps us learn from fugitives who struggled against state terror for freedom.

Fugitivity as an Approach

In "Venus in Two Acts," Hartman asks: "Is it possible to . . . resurrect lives from the ruins? Can beauty provide an antidote to dishonor . . . ?"[28] None Conceptual artist Glen Ligon read "Box" Brown's writing and felt inspired, not simply "to recreate it" as some have chosen to, but by "positioning myself against a certain historical experience and trying to find the connections between it and who I am."[29] In *To Disembark* (1993), Ligon deploys symmetrical arrangements of prints with delicate, stylized fonts on creamy cardstocks as restorative beauty by playing with the conventions forced on Jacobs and "Box" Brown to show their constraints and limits. The work suggests both the suffering induced by these demands and institutions but also the cruel idiocy of ideologies that enslave, commodify, auction, and so on. The name of the exhibit cites a 1981 book of poems by Gwendolyn Brooks. The word "disembark" means to leave a ship (alluding to ships in the thousands that crossed the Atlantic). What did it mean to come to the gallery and read runaway posters in 1993? What might it mean now? The exhibit included a sound installation that typifies fugitive sound art: nine art shipping crates complete with fragile and right-side-up stamps, each containing a recording of jazz, reggae, disco, rap, work songs, and even Ligon reading from "Box" Brown's book. The cacophony denied the quiet we expect at the gallery. In *Salvage: Readings from the Wreck*, scholar Dionne Brand writes: "Sound has the quality of duration; even when not immediate, a song is present and its effects can seem fully reprised: the day you heard it, where you were, the events of that day into which the sound interpolated."[30] Ligon touches visitors with his voice and music and each person's experience is unique to their experiences (or lack of experiences) in relation to each sound. Dyson parallels Ligon by seeing herself in connection to fugitives and similarly intuits that she can understand something important, some solutions, through that connection. She wrote: "My efforts are focused on developing a distilled abstract drawing practice in the language of architectural and infrastructural representation that lends itself to participation in spatial development and more livable geographies."[31]

In *Wayward Lives, Beautiful Experiments*, Hartman observes "black folks had been owned, and being an object of property, they were radically disenchanted with the idea of property"[32]—their "experiments" living free offer us with tools, practices, and philosophies. Barbara London, co-organizer of Museum of Modern Art's first sound art show, explains how experimentation in the sixties produced time-based art practices like performance, video, and sound developed in opposition to the gallery: "In the spirit of counterculture and revolution, artists were experimenting with time-based art that was intangible and difficult to commodify and collect."[33] Fugitivity and sound art share a resistance to monetization or commodification.

Before we move on, it's worth noting that visual artists make stunning works derived from fugitives' lives, such as Leticia Huckaby's silhouettes or Erin Batiste's collages. Art writing on their work ought to consider how and why fugitive figures of the past remain relevant to these artists and their lives in today's (art) world. Some contemporary artists centre incarceration in their work like Sable Elyse Smith; she is personally connected to the carceral system through her father. In a way, he collaborates through recordings she made of their calls. We must also consider any works by artists who are themselves incarcerated or formerly incarcerated and the systemic barriers they face should they want to show their work. The 2024 short film *The Quilters* tells the story of the textile artists imprisoned at a Missouri maximum security prison who craft intricately patterned quilts for children in foster care. They possess skill and care that would likely make a fourth generation Gee's Bend quilter (a descendant of captives and fugitives) smile.

There is a kind of doubling or overflowing possible—or what poet Alexis Pauline Gumbs might call spilling: Leigh and Moor Mother's sound art is fugitive and abolitionist because they amplify the subject position of the incarcerated. When their experience resounds in the gallery, free people have an opportunity to listen and be changed (changed meaning able to think about incarcerated people as human beings who deserve to be heard). Fugitivity is a theoretical framework much like intersectionality: a conceptual mode of analysis from the lived experience of the margins or periphery. However, fugitivity flies where intersectionality can fail when we don't factor in class, capitalism, carcerality, and imperialism. Black feminism is defined by Angela Davis as a layered analysis that connects movements from here to Palestine. The exact point where we rationalize a Black woman acting as a tool of empire marks the shift away from fugitivity toward intersectionality. I am less interested in visual or token representation and more interested in how (lived experience) works toward freedom from the oppressive systems that the Combahee River Collective named in their 1977 statement: "racial, sexual, heterosexual, and class oppression" or "the manifold and simultaneous oppressions that all women of color face."

Fugitivity can equip art writers to read into the depth of works that involve fugitives like Brent, but this approach also requires us to perceive how, or if, the artist points audiences toward freedom from enslavement, incarceration, colonialism, imperialism, and so on, right now. Then we can build solidarity by learning across our distinct experiences of resilience against genocide, state violence, and facism. Sound artists Jeneen Frei Njootl and Soledad Fatima Muñoz centre refusal and reverence for freedom fighters in their work. Both create in collaboration and community as well as in sound and textile. Their work can be misread with vague, shallow terms like "experimental" or described through identity in ways that narrow instead of reveal. Or, all too often, art writers reference conventional, canonical sound studies (and sound art studies), texts, and figures that dominate the discourse. Alternatively, we can recognize sound art as fugitive to highlight refusal in Frei's performances and memory work in Muñoz's installations.

Fugitive Sound Art

Fugitive sound art can describe Leigh and Ligon's sound works as well as describe artist Kevin Beasley's installation, *A View of a Landscape: A Cotton Gin Motor* (2012–2018). Beasley sends the audio from a cotton gin motor sealed in one room into another room where there is nothing but the relentless sound of the plantation, a ghostly, hollow whirring. By bringing the past to the present in an empty room (save the bodies brave enough to stay), he transports us in time through sound, much like Moor Mother and Leigh's collaboration. Similarly, sound artist Shilpa Gupta's installation *For, In Your Tongue, I Cannot Fit* (2017–2019) unsilences the voices of one hundred people who were detained, imprisoned, and/or executed dating back centuries. Gupta suspends one hundred microphones from the ceiling over metal stakes; each stake impales a slip of paper that holds the writing we listen to through the microphone in several different languages.

Some sound artists respond to incarceration in the contemporary setting. Lawrence Abu Hamdan's project *Earwitness Inventory* (2018–ongoing) documents torture in the notorious Saydnaya prison in Syria. His work brings us in connection with former captives of the oppressive Assad regime so that we can empathize with their memories of torture. Listeners hear one voice recall, "In Saydnaya, silence is the master." Laura Poitras and Sean Vegezzi's collaboration work *Edgelands* (2021) takes the listener to a floating prison on New York's East River. The chilling audioscape includes transmissions picked up from the ship, layered over a heartbeat. In a 2023 interview, Vegezzi shared that the people detained there specifically compare the site to the hold of transatlantic slave ships. The conditions of captivity now are too similar to despair; sound is a portal and fugitivity offers insights we need now.

Muñoz and Frei Njootli both fill the gallery with sound strategically. Describing one of Frei Njootli's performances, curator and artist Angela Marie Schenstead concludes that

> By activating the vibrations of the steel sheets with the bodies that were in attendance during the performance, Frei Njootli refused to make her own body and voice a spectacle. The performance was an offering to the non-human and formless beings through sound—a gesture that undermines and renders irrelevant the colonial control and racist expectations of Canadian art institutions and audiences.[34]

Because Campt defines fugitivity as a wide range of possibilities that share one quality, that of "undermin[ing] the category of the dominant," Frei Njootli's work is exemplary. They can be read as fugitive because they refuse to become a spectacle, reverse the relationship of labour with the spectator, make an offering to beings that have withstood genocide for centuries, and push back against the colonial, racist ideologies within the institution itself. Frei Njootli's installation *from strength to this question* (2019) features the sounds of vocalizations, Ski-Doos, and beads. Frei Njootli states that "I like to work with sound as a tool of disruption, thinking about how it can change someone's experiences of the space…how sound bleeds and navigates this rectilineal space."[35] The use of "sound as a tool of disruption" is the same as the people who protested at Bedford Hill

Reformatory and Metropolitan Detention Center in 1919 and 2019. Frei Njootli disrupts the gallery space with the sounds from the north, shifting the balance of power. Their sonic landscape spills into the centre, asserting who was here before and who will be here after.

Muñoz, like Frei Njootli, works with sound and textiles. Her latest project, *Woven Memory* (2021) comprises four site-specific installations across Chile made from portraits of people who were disappeared in detention during Pinochet's rule. Muñoz collaborated with a team to work with the families of the disappeared to present massive public works at former sites of repression. She describes the project as pedagogical, complete with booklets, kits, and archive search engines. Local communities who continue to be affected by Pinochet's reign of terror have organized for decades in groups across these sites and describe their role as *trabajadores de memoria*, or memory workers. Muñoz and her collaborators repeatedly asked themselves one question—"what can the object do?"—meaning, how can we mobilize this object and this opportunity for redress and repair? Praising function this way rejects the high–low separation endemic to the art world. Muñoz's work can be interpreted as fugitive sound art because each panel or portrait memorializes someone the state tried to erase from memory. The detained and disappeared were tortured by state thugs like police and military who bombed grave sites in an attempt to destroy any evidence of the lives taken (disappear the disappearance). Muñoz explains they were targeted because "They were fighting for our earth! Our land!"[36] She weaves to continue their work and keep their memory alive.

Like Frei Njootli, Muñoz's materials act as antennae and filter the sounds around through whatever is present, including viewers. Like Beasley's cotton gin motor, Muñoz's portraits emit an ongoing tonal composition with no beginning, no end. She has learned that sound can "make tangible the intangible." In 2021, visitors to the installation at a former site of torture known as "Londres 38" in Santiago heard the same church bells and street sounds that the blindfolded detainees would have heard while being held hostage decades ago. Muñoz activates sound to time travel and touch the experience of torture in detention. The panels' tones resound in place of the people they depict and through the frequencies. I hope those ancestors sense that we will never forget their sacrifice. Our reverence for them "undermines" the state terror they fought against and the land they fought for. The artist is always working in community and collaboration. The families involved in the project describe visiting the installations as "restorative."[37] Through their work, one site has been reopened and the search for loved ones restarted.

Unfortunately, the art world does not always encourage outcomes like these. More often, artists' lived experiences are fetishized, cannibalized, and/or profited from in the art world. The failures of museums in and since 2020 to shift away from supremacist ideologies is alarming but even after reading "Box" Brown's autobiography in the nineties, Ligon felt prompted to ask himself:

> What are the conditions under which works by black artists enter the museum? Do we enter only when our "visible difference" is evident? Why do many shows with works by colored people (and rarely whites) have titles that include "race" and "identity?" Who is my work for and what do different audiences demand of it?[38]

These reflections are worthwhile for all of us from our distinct positionalities since 2020/2023, and now. Muñoz takes every opportunity to remind her "Canadian" audiences that our imperialist business interests are complicit in these disappearances. Muñoz venerates her ancestors through textile practices like arpillera and constant homage to their resistance. She states, "While in Chile people are experiencing the effects of neoliberalism, Canadians are perpetuating this oppression in many cases without even knowing about it. Art has the capability of being outside of language and communicating with both parts." Frei Njootli "undermines" colonial ideologies and institutions and Muñoz "undermines" imperialism, exploitation, terror—both direct us toward freedom for their lands and people.

Sound as Repair, a Method of Care

Muñoz's installations remind me of how scholar Fred Moten once described sound: "fugitive," "dispossessed," and "dispossessive," meaning impossible to restrain or always in the process of escape.[39] We cannot stop the soundwave once it is free. We cannot close our ears. Moten also defines Blackness as "fugitive...an ongoing refusal of standards imposed from elsewhere."[40] For Moten, sound and Blackness overlap in their fugitive quality. The term fugitive sound art helps us connect across race through a shared experience of struggle. Writer Alexander Weheliye asserts that sound is more sovereign: "When we analyze the role of vision as it relates to the mechanisms of racism, sound emerges as a space where Black subjectivity is not fixed by the look of white subjects but is instead articulated dynamically by Black subjects."[41] The gallery becomes an apt setting to create conditions for listening for every Other. Composer Tara Rodgers observes that feeling sound, or listening, can help us humanize each other,

> Vibrations—including that specific class of audible vibrations experienced as sound—present alternative ways of apprehending reality that can point toward political sensibilities that emphasize complexity, interconnection, and interdependence rather than modes of distancing and control.[42]

Listening is care like abolition is care—the key is who is listening to who. In *Undrowned: Black Feminist Lessons from Marine Mammals*, writer Alexis Pauline Gumbs notes, "Listening is not only about the normative ability to hear. It is a transformative and revolutionary resource that requires quieting down and tuning in."[43] More is happening than simply hearing during a work of sound art; Brand describes sound as a portal to a time for a time, and Campt observes that sound touches you. Sharpe shared that she wrote *In the Wake* because "I wanted to stay in the wake to sound an ordinary note of care,"[44] and describes a scene in Toni Morisson's *Beloved* where a character uses sound as a diversion to free almost fifty prisoners.

Abolition remains urgent, and sound can be a site of freedom-finding and care. Fugitive sound art points toward freedom from within an oppressive reality and materializes "care [as] an antidote to violence" through listening.[45] The art world has always invoked and invited the centre (the ultra wealthy of whatever moment). When Frei Njootli invites visitors to listen to the sounds of the periphery in the gallery, then their work is "transformative and revolutionary." When Muñoz and her team create public installations that honour the memory of union leaders and organizers who were silenced by the state and imperial interests, then their work is "transformative and revolutionary. These artists are planting notes of care for the land and all beings who protect the land. Fugitive sound art celebrates our common struggle, our flight toward freedom, together.

Selected References

Bailey, Moya. *Misogynoir Transformed: Black Women's Digital Resistance*. New York University Press, 2021.

Bell, Karen Cook. *Running from Bondage: Enslaved Women and Their Remarkable Fight for Freedom in Revolutionary America*. Cambridge University Press, 2021.

Brand, Dionne. *Map to The Door of No Return: Notes to Belonging*. Vintage Canada, 2002.

Brand, Dionne. *Salvage: Readings from the Wreck*. Farrar, Straus & Giroux. 2024.

Brooks, Daphne. *Bodies in Dissent: Spectacular Performances of Race and Freedom, 1850–1910*. Duke University Press, 2006.

Brucato, Ben. *Race and Police: The Origin of Our Peculiar Institutions*. Rutgers University Press, 2023.

Campt, Tina. "Black Feminist Futures and the Practice of Fugitivity." October 7, 2014, Barnard College, New York City. Lecture.

Campt, Tina. *Listening to Images*. Duke University Press, 2017.

Cebek, Daphne. "In Studio with Torkwase Dyson" *GRAY*. Vimeo, November 11, 2021, https://vimeo.com/644828076.

Copeland, Huey. *Bound to Appear: Art, Slavery, and the Site of Blackness in Multicultural America*. University of Chicago Press, 2013.

Davis, Angela Y. *Freedom Is a Constant Struggle: Ferguson, Palestine, and the Foundation of a Movement*. Edited by Frank Barat. Haymart Books, 2016.

Drake, Kimberly. *The Slave Narrative*. Edited by Kimberly Drake. Salem Press, 2014.

Douglass, Frederick. *My Bondage and My Freedom*. Miller, Orton and Mulligan, 1855.

Dover, Caitlin. "Simone Leigh on Her Powerful Sound Installation at the Guggenheim" *Guggenheim Checklist*, May 13, 2019.

Dyson, Torkwase. "Black Interiority: Notes on Architecture, Infrastructure, Environmental Justice, and Abstract Drawing." *Pelican Bomb*, January 9, 2017.

Dyson, Torkwase. "Torkwase Dyson Reflects on Hypershapes," *Metropolis Magazine*, August 21, 2021.

Erickson, Peter. "Black Like Me: Reconfiguring Blackface in the Art of Glenn Ligon and Fred Wilson." *Nka: Journal of Contemporary African Art* 25 (Winter 2009): 30–47.

Farrington, Lisa E. *Creating Their Own Image: The History of African-American Women Artists*. Oxford University Press, 2005.

Finkelman, Paul. "Burns, Anthony." *The Dictionary of Virginia Biography*. Sara B. Bearss, John T. Kneebone, J. Jefferson Looney, Brent Tarter, and Sandra Gioia Treadway, eds. Richmond: The Library of Virginia, 2001. 2:417–418.

Fisch, Audrey A. "'Negrophilism' and Nationalism: The Spectacle of the African-American Abolitionist." In *American Slaves in Victorian England: Abolitionist Politics in Popular Literature and Culture*. Cambridge University Press, 2000, 69–90.

"GIRLS ON 'NOISE' STRIKE: Inmates of Bedford Reformatory Jangle Cell Doors and Scream." *The New York Times*, January 25, 1920, 19.

Green, Charles C. The Nubian Slave. "Nubian Slave." Online Exhibitions, Library of Virginia, https://www.virginiamemory.com/online-exhibitions/items/show/372.

Gumbs, Alexis Pauline. *Undrowned: Black Feminist Lessons from Marine Mammals*. AK Press, 2020.

Hartman, Saidiya. "The Belly of the World: A Note on Black Women's Labors." *Souls* (Boulder, Colo.), vol. 18, no. 1, 2016, 166–73.

Hartman, Saidiya. "In the Wake: A Salon in Honor of Christina Sharpe" February 2, 2017, Barnard College, New York City. Salon. https://bcrw.barnard.edu/videos/in-the-wake-a-salon-in-honor-of-christina-sharpe.

Hartman, Saidiya. "Venus in Two Acts." *Small Axe* 26.2 (June 2008): 1–14.

Hartman, Saidiya. *Wayward Lives, Beautiful Experiments: Intimate Histories of Riotous Black Girls, Troublesome Women, and Queer Radicals*. W.W. Norton & Company, 2020.

Heard, William H. (William Henry), *1850-1937 From Slavery to the Bishopric in the A.M.E. Church. An Autobiography*. Philadelphia: The A.M.E. Book Concern, 1924.

Jackson, Kellie Carter. "'Dare You Meet a Woman': Black Women, Abolitionism, and Protective Violence, 1850–1859." *Slavery & Abolition* 42, no. 2 (2021): 269–92.

Jacobs, Harriet A. *Incidents in the Life of a Slave Girl. Written by Herself*. Boston, 1861.

James, Joy. "The Womb of Western Theory: Trauma, Time Theft and the Captive Maternal," *Carceral Notebooks*, Vol. 12, 2016.

Kaba, Mariame. "Free Us All Participatory Defense Campaigns as Abolitionist Organizing." *The New Inquiry*, May 8, 2017.

London, Barbara. *Soundings: A Contemporary Score*. Museum of Metropolitan Art, 2013.

Martineau, Jarrett, and Eric Ritskes. "Fugitive Indigeneity: Reclaiming the Terrain of Decolonial Struggle through Indigenous Art." *Decolonization: Indigeneity, Education & Society* 3, no. 1 (2014): i-xii.

McKittrick, Katherine. *Demonic Grounds: Black Women and the Cartographies of Struggle*. 1st ed. University of Minnesota Press, 2006.

Mercer, Kobena. "Black Art and the Burden of Representation." *Third Text* 4, no. 10 (1990): 61–78.

Moten, Fred. "Black Kant (Pronounced Chant)." February 27, 2007, University of Pennsylvania, Philadelphia. Lecture.

Millar, Jeremy. "Lawrence Abu Hamdan's 'Earwitness Theatre.'" *e-flux Criticism*, November 28, 2018.

Muñoz, Soledad Fatima. Interview. Conducted by jamilah malika abu-bakare, December 2024.

Nhat Hanh, Thich. "The Fourth Precept: Deep Listening and Loving Speech." In *For a Future to Be Possible: Commentaries on the Five Wonderful Precepts*. Parallax Press, 1993.

Nunley, Tamika. *At the Threshold of Liberty: Women, Slavery, and Shifting Identities in Washington, DC*. University of North Carolina Press, 2021.

Olufemi, Anisa. "WATCHING ME: On Being a Black Woman in a Surveillance State." May 27, 2021, The University of Oregon, Eugene, Oregon. Lecture.

Pilkington, Ed. "Born in a Cell: The Extraordinary Tale of the Black Liberation Orphan." *The Guardian*, July 31, 2018.

The Quilters. Produced and Directed by Jenifer McShane, Netflix, 2024.

Quashie, Kevin Everod. *The Sovereignty of Quiet: Beyond Resistance in Black Culture*. 1st ed. Rutgers University Press, 2012

Rodgers, Tara. "Approaching Sound." *The Routledge Companion to Media Studies and Digital Humanities*. Edited by Jentery Sayers, First edition. Taylor and Francis, 2017.

Rogan, Ali. "The Largely Forgotten History of Philadelphia's Police Bombing of Black Organization MOVE," *PBS News Weekend*, May 17, 2025.

Schendstead, Angela Marie. "Dirty Words: Burnout." *Canadian Art*, May 28, 2018. https://canadianart.ca/features/dirty-words-burnout.

Sharpe, Christina Elizabeth. *In the Wake: On Blackness and Being*. Duke University Press, 2016.

Sharpe, Christina Elizabeth. *Ordinary Notes*. Knopf Canada, 2023.

Smith, Barbara, Beverly Smith, and Demita Frazier. *Combahee River Collective Statement*, 1977.

Spillers, Hortense. "Mama's Baby, Papa's Maybe: An American Grammar Book." *Diacritics* 17, no. 2 (1987): 65–81.

Stone, Mee-Lai. "Joan Didion to David Hockney: Facing Up to the Art Stars—in Pictures." *The Guardian*, January 26, 2023. https://www.theguardian.com/

artanddesign/gallery/2023/jan/26/joan-didion-to-david-hockney-facing-up-to-the-art-stars-in-pictures.

Wallace, David S. "Fred Moten's Radical Critique of the Present." *The New Yorker*, April 30, 2018.

Weheliye, Alexander. "In the Mix: Hearing the Souls of Black Folk." *Amerikastudien* 45, no. 4 (2000): 535–54.

Notes

1 Farrington, *Creating Their Own Image*, 9.
2 Martineau and Ritskes, "Fugitive Indigeneity," ix.
3 Brucato, *Race and Police*, 69.
4 Jacobs, *Incident in the Life*, 146.
5 Hartman, "The Belly of the World," 167.
6 Jacobs, *Incidents in the Life*, 173.
7 McKittrick, *Demonic Grounds*, 43.
8 Heard, *1850–1937 From Slavery*, 31.
9 Jacobs, *Incidents in the Life*, 6.
10 Joy Jacobs, *Womb of Western Territory*, 173.
11 Campt, *Listening to Images*, 7.
12 Pilkington, "Born in a Cell."
13 Simone Leigh, *Loophole of Retreat*, Guggenheim Museum, 2019. See Dover, "Simone Leigh on Her Powerful Sound Installation."
14 "GIRLS ON 'NOISE' STRIKE."
15 James, "The Womb of Western Theory," 65.
16 Drake, *The Slave Narrative*, xxiv.
17 Douglass, *My Bondage and My Freedom*, 320.
18 Olufemi, "WATCHING ME."
19 Brand, *Map to The Door*, 50.
20 Green, *The Nubian Slave*.
21 Fisch, "'Negrophilism' and Nationalism," 75–76.
22 Mercer, "Black Art," 62.
23 Dyson, "Torkwase Dyson Reflects on Hypershapes."
24 Dyson, "Torkwase Dyson Reflects on Hypershapes."
25 Finkelman, "Burns, Anthony," 417–418.
26 Letter from Anthony Burns to the Baptist Church, 1855.
27 Dyson, "Torkwase Dyson Reflects on Hypers Shapes."
28 Hartman, "Venus in Two Acts," 3
29 Glenn Ligon, quoted in Erickson, "Black Like Me," 37.
30 Brand, *Salvage*, 160–161.
31 Dyson, "Black Interiority."
32 Hartman, *Wayward Lives*, 270.
33 London, *Soundings: A Contemporary Score*, 8.
34 Schendstead, "Dirty Words: Burnout."

35 Frei Njootli, *from strength to this question*, Remai Modern Gallery (2019).
36 Muñoz, Interview.
37 Muñoz, Interview.
38 Glenn Ligon, quoted in Stone, "Joan Didion to David Hockney."
39 Moten, "Black Kant."
40 Wallace, "Fred Moten's Radical Critique."
41 Weheliye, "In the Mix," 536.
42 Rodgers, "Approaching Sound," 234.
43 Gumbs, *Undrowned: Black Feminist Lessons*, 15.
44 Sharpe, *In the Wake*, 132.
45 Hartman, "In the Wake."

UNHEARD VOICES

Theatre and the Black Deaf Experience

by **Natasha "Courage" Bacchus**

in conversation with

Dr. Syrus Marcus Ware *and*

Dr. Ra'anaa Yaminah Ekundayo (ABD)

IN THIS CONVERSATION, FORMER PARALYMPIAN AND acclaimed Deaf artist Courage Bacchus explores the intersection of Blackness and disability through the arts. Highlighting triumphs and challenges across all realms, she discusses the transformative platform of theatrical arts and her trajectory from field to field. Through observing the potential of speculative futures, editors Syrus Marcus Ware and Ra'anaa Yaminah Ekundayo join Courage on a journey through hope, growth, and Blackness in tomorrow.

Syrus Marcus Ware (SMW): Thinking about some of the incredible organizing and art and creation that's happened since the uprisings of 2020 and all that activism, we would love to chat with you about your practice and about what you've been up to because you've been so busy in the last couple of years. We would love to chat with you about *21 Black Futures* and about other creative projects that you've been working on since 2020.

Courage Bacchus (CB): Great! From January to June 2024, I will be in the Black Theatre Workshop (BTW). I've been with them learning about mentoring and writing scripts, and the formats for different story development and how that works and what that process looks like, so I've been working on that. I've been learning with them, on the craft of theatre and what that looks like and how to write scripts, as I mentioned. Also, the *Canadian Theater Review* has been partnering with them on my story. It's the four of us. We're called the Survivance Collective. We're a group of four Black, Deaf artists. This year we have some projects in the works, so I'm new to working with them.

I also have a small project upcoming—I believe the word is diaspora—regarding the Black diaspora that should be coming out next summertime, in 2025. Are you aware of *21 Black Futures*? They had just commissioned a book, which was quite nice, so I was part of that project as well. I'm part of a Deaf theatre collective, and I'm just counting, I believe there are seven of us. There's me and—let me just count— eight, nine theatre makers. We'll be going to Scotland to the city of Edinburgh to perform. They're having their annual festival that happens in August, and they have a special troupe this year, so I'll be flying to Scotland this summer.

I've been working with Sandy Hudson on a new offering for her upcoming book. Syrus and I will be working together for a residency later this year involving Deaf, Mad, and disabled Black and Indigenous artists called *Put Your Roots Down Residency* with Theo Walker Robinson. Two projects this year that began last year: The first one is an artist presentation, and the second one is a short documentary.

SMW: You're so prolific and doing so many projects; that's amazing to hear about. We'd love to chat and go back a little bit to 2020. I would love to hear a little bit about your experience doing *21 Black Futures*. You were one of the actors. Obsidian Theatre and CBC Gem brought together twenty-one actors, twenty-one playwrights, and twenty-one directors to make new work responding to that current. You were the main actor for your piece. I would love to hear a little bit about that experience!

CB: Wow. That was so exciting to be a part of. It was challenging as well as exciting, but what a learning experience. It was all new to me. I didn't understand the concept of *21 Black Futures*, so a meeting was set up to explain the concept and wow. As you mentioned, twenty-one directors and actors from across Canada got together for this project. It was a great experience being an actress. But the timing was quite challenging because we had to run through everything and at times, I was feeling overwhelmed, but overall, a good experience. That was good.

SMW: Amazing. I wonder, Courage, if you could talk a little bit about what you see being different now in 2024 for Black, Deaf artists compared to say 2019 and what was happening before the pandemic? What's different now if anything?

CB: About two years ago I hosted a Black-Deaf residency, the first time that I was part of something like this. It was really to uplift and strengthen the confidence of members of the community and help them grow in this field of art. Of course, as you know, with 2020 and the George Floyd murder, many Black, Deaf people across Canada wanted to meet up, and we got in contact with one another. We came from various backgrounds and genres, and we were really very supportive of one another through that very difficult time in that experience, I saw the art really take shape and grow. I saw new faces come onto the screen. Now in 2024, you see different people than you saw in 2019. The challenging part is finding out where the young people are and helping them to grow as well. It's having to search them out and support them in their careers. That's the most challenging thing right now.

Ra'anaa Yaminah Ekundayo (RYE): How would you say it has evolved from being an Olympian to being an artist to where you're at now in your career and how 2020 was this big, shifting moment? I was wondering if you could talk about your trajectory in terms of the arts.

CB: It's very overwhelming. I can't stress that enough. I didn't expect this journey to turn out the way that it has. The trajectory has been, I think, quite unexpected. I was involved with the Black performance *19*. From there my career just took off. I got involved with various projects as a mentor, and I realized that this helped my creative process. I became more creative because of the opportunities that I had. In terms of focusing on my physical business and being very serious about that, I have done that and switched to the art world and acting, but really, I take the time to rest. I recognize that work-life balance is very important. Whatever you have going on in your life and the physical fitness aspect of my life, great. The acting side is also great for my creativity, but I do need a bit of both, so that both sides can benefit. I'm understanding how to find that balance now. I used to be a track runner, but there wasn't a whole lot of expression in that field.

SMW: Whereas now you get to follow your interest, your questions, and you get to express yourself differently, I'm assuming, in the arts.

CB: Yeah, that's right. Not much expression in track and running, but in the arts, definitely! With track, it was all very competitive, and you had to work very hard, and the goal is to win and get medals. There wasn't a whole lot of socialization going on. It was all about me and making sure I was the best athlete possible. But I realized the importance of rest and recovery and taking that time for oneself to reflect on what you've done, rather than just go, go, go. Just for the interpreter. In elementary school in Grade 8, I had some classmates or one in particular. Not a whole network of people because I moved and didn't have that chance to get integrated into the community. When I look back on photos from that year, I realize what's changed. Before I was a track star and now, I'm an actor and people don't recognize me because it's been quite the switch. It's very surprising to look back on old photos with my classmate from elementary school and see how I've changed.

RYE: That's so beautiful to see that transition. I love the way you talk about really bringing care into your work and care into your practice and taking care of your body as a vessel, which you use to produce your art. Can you talk about areas in which you would like to see more care? Or how you think the realm of the arts across so-called Canada can further bring in care not just for Black people, for Deaf people, but for queer or femme, other people, all kinds of marginalized people; how we can bring or how you would want to see more forms of care prioritized?

CB: Well, I'm always being reminded that I'm not alone and neither is anyone else. We're all part of a collective group and a community. I think it's about building those comfort zones amongst ourselves and realizing that with one another's support and taking care of ourselves, we can overcome anything. We must learn that we have value and then let that guide our actions so that we can stand up for ourselves. Make sure that we have what we need to see us through and navigate this challenging world.

SMW: I'm wondering, Courage, if you could talk a little bit about your ideal Black future, if you were imagining 2030, 2040, or 2045 as a year, what does it look like? What does it feel like if we get to the places that we're hoping to get to where we're all a bit freer? What does it look like?

CB: I think any Black future whether it be 2050 or 2060, could be hearing, Deaf, or disabled. I want to see us come together as a community rather than be divided like the Black Deaf versus the Black hearing versus Black disabled and help one another to... I'm trying to find the right word here. I'm just thinking of what word really encapsulates this. What's the word I'm looking for? Ever since I was a little girl, I understood that there is a division across the Black community. You have hearing and then you have hard-of-hearing and then you have Deaf people, and we're all separated. I guess what I'm imagining is that there are no barriers to access. I don't have to worry about having an interpreter there. Everyone would sign. We'd all be able to communicate with one another. We'd all be using the same language, basically. And that means how we connect with one another. No barriers would exist, that's what I imagine.

SMW: That's so exciting. That makes me excited! The possibility that we might come closer together. That we might turn toward each other. That we might all learn. I mean, imagine if we had the opportunity to speak together and to be together and to live together and to do activism together because we were all able to communicate in the same language. This is why I'm so interested in these programs that we're seeing in the community coming up, where people can learn ASL and Black ASL and all these things to be able to increase our opportunity to communicate together. It makes me think about this moment in 2020 when the uprisings were happening, and there had been killings by the police and it was ongoing throughout the summer, and we were organizing on the street. We did ASL, some preliminary ASL training, so that we could get a message quickly. We need to go in this direction away from the cops, or we need to quickly get behind this fencing or whatever. If we didn't know some of those basic signs like we're coming together, we need to go, let's go quickly or whatever, we would not be creating a very safe environment for all of us. That's our goal in activism is how do we do this in the safest possible way, so that we can all get into the action and get out of the action and home safely.

I hope by 2050, so many more of us hearing folks will have learned enough ASL to be able to communicate together. That, of course, makes me think about all the other things that we're also thinking through. Like having audio descriptions and verbal descriptions for blind and low-vision comrades who are organizing with us. How do we work across differences together to build these kinds of futures? I'm excited about being shoulder to shoulder with you in this fight and where we might get to. I think what I love about your practice is that so much of this dreaming into a future is told through your artmaking. You take us on a journey in the characters that you create. You take us on a journey in the performances that you create where we can't help but want to get involved, so I'm excited about what's coming together toward the future. Ra'anaa, I know you were organizing in the streets in 2020 as well. Don't know how connected or interconnected hearing and Deaf communities are in the communities that you were organizing in 2020. But it seems like such a beautiful vision that you've laid forward, Courage. We need to get on the same page so that we can communicate, we can dream together, and build together, which feels exciting.

CB: Yes. Yes. I think that we are already setting up a system where we break down barriers. Whatever language it is that we're using, it's really dividing us. We all have a very similar experience. We're all part of the rainbow community. Why are we so separate based on language alone? Even the Deaf and hard-of-hearing communities aren't unified. We all need to get together for our own safety and empowerment. I think we need to share a language, whatever that looks like, or even a code. For example, we can have symbols or gestures that we share amongst one another and develop our own language or communicate, so that we can help one another. For example, like a wink or showing a wrist to say, time to do something. Kind of the way that you have this in a community where they have their own language, they know just by a look or gesture what they mean. Otherwise, where is the communication? That does harm to the disabled community when there are communication barriers. Especially when you have the cops involved and they're all doing their thing and speaking and yelling and like you said, "To keep everyone safe we need to be able to communicate so that we can all protect one another."

SMW: Absolutely. Of course, what we've seen with the cops again and again, is that they don't seem interested in learning ASL at all. When meeting Deaf people on the street, they just keep talking louder rather than communicating in ASL. Right? I saw it during the G20 protests in 2010. Then I remembered in 2020 when they just would not communicate with a Deaf person in an appropriate way, and then as a result, escalated their tactics because the person wasn't responding. The person wasn't responding because the cops weren't communicating in ASL, which was the language that the person used. How do we keep each other safe? We say we keep ourselves safe, how do we do it? Part of how we do it is, I think as you say, we learn some shared testers that will allow us to be able to communicate quickly.

CB: Yeah, because somebody asked that. You have Black gangs. They have their own system to protect one another against the cops, so perhaps we could borrow their techniques of how to communicate with one another. I mean, I'm not part of a gang, but I'm aware that they do have a system and anyone who joins the gang is introduced to the system, but also a way of protection. They use some words or signs or symbols or something, or maybe a tap on the shoulder has a meaning, whatever people are comfortable with. Then they all vote and agree on which signs and gestures they're going to use, and that becomes standard in the community. For example, if you have someone who's in a wheelchair, they will be protected because they are part of the communication system that was agreed upon. It doesn't matter if you're from the disabled community or the Deaf community, you all agree on the same way to communicate. Very powerful to see that, especially in response to police action. When the cops escalate, as you say, having that shared language just gives that extra bit of power to the group.

SMW: I think about when we were organizing in the summer of 2020, there were moments when we had to make quick decisions and had to move people quickly from one place to another. Well, how do you do that in a way that everybody gets the info in a timely way so that they can also move safely? It's such a big thing that you're not only talking up at the top, at the highest, tallest person. But you're also talking at multiple levels so that people who are sitting down can get the information as well. Thank you for that. I would love to chat with you both about the fellowship at Wildseed Centre for Art & Activism. You're both fellows for Wildseed for the Black Arts Fellowship. Courage, I know you were one of the inaugural fellows in the first year. We would love to hear a little bit about your creative project and what it is that you're presenting at Wildseed.

CB: Yes, Oluseye. I saw their presentation and their work, and we all took turns as part of our fellowship. When it was my turn, I didn't really know. I have these medals that are just collecting dust in a box somewhere. They proposed the idea of why not turn it into an artistic piece, something I'd never thought of. Okay, I can try. You'll see the fruition of my work. The first one was used in mixed media, and I wasn't quite sure how to put it together. Should I paint it blue? I was trying to figure out how to bring this piece alive, and Oluseye gave me some ideas, which I incorporated into this artistic piece, and you'll see that tomorrow. I'm looking at it right now. It's just over to my right here, and it's all 3D. You'll see it tomorrow if you're going to be there. My family's like, "Wow, you did that?" Yeah. Well, a friend helped me, but my family was so impressed that I was able to make this. It's great and it's very inspirational in that way. I do miss track. When I look at this sculpture and see my medals, I miss my track life, but that's life.

SMW: Do you think you would ever do track again? I know that track stars often are usually in the earlier part of their life when they're doing the running and the hurdling, but I also know that some people run up until they're one hundred. Would you ever consider continuing—

CB: Yeah, I saw it at the, let me just spell it out, the Master's Game for people who are above the age of fifty-five to one hundred. I think it was 2014 to 2016, so about a two-and-a-half-year period that I saw this woman. She was a hundred years old, and she was still running. I witnessed it. There was an older man who was doing the javelin, and one was doing shot put. They were all an advanced age, as you would say, but they were in such good shape. I was impressed by them. I added that to my sculpture, the period for the timeline when I received all my medals from high school to postsecondary age. I have a timeline of all my medals incorporated into this sculpture.

RYE: I'm just really fascinated by how you are bringing this completely other side of your life into the arts. Melding the world of track and arts, and really doing this unique, multidisciplinary approach. I guess, maybe the question there is, is there more collaboration between track and arts in your future? Or how in other ways have you seen your track history really start to emanate into your artistic practice?

CB: Both. I see them coming together again. This sculpture I did has given me the courage to do something else. I had forgotten that I had made a video of my project, and it was a metaphorical story I shared. I mean, track and what that means. For example, I've noticed there are often awards for MVP, the most valuable player, those types of things are fairly common, and I think, why not reward myself for being in good shape? For maintaining my health or something like that? But awards are always about exposure and money and something that's external to yourself, not to be very much what the Olympics and other sporting events are all like. It's about how you show yourself to the world for other people and Deaf or hard-of-hearing people. Usually, the award is somehow designed in their likeness, something that speaks to who they are as a person, so they're not getting an award for other people's participation. It's partly because of who they are, and the award is designed based on that. I was just thinking about this metaphorically and how to award a team and the larger community and what they mean to the Deaf and hard-of-hearing community. When I was younger, I was so innocent. I was colonized, and I thought, I need to win awards, too, because that's the thing to do. Now I realize that awards can mean so much more and be related to the person and not the society.

RYE: That's such a beautiful sentiment. Thank you so much for that. I think that's inspiring. For myself as an emerging practitioner, I feel like I just took so much from that. I'm going to hold on to that nugget of just beautiful, creative wisdom, so thank you for sharing that.

SMW: It's been so wonderful to get to experience your practice. Since I got introduced to it in maybe 2019, and now with so much of your work out there everywhere, it's exciting to be able to chat with you today about your process and projects. You started today telling us about all the projects that you have that are coming up, which is so inspirational and exciting. If there was one project that you're most looking forward to that you could tell us a little bit more about, which one would it be?

CB: Well, flying to Scotland. The reason is that last year, the same performing troop that I'm part of went there. They toured Edmonton. They were in Ontario—Ottawa, Kingston, and Southern and Eastern Ontario. They went to schools for the Deaf to perform for children, and they saw the enormous impact it had on those Deaf students. To go to Scotland, it's an honour because it recognizes the work that this troupe has done, and they were invited back this year again. Obviously, there was an impact on the community over there as well. It's largely a hearing audience, not a Deaf audience, so that's quite something to have an impact there. Obviously, having the Deaf youth be inspired by the work of this performing troupe is the ultimate. But having others outside of our community, outside of this country, recognizing what we do is also amazing. But I think it's really about the youth, the fact that they see Deaf adults who are performing, maybe it gives them a sense of self-worth.

Maybe they realize that they do have value, even though they're surrounded by people who tell them they don't. It might initiate a conversation with their parents and just get encouraged to respell something. Thank you. Yes. For the people who are from the Caribbean or West Indies, families or communities, we've never seen anything quite like this before. To see someone like me or someone who looks like them in this role gives them a feeling of confidence. Maybe they're shy. They're not comfortable expressing themselves, and then they see someone like me, and it gives them that permission to be who they are. I think as Deaf people, we need to work together, not against one another. Regardless of what generations we came from or the communities in which we grew up, we must recognize where we exist in whatever diaspora we find ourselves in and work together.

SMW: Thank you, Courage!

TOTAL

An Excerpt

by **Aisha Sasha John**

LEARN TO LOVE YOUR LITTLE WHOLE

WHEN I DISCOVER ITS POINT I'LL TELL

HOW MANY TIMES A DAY SKINNY PEOPLE SHIT

WHAT I FEEL THROUGH FLEEING

OF MONTHS, I AM NOVEMBER AND DECEMBER

MUST, NEED, HAVE TO, WILL

A BURSTING IN OF JOY

SILENCE AND TALKING

AUNTY CATHY' DAUGHTER (ME)

BLOOD HIGHWAY

CHAKRA BLUE RATTLE, CLAW SWORD, AND A FRESH
PILE OF SOFT SOIL

"ME FIRST" SHIRT

ROOT INCHES

SOUL

ALLIGATOR AND OWL

STARED AT ON THE SUBWAY

IS THERE SOMETHING I DON'T KNOW BECAUSE I'M...UNINFORMED?

PEANUT BUTTER AND BLACK GRAPES

JOY

YELLOW HANGING FLOWERS

NONDUAL MINDFULNESS

I WANTED TO TALK ABOUT WHAT I HAVE TO LIVE DESPITE

THOUGHT AS (MERELY) MENTAL SENSATION

COLOURS OF IRON AND RUST

THE NEXT DAY THE BITCH CAME

A BLAZE IN THE VALLEY

A NEAR-EMPTY PARK AND I

TIRZAH IN THE PARK AND TEXTING

THE WIND ROARED AS DIRECTION

A SHEPHERD ESSENTIALLY

IRMA VEP

MAGGIE CHEUNG

MORNING MILDLY HORNY

SYLVIA WYNTER RETURN

THE INFLUENCE OF AROUSAL

THAT WHICH KEEPS YOUR POWER SECRET FROM ITSELF

THE HURRICANE VS MY MOTHER'S COUNTRY

THE FAT OF MY AUNTY'S ARMS

ON LUCK

OCEAN OF PRIOR CAUSES

OPPORTUNITIES TO EAT MAYONNAISE

WHY I ASKED WHAT AN ARROW'S OPPOSITE IS

FROM 35 TO GASP

THE SOFT GREY COTTON ONE PLUS ANOTHER I CAN BLINK BEHIND

LAVISH ABSENCE'S ARRIVAL

BABY'S FIRST BLENDER

INAUGURAL SMOOTHIE

STUDFINDER

SPELLING CEILING

IF THERE WERE SUN, I WOULD MAKE MYSELF BLACK BY IT

THE PRAYER OF DAWN

IN CYCLES AND CIRCLES

AFRO-COLOMBIAN ANGEL

PRODDING 40

THE PLACE ELEGANCE ARGUES GRACE

SOMEONE PUT A SMALL SQUARE OF BLACK FABRIC ON THE DEAD POSSUM LYING ON THE CURB SOUTH ON BROCK STREET

SPOTLIGHT, SHADE

THAT I AM A BAT AND I CAVE

YELLOW FLOWERS

THE LUMINARIES

DAY OF REST AND WEEK

CAT VS. LAMB

BLOOD RED MEN'S T-SHIRT BACKWARDS

WAR WITH WHAT'S RAVENOUS IN ME

I AM NOT HOW I HAVE BEEN INSATIABLE

EATING FAST IS LIKE TAKING DRUGS

BREAD OR SOMETHING I HAVE TO COOK

DISCOVER THE VERSATILITY OF TEMPEH–NO

IMAGINATION INJURY

IMAGINATION AMELIORATION

IMAGINATION REPAIR

FOUR RAISINS

FOUR RAISINS WILL LAST AS LONG AS A BOX IF YOU EAT THEM AS A PRAYER

HE RECOMMENDS MINDFUL SMOKING

OKAY I JUST FIGURED OUT WHAT JESUS IS A METAPHOR FOR

BUSINESS DAWN

DID YOU HEAR THE ONE ABOUT THE SUFI SAINT?

RABIA OF BASRA:

"ONE DAY, SHE WAS SEEN RUNNING THROUGH THE STREETS OF BASRA CARRYING A POT OF FIRE IN ONE HAND AND A BUCKET OF WATER IN THE OTHER. WHEN ASKED WHAT SHE WAS DOING, SHE SAID, 'I WANT TO PUT OUT THE FIRES OF HELL AND BURN DOWN THE REWARDS OF PARADISE. THEY BLOCK THE WAY TO ALLAH. I DO NOT WANT TO WORSHIP FROM FEAR OF PUNISHMENT OR FOR THE PROMISE OF REWARD, BUT SIMPLY FOR THE LOVE OF ALLAH.'"

TERRIBLE, MOREOVER, AND LIGHT

IMMEDIATE, CLOSE, PROXIMAL, HERE

THAT MY RAGE MODELS HAVE BEEN MALE RAPPERS

THE BRIM

THE VERGE

VS.

THE GREAT GIVING UP

DEAR GOD: WHO AM ME?

THE CAT UPCHUCKED AND RE-ATE HER CHICKEN
TREAT

CANADIAN APARTHEID

THIS COUNTRY IS SICK AMIRITE?

CROSS-COMMUNITY CRYING

A CRY-IN

CLASS PICTURE AND CRY

DREAM I HAVE BELLY BUTTON BETWEEN MY BREASTS
CLOAKED IN LABIA

FROM HEARING TO HEEDING

IN WHICH WHAT IS HARD IN ME SOFTENS

SHE PUT A STRING AROUND MY LOOSE TOOTH AND
SHUT THE DOOR

TO SWALLOW WHOLE AND SQUEEZE SOFT

THE SNAKEHOOD, THE PRIESTESS, THE SUPPLICANT, GOD

THAT YOU WERE NEVER BORN AND WILL NEVER DIE

FROM PERCEIVE TO PREDICT

I WOULD LIKE TO THANK LOVE

INTROSPECTIVE RETROSPECTIVE

by **Ravyn Wngz**
in conversation with
Dr. d'bi.young anitafrika

RAVYN WNGZ REFLECTS ON HER LIFE, PRACTICE, AND activism as a multidisciplinary Black trans artist.

d'bi.young anitafrika (d'bi): Welcome, Ravyn. It is always such a powerful and nourishing exchange when I get to share space with you. Thank you for taking the time to talk with me about your life and art in Northern Turtle Island. Could you start by talking about your intersecting identities as a multidisciplinary artist? How do you introduce yourself?

Ravyn Wngz (RW): My name is Ravyn Ariah Wngz. I am Afro Indigenous, Two Spirit, and a trans woman, born on the island of Bermuda. I grew up between Atlanta, Georgia, and Bermuda. I moved to Toronto, Northern Turtle Island, to pursue dance in 2004. I'm a dancer at heart and spirit and movement. I'm a descendant of abolitionists, and I feel like that's my purpose-filled roadmap, so to speak. I'm invested in creating dynamics in the communities I'm a part of that are intentional about how we treat each other in quiet moments when we're angry and when we have conflict. I'm really interested in unpacking and doing away with the punishments we've all received and experienced. I identify as Two Spirit and trans for many reasons. Being Indigenous and trans is a spectrum of experiences. I don't have a destination for my gender representation. That has been a beautiful process for me and a difficult one for people outside of me to understand. A lot of my artwork and practice invites people into that ceremony, bringing people into the process of how I move through life. Also, how I see life from numerous perspectives growing up in Atlanta, Georgia, and Bermuda; having specific Black experiences that I associate with those spaces; then moving here and choosing to look and dress differently.

d'bi: Could you tell us about your work with Black Lives Matter in Toronto and your experience of the life-changing speech you gave on Black trans realities within an anti-Black society in 2020?

RW: Absolutely. Throughout my dance and high school experience, I had to advocate for myself and the people around me. I was fortunate to grow up with a mother who was a deputy principal and was very adamant that I needed to be able to speak up for myself, speak clearly, and with conviction. As a Black queer trans person, I was socialized to believe that I wasn't the right representative for Black leadership. I focused on multicultural relationships within dance—how our intersecting oppressions were impacting each other, and how we could create work that highlighted that. It was really in a space of advocacy, less in a space of activism.

My community organizing through dance, creating affirming dance education, led Black Lives Matter–Toronto to invite me to take part in a Take Back the Night event. They asked me to choreograph a flash mob. It was the first time I used my choreography in this particular way. I had always wanted to be impactful in my community, especially growing up in Atlanta, Georgia, with Dr. Martin Luther King Jr.'s statues and all of that. It was presenting itself repeatedly. I think I was in a little bit of denial about what was happening because of my preconceived notions of leadership. I just wanted to be a dancer. Advocacy and activism for me are about fighting for my daily acts of living. It didn't feel like a political act; it was my life.

I participated in the Black Lives Matter–Toronto Tent City in 2016. I had done the Take Back the Night celebration and thought they were cool people. They were much different than how they were talked about in the media. At the rallies, there was so much care and thoughtfulness in who was included and how people were talking about trans people—in a Black space...that was very new to me. I watched hours of interviews of Sandy Hudson and Rodney Diverlus specifically, listening to what they were saying, unpacking systemic oppression and anti-Black racism that I couldn't see because I hadn't grown up understanding all the ways it was covert here in Canada. In Georgia, it was overt, so you didn't have questions about what something was or wasn't. Here, it was more insidious. That first night, we were attacked by the police. It was an extreme moment that I still think about because the most terrifying moment was watching people I just taught in a dance class get crushed to the ground. The officers looked terrified. For me, it was like, you are terrified of us, but you are the one creating body terrorism on us. It made me think beyond the police for the first time. I went back to the space the next day because I knew nobody could release that trauma without support. I did harm reduction, I stretched, and we did singing circles. I shared release strategies with folks. They took notice of what I was doing. I wasn't trying to be noticed or seen; I just wanted to be helpful.

They included me in a meeting to strategize some actions to get [Ontario's] Premier [Kathleen] Wynne to meet with us. It was my first time in a meeting like that. I thought, how did I get here? I'm a dancer. But I participated, and it was exciting and terrifying. I felt they knew what they were doing, so I went with it, and we got the results we wanted. It was at that time that you and I started working together, d'bi, on your play *She Mami Wata* from the Orisha Trilogy. What a beautiful experience. I felt like my life was really happening for the first time, especially as a trans person. This was some of the first times I was telling people that I was trans, sharing my pronouns, and being called Ravyn in public space. All of that was so new and challenging to navigate the switches and changes in how I was being related to. I remember it was after you had invited me to be a cast member in the third play of your Orisha Trilogy called *Bleeders* and I was sitting inside the rehearsal space when I received a text from one of the members asking if I would be interested in joining. I remember thinking to myself that here I was playing a character in an Afrofuturist play; a character who was a descendant of today's Black Lives Matter movement, and now I am being asked to be a part of the present movement. I trusted Spirit too much to not say yes to this invitation.

d'bi: You just brought me way back. Black Lives Matter inspired the entire Orisha Trilogy. *esu crossing the middle passage* was an ode to Black Lives Matter–Toronto's [BLM-TO] activism. I wrote specific scenes into the play that represented the ongoing revolutionary action that was happening, like at the Toronto Police Headquarters. Remember the talk-back session we had, that was for Black Lives Matter to come and speak to the theatre community about the urgency of getting involved in community interventions? The play's audience was so moved by their presence there, and I remember feeling like I was part of something transformative. The conversations about our role in society, the impact of our decisions on future generations, and how white supremacist systems impact the Earth and future generations were crucial. It was such a powerful moment working on *Bleeders* with you, Ravyn. You were playing one of the Ohosi Mino, the radical group of Black freedom fighters who protect the people in future in this Afrofuturist dystopia. I was thinking about Sandy, Syrus, Rodney, and the rest of the folks who were putting their bodies on the line for us to achieve emancipation—those folks in the future who are contending with the choices and ramifications of supremacist toxicities. For me, you were already one of those people. But I had no idea you got the invite while working on the show [laughs].

RW: When I first got the message, I said yes right away, but I was working with a spiritual clairvoyant healer at the time. I sat with her and said, BLM-TO asked me to join, but I don't know why they asked me. I haven't figured out what I offer to the team. They're brilliant. She said, "You are not there to do the same thing everyone else is there to do. You are the energy of healing. The dead have chosen you as a protector, a transitionary figure. This is why you are Two Spirit, that bridge. It's in the softness, in the healing. You are going to help the movement heal."

I focused on safety for the first two years. The group was curating safety for everyone except themselves. My influence was to think about how we were taking care of our bodies, spirits, minds, and the group container. We had uncomfortable conversations, but they were necessary. How can we ask people to treat each other better if we in this group aren't working through those dynamics? We must do inside what we want for our folx outside. That was influenced by working with you, d'bi. In creating *Bleeders* that centred the principles of your method such as *sacredness* and *integrity*, the process of creating a safe container also had to embody those principles. It was difficult, but I found myself sitting with families, taking in their information, letting them know what we can provide as BLM, and being transparent about what they might experience. It was difficult because many other Black people didn't expect me to be in this group. I had to navigate that, and as someone newly out as a trans person, I didn't know how to ask for support around it. I had to learn articulation of my own safety strategies with the group.

I'm grateful for Syrus, who had twenty-five years of activism practice before ever joining BLM. It was helpful to lean on Syrus to figure out how to do this and live this experience while also pursuing a dance career. Fast forward, the first two years of BLM, I was in study mode. I went to every union, high school, or event I could speak at to work through public speaking. I developed a way of speaking and doing speeches that allowed people to enter from wherever they were. When 2020 happened, the pandemic was in full force, and it was scary. The continuation of policing impacts on our bodies with George Floyd, Breonna Taylor—Korchinski-Paquet here in Toronto, so many names, so many families. I didn't have time to be scared about the pandemic. I had to be safe around it, but I didn't let myself feel the pandemic at all. I pushed and created vigils and did all those things.

When the action happened that led to three of our members being detained, it shocked my system because we had never had arrests in our movement. We had to re-strategize and figure out the whole thing. I was in organizer mode. We had to do a press conference to explain what happened and bring the public in. Public protest is a kind of performance that brings people into the conversation. I didn't want to be there the morning I woke up. I sent a message to the group saying I wasn't going to make it. I was feeling resentment, frustration, anger, and a soul tiredness that felt unfair. Syrus said this is our duty, what we committed to doing. Let's show up. So, I showed up and did the speech. The speech I prepared, not many people have heard that. I started with a quote from Amanda Seales about being the change you want to see. I was in this inspirational place of art as activism and practice. After everyone did their brilliant thing, a reporter asked a question that made me so angry. I was like, I'm not holding my tongue today. I said what was on my mind, shooting it off. It was a rant for me. Rodney was holding the small of my back because I was rocking.

The next morning, I woke up to 10,000 new followers on Instagram. It was shocking. My speech was being shared around. I did an Instagram live to tag the people I quoted. I wasn't trying to take their words. I was talking to Syrus throughout the experience; my marriage was also ending. My partner had left two days before the speech went viral. I wasn't in a physical, emotional, or spiritual place to receive it all. It was almost like window shopping. I thought, I can't do this. It was almost debilitating. It was already scary being on the subway because I didn't know who knew who I was or how they would treat me. My back was already up against the walls. Then OVO 40 posted my video, and I started receiving messages from folks in the hip hop community who were immediately transphobic. They were saying things like, we went from Martin Luther King Jr. to this. This was one of the statements that stuck in my brain. I was so mad.

I never wanted to be a famous activist. I'm not interested in that kind of thing. I hadn't even posted the video on my own page. It took about a year before I finally posted it. I remember telling Syrus that I wanted to disappear. I needed to stop because there was too much happening, and I didn't think I could handle it. Syrus said, "They're finally listening to us trans people, and it's you. There are ways you can do it, but it's you."

So, I fell into duty. I showed up on Instagram, did my Lives, and started sharing my stories and how I came to these understandings. Thousands of people began sharing my stuff, and then Rihanna started following me. I didn't even notice at first. My twin brother told me, "Hey, Rihanna's following you, and she only follows 1,400 people." I was like, "What?" It was bizarre. Viola Davis... this person, that person—it was overwhelming.

Then Madonna posted my video on her page. Two or three million people saw it. Still, I hadn't posted it on my own page. She sent me a voice note saying, "Thank you for being so brave. This is really powerful." I was like, "Am I having a conversation with Madonna?" I have so many critiques, but what is happening right now? I kept saying that to my friends. It was overwhelming, and it took a while to get through that.

Then I started getting offers to write. "Can you write for the LA *Chronicle*? Can you write for *Maclean's* magazine? Can you speak at this scholar leadership conference? Can you do this UN thing?" I was like, "What?" It was so much, an out-of-body autopilot experience. Only now can I reflect and realize there were some important things for me to learn about myself, about what I had believed and accepted about my realities. I realized I could dream bigger, that I could have the impact I wanted when I was ten years old. It was showing up in a different way than I had planned, but I did want this. I was one of those kids who wanted to be like Michael Jackson so I could influence the world. If that meant activism, then that's what it is.

But then I started getting attacks from people who had been marching with us, people who were formerly on my team. That was scary because they knew intimacies about me, where I lived, and there were threats to my life as well. I was both celebrated and unprotected because of the visibility. People's relationship to fame is so dangerous and dehumanizing. I found people kept saying, "I love your work," and I would ask, "Explain that to me." I found myself becoming aggressive, but then I realized people were appreciating my work. I needed to sit and reflect. My nervous system was out of control. I leaned back into my movement practice and developed a method to take care of myself. Burlesque was also part of that as a body politic and a way to release these stories.

Now I'm figuring out a better balance—how to do this kind of work and my creative work and have them feed each other. I feel fulfilled, but it took a while to figure this out. No trans person in this movement has experienced what I experienced—this kind of fame, especially in Canadian activism. There weren't many people I could turn to for advice. I did receive some support, though. Amanda Seales was helpful and used her platform to interrupt the transphobia coming at me. She asked, "Did you listen to the message, or did you pause at the messenger?" It meant so much to me that Amanda and others like Indya Moore and Angelica Ross were supporting me publicly.

d'bi: Ravyn, that's a journey and a half. I am so appreciative of the people you were in circle with to support you through such a life-altering experience. Where do you find the inner strength to hold yourself steadily through all the experiences of harm, of violence? How do you celebrate? Where does that commitment to truly live your life come from?

RW: My mom encouraged and supported me to be my individual self, especially as a dark-skinned, male-assumed person. My mother was a single mom raising two Black, dark-skinned kids, and she understood that we would be treated differently in the world. She taught us to walk tall and present ourselves confidently, even if we weren't. That almost feels natural to me now. I was working in community, sharing my art in Black and trans BIPOC [Black Indigenous and People of Colour] spaces where I was celebrated for who I was on stage. That kind of enrichment supported my confidence. I celebrated myself because I was celebrated in those spaces. I've taken people's reactions to me personally, but I don't anymore. It is a choice.

I know I have the privilege of living in Toronto, even though there are hardships. There is a particular kind of privilege in being able to present myself as myself. That's also why I do it. Someone needs to know I existed in this. When I learned Bayard Rustin was a Black gay man who organized the March on Washington, it was life-changing for me. James Baldwin and Dr. Maya Angelou were friends. Nikki Giovanni, they were friends. They were prolific and brilliant but just regular people to themselves. I realized my work is about trying to become more human to people, to share the different kinds of humanities we can exist with, especially as a two-spirit person on Turtle Island. As a two-spirit person, I'm a memory keeper. It's important for me to use my art to share the history of how we got here and where we're going.

d'bi: Ravyn, I would like us to shift attention to the exciting work you have been doing celebrating the legacy of the legendary Jackie Shane. How did you come to learn about Jackie Shane?

RW: Miss Jackie Shane is a huge part of why I live so boldly now. She was an incredible artist, performer, and musician—charismatic and beautiful. She was very intelligent, writing her autobiography, and the title of her book was similar to a play I was writing in 2012. There's a deep connection between us—spiritual and ancestral. Everyone who talks about meeting her was moved by her. When I learned about her in 2017, when it was announced that she had been nominated for a Grammy, I realized that I had been writing her story without even knowing it. Maybe she was speaking to me all along. I met Nicky Lawrence, who performed one of her songs, and she told me I looked like Jackie Shane. That was the greatest compliment I've ever received. Nicky invited me to emulate Jackie Shane on stage, but I didn't see myself as a drag queen. Instead, I offered a movement experience that was like her image.

Then suddenly, Jackie Shane stories started showing up everywhere—a mural on Massey Hall, a documentary by Elliot Page. She was returning to tell her story, and for some reason, she chose me to be the person who does some of that storytelling. So, I must honour it. When the Heritage Minute about her was announced, I initially didn't want to audition. I didn't know how to audition, and I felt like they didn't want me. But then I got one more ask, and I finally auditioned. They asked me to re-audition, and the process was beautiful. I made the decision not to see myself until the Heritage Minute was released. I wanted to trust the team to be brilliant and to perform that brilliance.

The most celebrated I've been was through my performance of Jackie Shane, and there's something about that that feels special and beautiful. It feels beautiful to be able to tell her stories, especially as a dark-skinned trans woman. If she was doing it in the sixties and seventies, I'm going to do it now.

There are two projects: A Jackie Shane musical that I'm working on, which is a cross between her story and mine. Through six or seven of her songs, you can piece

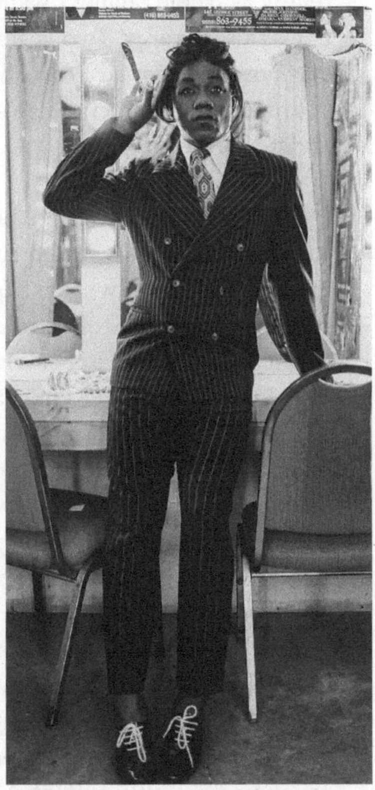

Ravyn Wngz on set as Jackie Shane. Photograph by Wade Muir. Courtesy of Ravyn Wngz.

together some of her thoughts and feelings. We're going to use those songs to draw the skeleton and then correlate them with six or seven of my own stories to create an experience for Miss Jackie Shane. I'm really excited about that.

Another project I'm going to do as my own entity is something she was planning before she passed away. She wanted to do a tour starting in Toronto, then going to New York and LA—only three places—but she wanted two nights of her songs for her fans. I want to do that for Jackie Shane Day next year. I'm working on her songs for a two-night concert and bringing in other artists to share their stories and the legacy of her influence. That's what I'm working on for Miss Jackie.

d'bi: Oh, that's incredible, Ravyn! I cannot wait to experience your storytelling as Jackie Shane! I want to shift now to talking about your practice as a storyteller. Two years ago, we had a conversation at the Black Womyn's Decolonial Praxis Symposium. Could you share a bit about your methods of practice as a storyteller, theatre maker, choreographer, and performing artist?

RW: Finding the connection between different modes of storytelling such as things that can be spoken, sung, or danced to tell the story most effectively is what intrigues me—how those different mediums support the fullness of the story. I plan for a feeling across all the different things I create. For instance, I'm performing soon for a queer Indigenous event, and I'm sharing my experience of being hunted as a "pretend Indian." It's important for me to share that experience with people who are seeing and celebrating me in different capacities. The feeling I want folks to walk away with is a sense of responsibility—for their participation, for not paying attention, for taking positions when things like that happen. It's not about shame but about sharing my reality with them so people start treating me as if I exist in real time. That's really what's driving my work now. Part of what I love about storytelling is that it can change your life when done with integrity and intention. It is life-altering.

When I saw Heather Headley, from Trinidad and Tobago, who originated the title role of Aida, performing the story on Broadway, and she opened her entire chest and sang that song, I knew I had to perform. I was training to be in the Olympics as a track athlete, but that moment made me realize I needed to be on stage. I didn't know how, but I thought, "I have some rhythm, I'll be a dancer first, and then a singer. That's how I'll get there. That's how I'll do those musicals."

These moments can change your life, and that's what theatre has the power to do. When I saw your play *Word! Sound! Power!* from the Sankofa Trilogy—it was life-changing for me in multiple ways. Watching you tell those stories, share those characters and experiences—it was thrilling, thought-provoking, and heart-enriching. I remember coming up to you after the show and saying, "Thank you. I feel like you gave me my ancestors back." I didn't think I could have that. People told me, "You're either Black or you're queer," but when you looked at me, you said, so matter-of-factly, "Don't listen to people," and I thought, "Who are you?" Since then, I've been a fan and now a friend, which I cherish deeply.

Before, I was so focused on form. Now, I'm not as focused on form as I used to be. I came here to be a dancer, and I thought I should be dancing. But I'm not in charge of how people encounter my work, so whether it's singing, acting, or writing, it's a celebration of me coming back together as an artist. As African people through many diasporas, we've been forced to siphon ourselves between categories. But if we really think about it, how can you tell a story without music, without singing and dancing, and without the collaboration of the audience you're talking to? It feels like ancestral veneration, that ritualistic space. I'm working on engaging my ancestors, not just in struggle but also inviting them to tea to enjoy this moment of celebration, to come with me to the award show, to go to this movie, but also to sit in the things I don't understand yet. That's really the work of me as the Black Widow of Burlesque—that's my tagline as an artist. Essentially, it's a mixture of my name, Ravyn, and my mission. I'm a messenger and harbinger of truth—that's Ravyn. I'm also a glamour weapon against oppression, using the tools of glamour, beauty, and the politics of desirability to bring people into my sensitivity.

d'bi: Yes! When I see you perform, the embodiment of and possibility for joy to conjure new futures, it feels so palpable in the moment. It activates every cell within my body when I see you perform.

RW: Thank you for saying that. That means a lot to me.

d'bi: What is your hope, both for yourself and for the community of Black arts activists? What is your hope for us as we move into our futures?

RW: My hope is that people will come to the realization and practice of collective freedom and liberation, understanding that those two tenets are often talked about in individualistic ways, but no one can be free alone. I hope that as artists, we understand our value, the medicine we offer through our work, and that we, in turn, give ourselves the medicine we're giving out. I hope we'll be in a place where artists are appreciated for how we interpret the world, how we help to carve and shape and document these moments in time. When you look at any time in history, you look at the art—what they were drawing, painting, the sculptures, the songs of that time. They document these periods in time.

I hope Black artists particularly will not just be lecturers of our history but will help hold and be held in these spaces of creation. What I understand about right now is that we're in a global paradigm shift, and we have been in that. One thing I took away from the pandemic is that we are much more connected than we thought we were. We impact each other in ways that none of us might have fully understood. I hope we create more works that are about a return to land, land as a concept of how we treat our bodies, how we treat each other, and that we walk gently on the earth. That's my true hope, and I believe there are those of us who are already practising it. We're already practising the future that we want to experience and drive.

d'bi: Ravyn, you give me infinite hope. Thank you for sharing your time, your optimism, your honesty, your stories, and your love with me today. Your words will continue to form concentric circles of possibilities throughout my consciousness for time to come. Have a magical rest of your day, old friend. I love you.

RW: I love you too, so much, d'bi. Thank you.

PART THREE

LIVING AS IF WE'RE ALREADY THERE

ON WRITING 2025

Light Years from Now

by **Dr. Syrus Marcus Ware**

The dominance of language and writing has come to stand for meaning itself. Live, embodied practices not based in linguistic or literary codes, we must assume, have no claims on meaning... It's imperative now, however overdue, to pay attention to the repertoire.

—DIANA TAYLOR
The Archive and the Repertoire: Performing Cultural Memory in the Americas

IT'S 2025.

I'm running, as usual. The time it takes to get to the water station leaves me with little time to get back to the group before our nightly gathering. I really don't need to sign up for the water shift as often as I do—there are enough people in our pod to share all the tasks. But I love the journey, the time alone to think, to be, to be solo. One of the hardest things about the *Changes* is the lack of alone time, the lack of individual moments of quiet to think and to feel free. I mean, we have a bigger *Freedom*—one that makes the lack of personal space and alone time feel relatively manageable—but I still miss the general "aloneness" of life before the revolution.

I slow my pace and adjust the water carrier on my back. I feel the weight of it—the heaviness of the water, but also of what it represents. We fought with our people at Standing Rock and in New Orleans and on Haida Gwaii and in Attawapiskat to protect this water, which has come to mean everything in life after the *Changes*. I should have brought something to read. I can remember before the *Changes*; I'm old enough to remember details that many in our pod can't imagine in their wildest dreams.

I recall travelling far to go to school, to go to work... trying to read to make the time go faster. I used to walk home from the 52 Lawrence bus in Weston, carefully planning my route to allow me to read and walk. I'd hold my paperback book and try to focus on the words swimming around on the page, moving with each of my steps. Now, we have the retinal share-a-book implants that were from an earlier time in the *Movement* when we had to share information quickly. Somehow it just doesn't feel the same.

I used to love reading about art, about creative practice. We were making so many things back then: objects, paintings, and interactions. More and more artists were creating within activist contexts. Yet, I rarely saw writing about our art-based movements. This was back when those in power still thought art was something that needed to be put inside elaborately air-conditioned buildings. Back when they thought that art was something to be seen by a select few—so few that they made sure that admission to their buildings was prohibitively expensive. Back when they knew that this act would keep the creative brilliance inside their walls and away from those who needed its beauty to ignite something in their souls.

I remember this time. I remember when those who wrote about art wrote about the things hanging and stacked inside the air-conditioned buildings, willfully ignoring everything else happening on every single inch of the walls, ground, space outside of those walls.

Back in 2016, when the fires that would bring in the *Big Change* were just beginning, we made an art gallery on the street in front of the police station in Toronto. We held a fifteen-day occupation that saw the creation of twenty-foot textile installations, countless works on paper, paintings, performance art showcases, and dances. We called for an end to anti-Blackness, an end to targeted policing—we called for change through our songs, our drawings, our bodies moving in rhythm.

It was nine years ago, but I remember it like it was happening right now—as if we were still there, singing, dancing and singing: "I believe that we will win." Smoke from traditional medicines being kissed by the fire of elders, syncopated chants fading in and out of my perception. Dancers practising their routines for the rally later that night, curators moving the art around on the walls of the public gallery. Large-scale paper ephemera from the earlier performance action at city hall: the Special Investigations Unit (SIU) report in Andrew Loku's[1] case wheatpasted to the entrance of police headquarters.

In these old memories, everything feels timeless—perhaps what Michelle M. Wright[2] wrote about the physics of Blackness has been laced through my thoughts. We exist inside and outside of time and timelines. It is as if today it is nine years ago, and we are waking up at the Black Lives Matter #TentCity to the smell of communal pancakes being cooked as if part of some magically useful social practice art project. But it is also nighttime, and there are ciphers made up of hundreds of dancers moving in ecstatic rebellion to the DJs' beats and the MCs' rhymes. Mustafa the Poet[3] is there, on a flatbed truck, his face lit up by the glorious sunset, telling us that "as long as the sun rises, so shall I."

But this isn't now; it was then: back when we stood in the middle of the largest Pride march in the country, dropped rainbow smoke bombs with dramatic flair to begin our performance, and held an audience of millions in a moment of rebellion, freedom, and calls for large-scale change. We set up an arts education hub in front of the SIU, delivering twelve hours of free community arts workshops about the prison industrial complex in Canada. We held a concert that night and rallied for the end of policing and for the start of community accountability. Artists. Activists. Performers. Political movements moving through elaborate choreography. These memories come flooding back through my cells, an embodied repertoire inside a human machine.

Maybe it was just what Diana Taylor wrote about the archive and the repertoire: how do you archive the unarchivable? Can you ever capture in writing, memory, or archive, the lived experience of a performance, really? Could we ever have captured these moments of activism blurred with art?

There was no writing about the art of this movement. There was no writing about the artists who were activists who were artists. So, we kept making our own writing. We wrote with fabric, scissors, gold threads pulled tight: "Which side of history are you on?" Because we knew which side we were on.

Funny that this is all now history. That we are here, now. In the *Changes*. In this time when we write our truths on the backs of maple leaves, spraying every surface with graffiti, spending entire days singing and dancing in hypnotic trances.

The dust picks up as I follow the bend in the road. From within swirls of dry clay dust I emerge and see my Black family celebrating in our field, singing, dancing, gathering. I pick up the pace of my run, bringing water with which to caress and bathe each other, to drink until we are never thirsty, to celebrate with our bodies, to create new life.

Originally published in *C Magazine*, issue 132 (C The Visual Arts Foundation, 2016). Reprinted by permission of the author.

Selected References

Cassisi, Anastasia. "Justice for All? An Analysis of Police Brutality in the United States, England & Canada." *Global Studies* (2016).

Mustafa the Poet. https://www.mustafathepoet.com.

Taylor, Diana. *The Archive and the Repertoire: Performing Cultural Memory in the Americas*. Duke University Press, 2003.

Wright, Michelle M. *Physics of Blackness: Beyond the Middle Passage Epistemology*. University of Minnesota Press, 2015.

Notes

1 Cassisi, "Justice for All?"

2 Wright, *Physics of Blackness*.

3 Mustafa the Poet.

THE AFROFUTURIST DREAMSCAPE

Black Cultural Identity

by **Yung Yemi**

in conversation with

Dr. Ra'anaa Yaminah Ekundayo (ABD)

IN THIS CONVERSATION, MULTIDISCIPLINARY ARTIST Yung Yemi shares his unique approach and understanding of Afrofuturism. Through a blend of styles, cultures, and historical elements, his community-oriented work fosters dialogue on Blackness, radicality, and the power of art. This interview reveals the trajectory of his practice from social work to social justice, touching on his mastery and his refusal of the societally imposed homogeneity of Blackness.

Ra'anaa Yaminah Ekundayo (RYE): Thank you so much for sitting down and chatting about your work with me today. I'd love it if you could start by describing your practice, what brought you to this kind of work, the themes that are present in your work, and how your practice is integrated into your life.

Yung Yemi (YY): I guess my practice at its core is sort of like remixology. I think there's a lot of parallels between what I do and remix culture. The reason I say that is because there's a very eclectic mix of influences in what I do both on a personal level and conceptually. On a personal level, not having a formal art background, like a technical training background, I've just figured things out on the fly. My educational background is in social work, so my education is rooted in social justice, research, and discourse. I have ten years of experience working in the field of youth outreach with primarily racialized youth here in Toronto.

I think I landed on Afrofuturism just because of the future-facing and speculative nature at its core. I just found that to be—it felt like just looking at a blank canvas, and that energy was very inspiring to me. My approach, my eclecticism, my remix approach is just my own personal way of trying to make sense of these experiences. It's hard to create something cohesive with all these disparate parts, but I think I found a way to do it, by approaching it through the lens of remixology. So, what I do at its core is collage, like everything—every piece of artwork I've made in some way I think could be described as a collage or an assemblage or what have you, in its most practical sense. Although I'm very content to play with the final aesthetic of the work that I do, it doesn't always ultimately appear as that, but that's what it is at its core.

RYE: Awesome! I love how you speak so intimately about your work. It's fascinating to see how all the different aspects of your life leading up to this moment impact your practice and how you can see the social justice and social work aspects, which is so beautiful. So, thank you for sharing that. In the vein of Afrofuturism, I'm an aspiring Afrofuturist, still learning a lot, and your work is truly one of the ones that have inspired me to learn more about Afrofuturism and lean into it. I was wondering if you could talk a bit about how you were exposed to Afrofuturism and how your experiences in merging the themes of Black creativity, liberation, speculative fiction, and technology have impacted your work and your trajectory as an artist.

YY: I guess my introduction to Afrofuturism as a concept, as a term, came around 2012, I want to say. It was directly from a Toronto-based artist, Danilo McCallum, at the time; he was working on doing some

Afrofuturist programming at OCAD University. Danilo created an exhibition called Black Future Month. I think he did the first one as a solo exhibition in 2012, I believe. We were all part of an artist collective, like an informal artist collective at the time. I was just involved in helping and supporting that process. The following year, he turned it into an open exhibition, a group exhibition that was hosted at OCAD University that I was a part of. So, I guess that exhibition was my first experience exhibiting Afrofuturist work and within that time frame that was my onboarding to the culture. I was just learning about the concept of it and how to express it.

I also found it really helped me find my voice, like going back to what I was saying about figuring out how to put these different experiences together. I think, again, with Afrofuturism and the fact that it embraces speculation and embraces alternate narratives I felt welcomed by that, into the genre. Even carrying everything that I carry with me, all these different experiences, it was a lane where it made sense to unpack all of that. That was my introduction to it. I think—was there a second part to that question that I didn't answer? [laughs]

RYE: I know you spoke a bit about it; it was just more talking about how you think bringing these themes of, you know, Black creativity and liberation, speculative fiction and technology have impacted your work and the continued trajectory. You spoke a bit about it, but if you want to add anything else about it…

YY: I think my greatest moments—or certainly my most important moments of inspiration and energy and freedom, I think, come through just being exposed to different forms of Afrocentric creativity, you know? I'm a child of hip hop! I was raised on hip hop, and I think there was a moment when I was old enough to remember when it was still really rooted in Afrocentricity and still really celebrated Afrocentricity. Then there was this shift as it became more commercially viable, more commercially powerful. There was a shift away from that rooting. That's how capitalism works. It's just an obvious evolution, unfortunately. I think I see a lot of that opportunity in Afrofuturism right now as a genre. I feel like it celebrates Black creativity in the same way that hip hop did and it's multidisciplinary in the same way that hip hop was. It has that same energy, but it just hasn't gone through that commercial transformation yet, at least not nearly to the full extent. So, you still have that opportunity to really revel in Black creativity and to celebrate it. We get to have these narratives and these experiences that are still rooted in Afrocentricity. Hopefully, we can stay here for a while. You never know how things will change once the big dollars start to come in. Once that train starts, it's impossible to stop it. But, at this moment, it still feels like we can guide the narrative as we see fit.

RYE: I appreciate your acknowledgement of how capitalism really is affecting all these things and how it's brought in and shifted the approaches and the outputs of Afrofuturism, particularly on a larger scale, you know. It's interesting how big Afrofuturism has gotten in the past couple of years just from Black Panther and everyone's like, "This is Afrofuturism," not realizing that there's so much more history rooted in it and so many more different outputs of it. I respect and appreciate how you define it and speak about how it can be so much more than how it's depicted. This leads me to the next question, you know, about your interpretations of Afrofuturism and I was wondering if you could speak to hybridity, and the Black diaspora as it emerges as this unique amalgamation of culture within your work.

YY: I think Pan-Africanism is central to my work because essentially, it's central to my life experience. My heritage is Nigerian and Swiss; that's my ethnic makeup. I wasn't raised in a big Nigerian community, but from a very young age, I gravitated to the other Black kids in my community. We just found each other and stuck together. But it was like, I would have a friend that's Eritrean and a friend that's Jamaican and a friend that's Guyanese/South African. So that was Pan-Africanism, you know, we were Pan-Africanism in effect! But, in our community, we were also seen as "the Black kids." So, it's like this interplay of making sense of having this incredible diversity within your friend group and your experiences but also making sense of the external lens of just being a homogeneous group.

It's just that's the reality of being Black in the diaspora. There's Blackness, as is defined both by our community and externally, and then there's actual ethnicity within the African diaspora, which, you know, is limitlessly diverse. I just see a value in finding unity across ethnicity, under the umbrella of Blackness. I guess that's the Pan-African element that's the vision of Marcus Garvey and, you know, the idea of strength in numbers and the importance of representation. But I also obviously see the potential for erasure if you don't, at every step, honour the diversity within Blackness. You can lose the individual for the whole. That's the core of this duality that exists, I guess, a little bit for all of us.

The series that I created, *Holding Space*, is a meditation on that. It's all these micro components that speak to specific ethnic experiences within the African diaspora, but it has this overall cohesive aesthetic that you know, if you're not paying attention to the details, then it just looks like it's all under one umbrella instead. I guess that's at the core of the work. That's the main inspiration for the work.

RYE: I was just wondering about bringing this—*(sighs)* I don't want to call it "Black individuality" into it, but we're not just homogeneous in our Blackness and there are similarities among the Black lived experience. It's a byproduct of colonization and all these things that are put upon us, but talking about like the diversity within Blackness and these Black communities and like you were saying about your friends growing up, you know, you shared something, but you came from such different backgrounds—

YY: Thank you. There's one other thing that's central to my approach and that is that within—due to the effects of colonization, due to the effects of historical erasure, there are a lot of Black people, specifically within the diaspora, that don't have that direct ethnic lineage or an ethnic history to connect to. I didn't grow up with my dad, I know my dad directly immigrated from Nigeria to Canada. I can trace my Black lineage directly back to a region in Nigeria. I have that and that's a form of privilege. My wife, for example, is Jamaican and she can trace that lineage directly back to Jamaica. There are a lot of people, though, that don't have that direct lineage. Something that I always think about in my work is also the intersection of privilege and I never want to make work or take steps in my practice that make what I do feel inaccessible to people that don't have that same privilege, that same level of access. I think that is another very key component when we speak about Blackness. It's crucially important to value and cherish the diversity within Blackness, but it's also crucially important to realize that not all of us have the same access to the history within our diversity. We need to make sure those people have a home as well within the movement.

RYE: What is your dream Afro future, whether that's specifically in terms of your practice or the world at large? And how do you draw from your vision of this in your practice, but, like, what motivates you in terms of what could be?

YY: I think my dream Afro future—it is kind of like a state where the historical erasures and the impacts of colonialism and capitalism and all the fractures within the Black experience, where those are repaired. I think that's obviously a utopic sentiment. But it's important to, as an artist, to be in touch with a very idealistic and dreamy vision, but I think in practice, in a practical sense, I think, it's about just having that level of appreciation and honouring those differences—the diversity that we have within Blackness. It's just finding ways to create cross-cultural connections within Blackness, to inspire curiosity and reverence, for each other even if we come from different ethnic backgrounds or what have you. I don't even know what a kid's experience would be like in Toronto in 2024; I think we live in one of the most culturally diverse places. I think that in itself is a huge form of privilege. But when I was growing up, African kids got made fun of, and me, for myself having an African name, I got made fun of a lot for that and there was just always a lot of infighting across cultural groups and stuff like that, and I think that's just a symptom of internalized oppression. We, especially in the diasporic sense, in these diasporic communities, you know, it's just a learned behaviour to turn on people that look like you, if that can align you with a bigger power structure. And it would be beautiful to see that inverted where we're not looking for differences to create distance, but we're looking at those differences from a place of reverence and, like, a shared value.

I guess my best example is just my little nuclear family unit, you know. I mean, me with my Nigerian heritage and my wife with her Jamaican heritage, and we want to learn about each other's heritage. Even though I'm not Jamaican, that's not my background, but I want to learn about that because we have a daughter now that has both of those lineages. Now we want to be able to raise her in a way where she can make sense of all of that and she can carry it; she can bring those sides together and create something even more powerful out of that. And that's the dream. That's what I would love to see us be able to do just in casual conversations and informal encounters. We can have a friend who's from a different background, but we can honour and cherish their history, and they can do the same for us. That's beautiful.

RYE: I've been thinking a lot about how 2020 was this big shifting moment in a lot of folks' work just based on the state of the world, the pandemic, the resurgence of BLM, you know, George Floyd, Regis, and all these things happening. What's next in your practice? How have these moments in time, like 2020 and 2012 and 2013 rallying around Trayvon Martin and everything—how have these moments really impacted your practice?

YY: I felt a surge of energy in that window—that 2012, 2013 time frame—there was a lot going on. It didn't feel as universal as it did after 2020, but, you know, if you're already tapped into the culture, I think you felt it in that window. There were just more conversations arising, people just taking, or being willing to take, more action. I think I definitely drew a lot of energy off of that and started moving more steadily in that direction and, you know what happened in 2020 was like a boiling over point of all that energy that had built all throughout the 2010s, I guess, and then just really boiled over with all the circumstances that arose in 2020, and that's led to this interesting moment that we're in right now where I think representation has just, in general in pop culture for Black people, has skyrocketed since 2020. There's been a lot of new doors open, a lot of opportunities have arisen. We know that this is how the system is designed. The system is designed to basically wait, to keep you out until the last possible moment and then right before the revolution hits or as the revolution is hitting, they open the gates and they say, "Come in," but they say, "Come in, but don't do too much." That's what I'm very wary about at this moment right now. It's like, I don't want to see complacency set in for myself or for anybody. I don't want to see this moment turn, like where we exchange our aesthetic representation for the opportunity to really affect change and to continue to push.

I'm working on a new body of work that's more personal too. As a Black artist, what translates in institutional settings and the art world at large is often something that has the edges sanded down a little bit to make it palatable to a "wider" audience. It has to be presented in a certain way. It has to have a certain aesthetic and language to it. I'm going to continue to keep fighting and try to create as much of that freedom work as I can with the time and the resources that I have. So yeah, that's basically what it comes down to. I just know when I'm creating, I know what has that 2013 energy in it and what doesn't. I want to continue to create from that place and make as much of that work that resonates with that energy as I can. Whether it finds a home or not, whether it fits into the, you know, to the greater art world dialogue or not. I'm going to continue to keep pushing in that direction and see what happens. 'Cuz I have been fortunate enough that even when I create things that don't necessarily resonate within the art world at large, they still resonate with me and my community. That always gives me far more validation and far more, you know, personal energy to keep moving, than that institutional recognition or anything like that. That's currently where I'm at. [laughs]

The Black Lives Matter mural that we did in Kensington Market in 2020 was a special project, just in the nature of how it came together. It was completely created by the Black artist community here in Toronto, completely self-funded. It completely relied on the scale and the labour of the Black artist community in Toronto, and I think, number one, it was an important example of the autonomy that we have and the ability to unify and mobilize. It was just a beautiful moment of all these artists coming together and paying out of pocket to make that happen and giving their time and their labour to make that happen. The response was also beautiful; we had a lot of people reach out and share a sense of pride that Toronto took part in that—in what was like a global movement, you know, that we had those street murals all around the world. It was kind of like a microcosm, it was like, a little bit of that same concept that I was talking about earlier of, you know, all these different backgrounds and practices coming together to create a unified thing. Because we have such an amazing Black artist community here in Toronto that has done some incredible things, and it's something that I just, like, I always want to keep in the forefront of our minds—is like the power and the strength that comes from collaboration and working together, having that unity, and as I just mentioned it again, it touches on that idea of Black as this umbrella. But also honouring the strength in that diversity and all these individual practices of these artists that came together and made that happen. So, yeah.

RYE: Thank you so much for taking the time to chat with me and sharing a lot about your practice. I'm so excited to see this chapter coming together and I was so excited when you said yes. So... [laughs]

YY: It's a huge honour. Honestly, thank you for inviting me and putting this together.

THE ARCHIVE AS LIVING ENTITY

Notes from Yamayeka

by **Kanika Gordon**

Until we meet again... the diasporic is an act of will and memory.

—BELL HOOKS
Art on My Mind

IT IS MARCH 2024. I'M LOOKING OUT THE WINDOW AT the mountains of Oaxaca state. I'm a visitor to the traditional lands of the Mixtec and Zapotec Peoples, just a short distance outside of Oaxaca City. The elders here have touched my heart in so many ways. I stop and talk to them in the streets—their kindness and generosity often make me want to weep. Growing up on Treaty 13 territory/Toronto/Tkaronto, I never had the opportunity to grow up near my grandparents. In fact, they passed away before I was born. Elders in the society I grew up in always appeared to me as discarded and left to be cared for by facilities, far away from family, their usefulness seemingly coming to an end. At the time, I didn't know that this disregard was not a global phenomenon, that there were many cultures that revered their elders for their knowledge and experience. I want my elders to know that I value their wisdom and intend to listen as deeply as I can. They have awakened a need within me to hold their stories with care. I find myself responding to my neighbours clumsily in Spanish.

It all began with my mother. She left our ancestral lands for opportunities at a time when Toronto/Tkaronto needed workers. The year was 1967. I often think of how easily a border can swing open depending on a few variables. How its hinges can be well oiled by its own need. But what is a border on stolen land? My mother's crossing of waters is lapping at my ankles. Do you hear your lands calling across space and time? I'm being called home. The time for reconnection is upon me. I long to put my feet on the soil and tend to the graves of my ascended dead. My mother's crossing has left me occupying a space of deep questioning. I want to know our ways. Give me your stories; let me keep them safe. I will share them with the others.

How far do memories travel? I find myself occupying multiple timelines at once, moving across the Indigi space-time continuum. I'm sitting at the kitchen table while simultaneously sixty years in the past as my mother shares her childhood memories. This interview is the first in an ongoing series, which by the time of this publishing, will be well underway into other manifestations.

These exploratory works intend to encompass visual, auditory, and written dimensions that establish sites of transmission that transcend linear time—bringing our peoples from across the vast expanse to this moment of recollection. With the body as a reservoir of ancestral memory, our most ancient of technologies, I am compelled to access deeper knowing through the memories of the Elders of Yamaye.[1]

I begin with folklore, stories of the trickster spider Anansi, a character (also a deity, but my mother doesn't know that, nor will I tell her as she is a Christian woman) that made its way from West Africa with our ancestors. I pull at the fibres of her consciousness—Anansi, a connection point to her youth—in hopes that my question will act as a pathway, a guide to unravel the threads of her memories. They pour from her in the form of stories and songs—I feel the warmth of her recollections coursing through the room. The weight of a deepening.

Kanika: Did you have any favourite Anansi Stories from your childhood?

Lillian (Mum): Ha! Him a ginal! You know, someone who is not to be trusted. We used to have books at school with his tales. They were meant to teach us important lessons. He was always getting into some mess. The stories also came on the radio. My mother would put the radio outside on the veranda so that the neighbours could come by and listen to the programs. We did this when we got a TV, too, as not everyone in the community had one. We would listen to Ms. Lou[2]

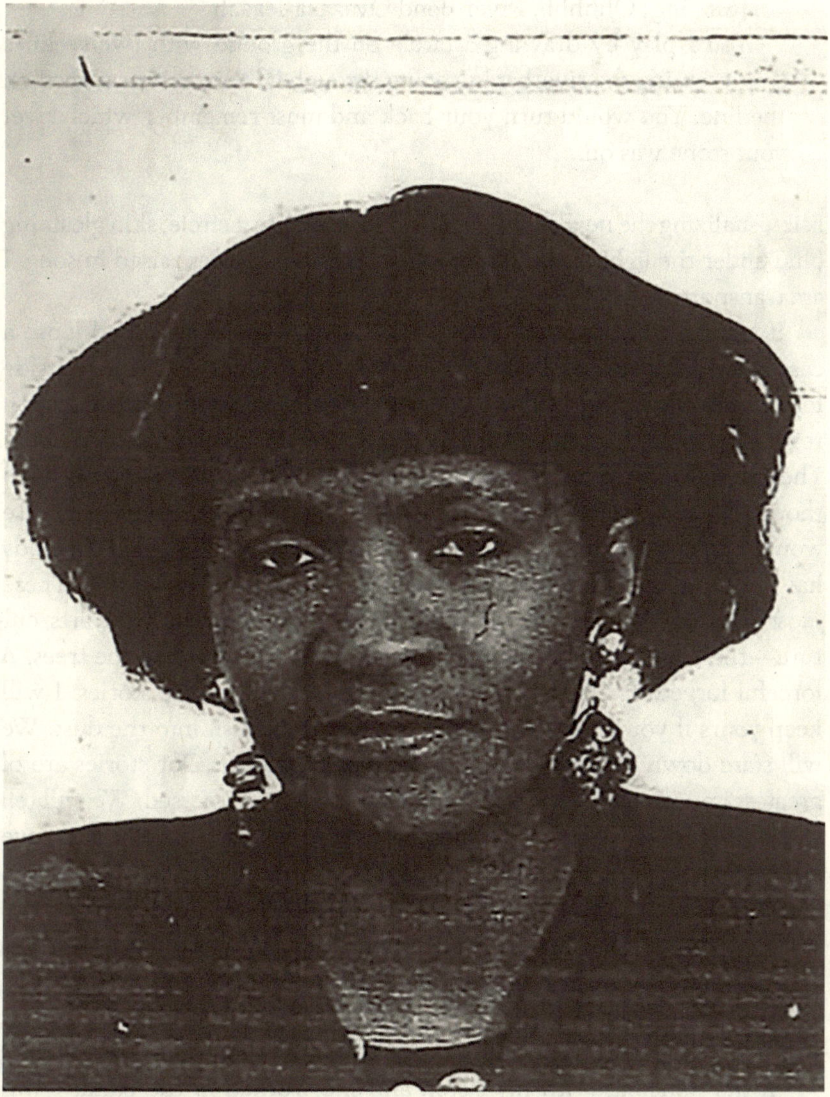

Mum in 1993. Courtesy of the Author.

too. Gosh, I remember that when people got married, the festivities lasted several days—the couple would dress up and go to both family homes. Performers would put on comedy shows for the community and everyone would eat.

And—on moonshine, all the neighbourhood kids would come out to play.

[Singing] Ohhhhh, River Bend Ovaaaaa-leaaah

You'd play by drawing a circle on the ground with twelve lines (representing the riverbanks) going through it. A stone was placed on the line. You would turn your back and must remember which river your stone was on.

I sit visualizing the neighbourhood kids, standing in a circle, skin gleaming blue under the light of the full moon. I hear their voices raised in song. I am transported.

It started with a small thing. This stream of memory pulled loose a cascading of memories. I see my grandmother placing the radio outside for the neighbours to listen to. Hear the community. This one question revealed so much. I am compelled by these stories. I must remember. They are anchors to my ancestral lands. They anchor me to myself, even though I am a great distance from my home. Dominant settler culture would have us forget. We must choose to remember. After all, the body has not forgotten. There are genocides happening as I write this. These most heinous of acts. An uprooting. The attempt to dismantle the arts, culture— the burning of books. Silence the poets, then destroy the trees. A forceful forgetting. There must be someone left to tell the stories. I will keep yours if you keep mine. I will not let you vanish into the dust. We will stare down the barrels of imperial guns together. Our stories are of greatest importance. We are the witnesses and the witnessed. We will tell it as we see it. As we know it. Tales in our own tongues—a refusal to have our stories told for us. We own our gaze.

K: What did you think of Canada when you first arrived? You were so young at the time, just twenty years old.

L: Well, I honestly didn't know anything about Canada. I was living in the Bahamas with my sister, and she worked in the bank. I was focused on my typing course at the time, and she was the one that came and told me that they were looking for workers. They were giving us problems with the papers and saying they would send people back to Jamaica—so I went to Canada. [laughs] They didn't even check your ID; whatever name you gave them they'd put it down on the paper and off you went.

K: Oh wow, they must've really needed people.

L: Yeah, they gave you your card to work. Your Social Insurance Number. The only thing you couldn't get was a bank account. They needed some time to get to know you. Then the government would call to tell you to come and get your permanent residency. Some people were afraid to go—they thought maybe they'd be sent back.

K: What made you decide on Canada over other places? Some of our family ended up in the US and the UK...

L: Well, at the time, we were considered British subjects—not now, but back then it was easy to go to both Canada and the UK for that reason.

K: What kinds of things helped you hold on to your home?

L: I'd go up to Eglinton if I wanted food from home.

K: Oh yeah. Little Jamaica.

L: There was a place we used to gather called the Wif Club. It seems they must've been upset because it was mostly Black folks gathering there. They must've burned it down.

I had of course never heard of the place. On my search I came across a scholarly paper by Keith McCuaig titled "Jamaican Canadian Music in Toronto in the 1970s and 1980s: A Preliminary History." It mentioned the venue, and its demise.

"During the 1960s and 1970s, Jamaican night clubs were a central gathering place for Jamaican Canadians in Toronto. The first Jamaican-owned nightclub in Toronto was the West Indian Federation Club, known affectionately as the Wif Club."[3] It went on to say that "Jamaican and

Trinidadian musicians were brought in to perform at the club, catering to the Caribbean Canadian population's desire for music from back home. The business underneath caught fire, destroying the club."

Home.

The way it travels vast distances to meet us where we are. In a time where people are being dispossessed of their homes, when the attempt to erase cultures, lineages—a heavy weight pressing us into the dust. I choose to remember. When I think of my childhood, growing up between Mississauga and Roncesvalles, I can still smell the musk incense, see the beaded room dividers and wooden giraffes surrounded by African masks. These signifiers occupy space as reminders in our homes away from homes. They have become important motifs in my work. The visual aesthetic, a transmission to be picked up, a signal for the others. This is the task of the memory keeper. We tell the story. We let it continue its trajectory through time, gaining its passage through our bodies across generations.

K: I'm often sad I didn't get to spend time with my grand or great grandparents. I feel there's so much I could have learned from them.

L: Oh yes, my grandmother could preserve yam for so long! I don't know how she did it. She would boil down the coconut shells to make oil. The leftovers would be turned into a custard.

It doesn't surprise me the way I feel completely rooted to the earth when I eat or drink certain foods. My grandfather grew yams, bananas, coconuts, cacao, callaloo, tomatoes, gungu peas, and all kinds of bush for tea. Do you feel the weight of embodiment when you eat the foods from your lands? When I learned of my grandparents' skill for gardening and farming it all made sense. The way warmth rolls over my flesh when I have cocoa, the way I am elevated after pressing the butter into my skin. It explains the vibrance that moves through my body at the taste of mango, coconut, and grapefruit. They speak to me through the earth, and across realms. I dream of my grandfather—he tells me to use stinging nettle to increase my iron. We sat in the late afternoon sun after a day of foraging. I never saw his face in this waking world—he gave up his flesh before I was born, and yet, he shows his care across timelines.

Yes, we occupy it all at once.

Black visual aesthetics engage us in the depths of our memory centres. It allows us the space to wield our narratives, awakening and piercing the stillness—seeping through the haze created by the amnesia that is the settler-colonial project. They would prefer to tell us who we are, who we've been, and who we will be. They attempted to strip us of our names, our origins, and our practices. The link can never be severed. Not if you can still encounter these sparks of knowing, internal working against the external.

K: When you first arrived, were you in community with other Caribbean peoples?

L: Yeah, you'd meet them on the street or at work. I had a friend, Shirley, and her brother that I knew from back home, so I stayed with them for a bit until I got a place. In those days you could pay ten to fifteen dollars a week for a furnished room. In the Portuguese or Italian communities sometimes they'd split a place in two and rent half the room to you and the other to someone else. Yeah, it was a wild life. [laughs]

K: Do you remember what area you first lived in?

L: Up on Bloor by the Honest Ed's, I used to go over to Kensington Market to do some shopping. I still like to go over there when I visit Toronto. I still have a pair of shoes I bought there. Blue velvet—they wrap around the ankle. If I ever felt homesick, I would go up to Eglinton to get some food. Of course you could always make it too.

K: They still have a ton of shops up there. There's this place that used to have a jerk chicken special. You'd get it with coleslaw and rice and peas.

Connection points to home. I take my place as witness, and record keeper.

L: After I got my work permit, I remember looking down over the land as it passed by from my window seat in the airplane. This lady was asking me what use I would have for the umbrella I had with me. I didn't know what to expect once I arrived. I had all kinds of weird jobs. This one where you'd wipe down beach chairs after they left the manufacturers. I was making 1.25 per hour. I packed boxes. I even worked at a toy factory. Grand N Toy.

K: I remember them!

L: Yeah, you'd paint the little figures. Give them a little red mouth. Paint the horses for the merry-go-round.

K: You've done a lot of different things!

L: Yeah, you'd go, and they'd just train you. I had taken typing courses in school in the Bahamas so then I went off to work in the offices.

K: I remember meeting up with our Rastafarian friends, playing with the kids—they had a shop near Bloor.

L: Yeah, we used to have a book club for you kids on Saturdays.

K: I don't remember the books, but I remember the kids. [laughs]

Every time I go into a Caribbean shop, I feel like I'm travelling home. The spices, cassava, breadfruit, and plantain. I used to go to a shop in Kensington called Caribbean Corner when I was feeling homesick.

L: [laughs] Homesick?

K: [laughing] I'm only a first-generation Canadian, so I'm more Jamaican than I am Canadian.

L: Well you have a ton of cousins down there, so if you want to move there you can go on.

We get on a call with our cousin Iris—the daughter of my grand aunt. We discussed meeting in Jamaica near the end of August. She speaks in rapid Patwa[4]—exclaiming how it's always a great time. How they'll make curried goat, oxtail, and gather all the family around. My mom reminds her she'll need some fish too. Neither of us eat meat anymore, but she's so excited we don't want to take away from the moment. Our ears hover over the earpiece of my mom's phone as we talk. I have a picture in my mind of this gathering. The family that stayed behind and the ones that returned from their years abroad. I tell my mom I want to visit the family land that I've been told has been long abandoned.

L: It has been decreed that the land is to never be sold. [In Patwa] Mine duppy come find you. Meaning—unless you'd like to be haunted by spirits. There's also money buried; it's said that it will come to the one who is meant to find it in a dream.

My grandparents, greats- and great-grands- are buried there. It is my intention to tend to them—to sweep the leaves from their headstones. To tell them I have returned. It's been nearly thirty years since I've stepped foot on our soil—and yet, I remember the air, the sounds, the feeling of home. How could the land not remember me too? I often wonder what I will dream about once I reach my home. This culture of dreaming has become a theme in my work. The revealing of speculative worlds while weaving Afrosurrealist iconography and sound.

K: I really want to go and listen to the stories, meet the people that have been living there. I didn't realize so much family was still there.

L: Everyone didn't leave for other lands. Well, I'm thankful to have had the opportunity for a better life. If I want to go and buy some of the land, I can. I don't know. I'll see.

K: I've heard the cost of living is high.

L: For them, yes, but you're making money over here. So, you'd be fine.

K: Yeah, seems like a lot of people moved back. They go, work, make their money, and move back home.

L: Yeah, you must be sure you have some ideas about how you'll survive there.

Survive.

Yes, we are a people that survived.

I have begun collecting the stories of the elders in my family. *A digital format of our oral traditions*. I recall the stories I've heard over the years about meeting family members that have passed on through dreams. The receiving of warnings and knowing of things to come. My intention is to move outward into the community and deepen my knowledge and understanding of the folklore, spiritual practices, and history of my island's peoples. Much of the magic and fantastical nature of our peoples has been deeply embedded into the culture—much of this richness is an obfuscation because of suppression during colonization. In my youth, one of the most prominent topics I heard among the elders was about dreams, prophetic in nature and often including encounters with the dead, stories about duppies,[5] and the practice of Obeah,[6] which involves spell work, ancestral veneration, and knowledge of Indigenous plants and their uses. Obeah became punishable by death in 1760, following a rebellion as practitioners had used this to strengthen their resolve and encourage their efforts to fight their oppressors.

So many of our people leave their homes for better opportunities because of the lasting violence of colonization, shifting the dynamics of power and access. Their oppressors' legacies are still in need of penance.

Our first peoples, the Taino, and Jamaican Maroons established a settlement in the seventeenth century, where they defended it, maintaining their sovereignty against the Spanish and then the British. The leaders were said to be practitioners of Obeah who used their practices to assist them in their battles of resistance.

▪ ▪ ▪

There are so many ways in which to resist. My resistance is rooted in love. And a belief in the unmeasurable value of our stories. We hold much more than what was done to us. Our bodies are the most sacred of Indigi technology—they are conduits for knowledge that span multitudes of generations.

In November 2023, I attended a talk hosted by Neema Gilthere, "a writer, artist and guerrilla theorist based in the digital diaspora whose work explores love and indigeneity in a time of algorithmic debris." I have found so much resonance in her offerings to this world. The talk discussed forms of content and media that could be used to support Palestinian liberation. This was one month into the horrifying genocide being carried out against the Palestinian people by the colonial state of Israel. To sit and discuss the art, culture, and narrative of a people who were, and are, simultaneously experiencing erasure in the most violent of ways made this moment beyond poignant, and of the utmost importance. I learned that the digital archive could be used as a space to counter misinformation and preserve the narrative of the people. To be focused on the voices of the often unheard—the colonized—is engaging in a form of resistance. This experience reshaped my view of archival work. I realized the archive was more than just an act of preservation—it is a digital format for our oral histories, but also a centring of all we hold dear. Our unmovable line in the sand. Our nonseverable truths.

I have often thought of Neemas's exploration of "diasporic embodiment in the age of Big Data" as something that greatly aligns with why this work is so compelling. To be anchored in our internal waters across time, in this ever-changing landscape, to remember where we have been, who we have been and are in an age of forced amnesia is a powerful act. In an interview for *Bomb Magazine*'s 2022 Spring Issue conducted by Ethel Tawe, Tawe states "Guerrilla theory puts an emphasis on oral history and non-written forms of documentation and preserves history that way. Something I like to think about is how we're holding memory in our bodies through music, dance, and other physical ways through which we carry history forward." To which Neema responds, "As an African, I feel the pain of our history being quite literally burned, erased, distorted, and weaponized against us. We are not able to rely on conventional archives. We don't have books from the 1300s written by us to tell stories of how we were living since time immemorial. But like you said, we do have oral histories and our bodies are repositories. We still store the memory within our flesh. So, a big part of my practice is just that: embodiment."

What is it to be a living embodiment of your lineages across time? I would have loved to learn how to cultivate the land from my grandparents. To make preserves. They come to me in the "other spaces," they share their knowledge unrestricted by limitations of linear existence, time or space.

▪ ▪ ▪

"I believe that we have memories that extend beyond what we have consciously experienced. That we carry within us ancestral memory."

—ALISON SAAR

■ ■ ■

In many Indigenous cultures, time is depicted as a circle, or a sphere. In the still image above, my mother looks forty years into the past. The image intends to explore the way the act of remembering becomes a vehicle for time travel and, thus, a passageway to the infinite. As memory travels through each of us, moving in all directions through time, it also goes through a process of decay, a metamorphosis. And yet, energy is never destroyed—only transformed.

When looking through archives, I am filled with questions that are so rarely answered. Questions like: Who were they? What were their stories? They are photographed as they look on. A crossing of gazes. I am dreaming of the Yamayeka archive, a living, breathing space in conversation

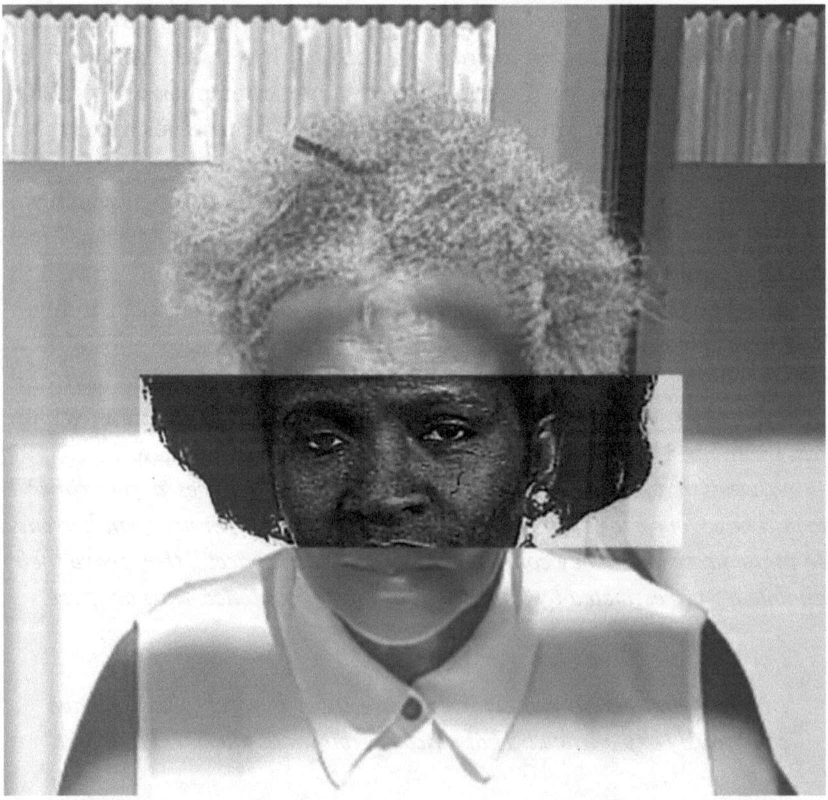

Kanika Gordon. "Coalescence." 2024. Colour collage/photocopy image of the author's mum. Courtesy of the Author.

with the viewer. A call and response. These collections of stories from our elders are transmissions to the generations that follow—have you turned your dial to the frequency? Let it be a space of warmth and safety, a conduit to care.

In the interview with Ethel Tawe[7] for *Bomb Magazine*, Neema states that

> Diaspora is the wound that is full of possibility. This feeling of dislocation and displacement necessitates the formation of new narratives and hybridization. I have this theory that when you set foot on a soil, you are connected to all the ancestors that have set foot there as well, and all their gods. It becomes this meeting in the skies with all the forces that have tended to that land and all the forces you carry within your body.

Indeed, the reservoir of our body knowledge runs deep.

The archive: both receptacle and tool. The placing of our stories inside it is a liberatory action across Northern Turtle Island and beyond.

Let these stories remind you of who you are.
Let these stories remind you of who you've been.
May all we know guide us.

Selected References

hooks, bell. *Art on My Mind: Visual Politics*. The New Press, 1995.

Notes

1 Commonly referred to as Jamaica, meaning "Land of Wood and Water" as claimed by pro-slavery, Anglican clergyman G.W. Bridges in 1928, stating two Arawak words had been found in Florida. According to descendants of the Taino, the peoples of this island are referred to as Yamayeka, People of the Coast of Great Spirit with Yamaye, meaning Coast of Great Spirit. The area of what is now Eastern Portland was named after a Great Chief Aomaoqueque. Likely pronounced as Yamowkeke in English. The closeness to the word Xaymaka or Yamaya as the earliest forms of Jamaica is of relevance.

2 A folklorist, writer, poet, and educator. I hadn't heard of Ms. Lou, so I made sure to note down her name for later. As it turns out she was one of our island's icons. One of my favourite works of hers titled "Jamaica Language" is a live performance where she reiterated that Jamaican Patwa is worthy of respect. She does it with so much charm—she is funny, lighthearted, and poignant, instilling pride in all those that hear it. In a segment, she refers to her aunt, who gets upset when anyone tries to say our Patwa is not a language, and that if English can be "derived" from Norse, Greek, Latin, then so can Patwa—it is not corrupted English but "derived" from a number of languages.

3 Pronounced whiff.
4 Primarily made up of West and Central African vocabulary, which includes Twi, Yoruba, and Ewe among others. Influence can also be found through our first peoples, the Taino and Caribs, which spoke Arawak languages, then by the movements of people through indentured servitude via Hindi-speaking Indians, and the Irish. And, lastly, English, Spanish, and Portuguese through colonization.
5 Spirits.
6 Meaning wizard or witch in the Ashanti Twi language.
7 Image-maker, storyteller, and time-traveller, whose work involves examining archives and identity in Africa and the diaspora.

BLACK DIGITAL ANGELS

by **Kim Ninkuru**

BLACK DIGITAL ANGELS ARE THE MANY BLACK TRANS women you have dehumanized by either deifying or pitying them online.

A-N-G-E-L
looks like we only live url
A-N-G-E-L
she also has a story irl

Am I only allowed to exist when there's a screen between
me and you?
How many filters must my humanity go through for it to
have value?
Because it seems like as long as I'm logged in I am somebody
I am your muse, your goddess, your voice of reason
Somehow my face on your screen causes reflection
While my body in these streets faces eradication.
You scroll through my timelines looking for redemption
Liking every pic of mine as if that's how support functions
if you gotta lie please stay out of my mentions
this isn't real life, it's just an application

Question: how does a girl like me live her best life?
and I mean her real life. like her in real life, life.
She doesn't
A girl like me doesn't get to live her best life irl.
Instead, I only get to give it. Life.
And you tell me "You give me life"
Making it clear that my very existence is for you to consume
And you are right. I've been conditioned to perform to be allowed in any room
That's one thing you definitely can't tell me I don't know how to do
It's been my livelihood, girl
giving you life is literally my livelihood, girl
I literally give you life for a living, girl
Cause if I don't, I'm one more dead girl
I post on IG
You digitally frame me as this divine entity that soon becomes a distant memory once you're out of battery
Inquiry: do you canonize me online to ease the pain of my potential death offline?

Just asking, because from the way you tell me "You're so pretty" it looks like you're trying to convince yourself more than me
As if you're trying to hold on to a truth too big
A truth you would rather not see
So, you smile in my face to ease the pain you feel while you're killing me
And I'm here. giving you life.
irl a girl like me doesn't know love
Love that comes armed and ready to fight for you
Love that knows what it's doing
Love with no question asked
The type of love I get shows up unprepared
As if it's the first time it's coming to class and my lesson was a hundred years ago

My love (the love that is mine) always comes only with questions
It is weak and doesn't know how to fight for me
Maybe that's why girls like me prefer anger
cause she's always ready
No question asked.
URL tbh LOL WTF

Black digital angels open up their wings and, deeper inside the web, fly high high high
screaming on top of their heads: "how are you going to show me love without wifi?"
How are you going to show me love without wifi
What's a girl supposed to do with one more like
if more than anything she just wants love in real life
How will you show me love without wifi
URL
IRL
GIRL

WINTER | BLACK FUTURES

by **Kayode Jonathan Akande**

THIS COLLECTION OF WORKS REPRESENTS A PERIOD OF self-exploration and artistic experimentation mostly created around the fall of 2023. Through these pieces, I aim to capture vibrant emotions and experiences, blending elements of my heritage with cultural influences. Using bold colours, dynamic forms, and a touch of surrealism, I illustrate resilience and strength, providing an uplifting representation of BIPOC individuals and celebrating our beauty and unity. Each piece embodies a unique narrative that I withhold from fully explaining, inviting the audience to interpret and connect with the art in their own way.

OPPOSITE TOP: Kayode Jonathan Akande, *Winter / Black Futures: 1*, 2023.
OPPOSITE BOTTOM: Kayode Jonathan Akande, *Winter / Black Futures: 2*, 2023.

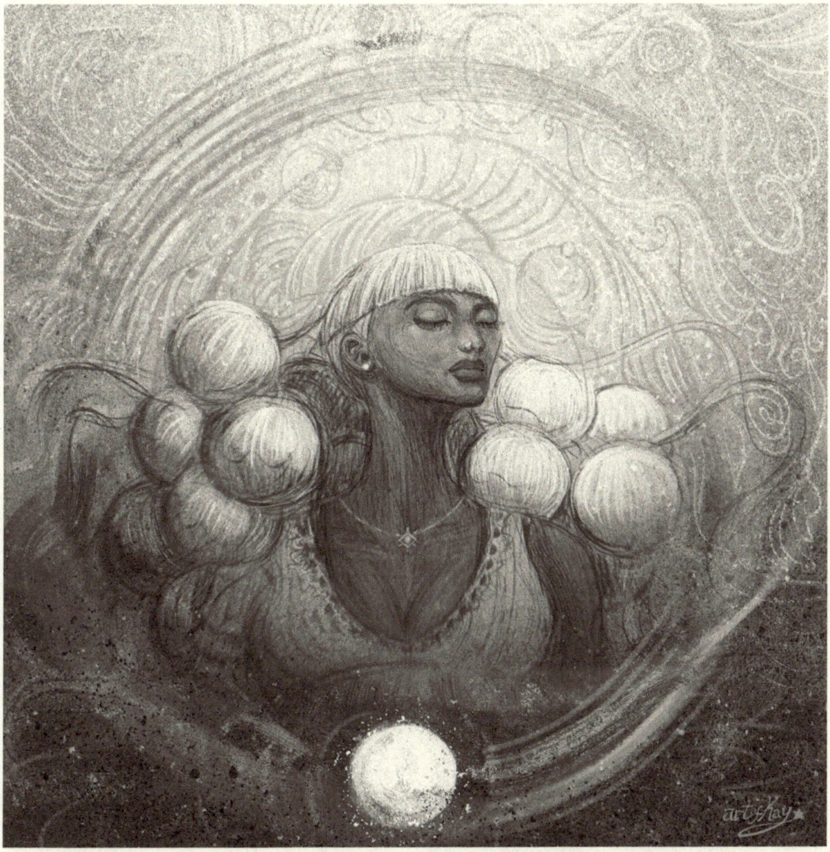
artofKay

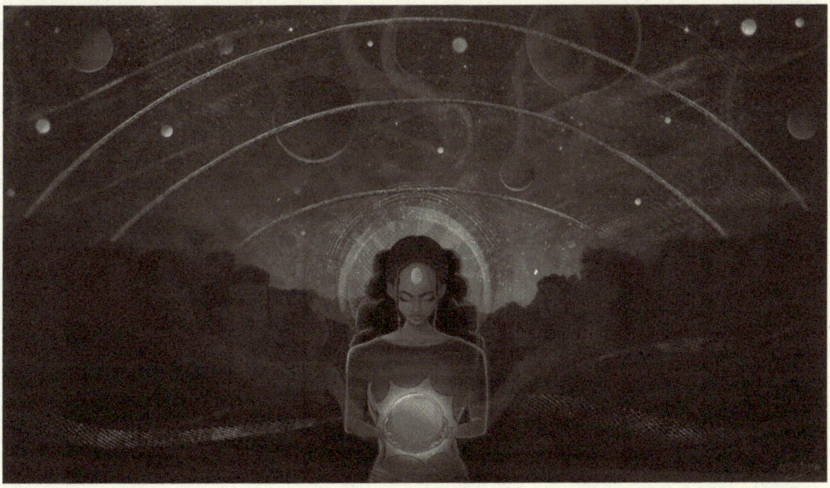

FORCE AND FORM

Doing What I Can't to Reshape the Discourse on Police Brutality

by **Pauline Lomami**

NATASHA MCKENNA, STEPHONE WATTS, KORRYN GAINES, Daniel Prude, Eric Smith, Quintonio LeGrier, Laquan McDonald, Kevin Matthews, Tamir Rice, Charleena Lyles, Freddie Gray, Sandra Bland, Eric Garner... These people were Black. They were all killed by the police in the United States of America. In Northern Turtle Island, there are more names: Regis Korchinski-Paquet, Jermaine Carby, Andrew Loku, Jamal Francique. All of them were disabled. Black, disabled, and killed after encounters with the police. I was seeing these names of people killed by police on my social media feeds. Sometimes, the names and tributes would completely take over the whole feed. Every new event of police violence experienced by Black or disabled people relayed in the news or on social media triggers memories of personal experiences or fears. Despite the large underlying issue of police brutality and violence in Canada and across the United States, the specific case of Black disabled people hasn't been part of a lot of mainstream analysis of policing. These folks were not only killed because they were Black but because they were disabled too. Since 2020, there has been more attention in public discourse and the media about how disability and ableism and saneism affect police violence toward Black people. For example, the Black Lives Matter movement has been a space where voices have risen to demand that we remember, acknowledge, and address Black disabled experiences and contributions.[1] Unfortunately, the media attention span to cover these issues does not typically last long. Targeted policing of Black disabled people reappears in the news, however, mostly because of continued violence by the police. Reporting on local violent incidents can attract media coverage back to the topic such as the case of Pradel Content in Montreal.[2]A deeper discussion needs to happen in Montreal, Quebec, where I am based, as these topics have not been profiled enough.

Police brutality has been a constant preoccupation in every country I've lived in. Like many, I was following cases in Europe and North America of police brutality after Trayvon Martin's killing in 2013. I joined local protests, including the first Black Lives Matter protest in Stockholm in 2016. I brought my kid brother to this first gathering, and together we called for Black justice and abolition. I've been in many marches and protests in Belgium before, such as radical left protests, youth cortege at the Pride, feminist demonstration, "Reclaiming the Night," World AIDS Day march, or even the group of Belgians going to Paris twice to join the march in support of the draft bill on marriage equality in France. I always maintained distance from the police as much as possible in these situations, and the few interactions I had would be stressful possibly because of the presence of an older white person, even if I was a co-organizer of some of these events. However, I would avoid anti-racist protests and other demonstrations explicitly addressing police and state violence because I expected the police to be more aggressive. My body can't promptly answer orders such as "Put your hands behind your back" or "Put your hands up," and a brutal handcuffing in my back could result in terrible and serious damage. So, for the first time, in Stockholm, I found myself facing the coexistence of the power of taking to the streets collectively and the vulnerability of being exposed to police presence. I was constantly negotiating my agency and the risks as a Black disabled person wanting to protest police brutality in the streets.

I was trying to find numbers and process statistics and understand probabilities. In the United States, Black people account for less than 13 percent of the population but are killed by police at more than twice the rate of white Americans,[3] between a third and a half of people killed by law enforcement are disabled,[4] and more than 55 percent of Black disabled people have been arrested by the time they turn twenty-eight.[5] Canadian statistics were harder to find and, for approximately 25 percent of cases of people killed by the police in Canada, it was impossible to confirm the race of the person killed as the information was not available.[6] I could still appreciate reported information related to Black people and disabled people separately. People with disabilities experience higher rates of violent victimization by police and a lower sense of safety toward police than people with no disabilities.[7] From 2000 through 2020, Black people form less than 3 percent of the population but 8.63 percent of deaths.[8] From 2000 to 2017, more than 70 percent of all victims suffered from mental health or substance abuse problems.[9] In Toronto, data from Special Investigations Unit (SIU) investigations show that despite making up only 8.8 percent of Toronto's population, Black people represent 70 percent of police shooting deaths between 2013 and 2017, twenty times more likely than white people.[10] During the same study period, Black men represented only 4 percent of the Toronto population but were complainants in 25 percent of all SIU investigations of sexual assault by the Toronto Police Service.[11] In Montreal, Black people are 4.3 times more likely to be stopped by the police than white people in 2006–2007.[12] Moreover, a study from 2017 suggests that more than half of people with developmental disability in Toronto had been stopped, handcuffed, and hurt, either emotionally or physically, during an interaction with the police at some point during their life, around 60 percent affirm that their experiences with the police influenced their day-to-day life; 70 percent add that it had influenced their mental health; and none of the participants indicated that the officer(s) were able to recognize their disability on their own.[13] In overall Canada, trust and confidence in the police is a real issue for Black people and disabled people. More than half of Black Canadians distrust the police.[14] The odds of having low confidence in the police are 30 percent higher for people who have a physical disability and 50 percent higher for people having a mental or cognitive disability than for people who don't have any disability (Ibrahim). We still miss public data for experiences involving all forms of disability.

As I was digesting these overwhelming figures, I was also looking at Black disabled people making numbers in the street and online. Two examples from the United States marked me at that time: a design work and a march from 2020 by and for Black disabled people protesting police violence. Currently based in Baltimore, Jennifer White-Johnson is an Afro Latina artist, designer, activist, and a Black mother—with Graves' disease and ADHD—of a young Black autistic son. Like many of us, after seeing the footage of the murder of George Floyd, another case of an unarmed Black person killed by the police on May 25, 2020, she felt emotionally exhausted by the weight of this repetitive event. She was also exhausted "knowing that Black disabled people would be excluded from the conversations around police brutality that were arousing out of the protest."[15] She thinks that being "Pro Neurodiversity is to be Anti Racist." On May 31, 2020, a week after the killing of George Floyd, she designed a graphic that is now largely widespread in marches and events in many countries, organizations from all sectors and on social media. The graphic merges the Black Power fist with the neurodiversity infinity symbol. Associating these symbols with each other conveys the message that Black Disabled Lives Matter, as inscribed in the forearm of the design. The Black Power fist symbol has been used by Black activists for decades, including by Black disabled activists such as Fannie Lou Hamer[16] and Brad Lomax.[17] Revisiting the Black Power fist, as Jennifer White-Johnson did, holds symbolic and historical meaning. She made her graphic into a poster that people can download for free, and her creation is now used all over the world in protest for Black Lives. Through her design and its dissemination, she virtually protested with the Black disabled community and called for the disability community to address racial justice and for Black communities to address disability issues. It even made its way to mainstream media: the *New York Times, Teen Vogue, Crip Camp, Rolling Stone,* and even Barack Obama's Twitter and Instagram feeds, in amplification of the thirtieth anniversary of the *Americans with Disabilities Act.* Her action is an intervention in public space that supports performative actions in the street as people hold the sign she created when marching against police brutality. According to her, "Black disabled artists and designers are reminding folks that collective liberation can't be created in a silo."[18] On June 15, 2020, two weeks after George Floyd's murder, one week after the release of the Black Disabled Lives Matter's design, a coalition of organizations in Detroit held a Black Disabled Lives Matter protest and march.[19] The organization of this event had the realities and concerns of Black disabled communities at the centre. Most large protests and marches are not accessible to people with disabilities; accessibility is a constant element and never put in contradiction with the critical reason for the gathering as we often see in regular ones. Moreover, because COVID-19 disproportionately impacts Black disabled people, the organizers planned, intentionally and explicitly, pandemic-related measures such as physical distancing and sanitation. The demands were the reflection of the priorities and values of those most impacted by police violence, and all featured speakers were Black and disabled. The protest was documented with photos, videos, and writing to palliate the fact that Black disabled stories are rarely covered by mainstream media. They also delivered training to volunteers who could help most appropriately by teaching them disability etiquette and language, suggestions for how to offer help to disabled participants, day-of expectations, and safety protocols. Moreover, they trained white, non-disabled accomplices to act as a buffer between marchers and the police. They planned and organized the event in a way that empowered protesters while acknowledging their vulnerability and acting in consideration (Teddy et al.). In the way this whole embodied intervention in public space has been organized and planned, we can see the coexistence of power and vulnerability and the negotiation of agency and risks taken by the Black disabled protesters. I am sharing these two examples not only because they marked me in 2020 but also because they are quick well-thought-out responses following police violence-related events, because they constitute communicative and performative intervention in public space, and because they interact with each other. The sign is a statement that addresses the issue to the viewer and targeted institutions. The protesting Black disabled body in public space combined with the protesting sign can evoke and resist what police violence can do to Black disabled people.

In a context where Black bodies are perceived as threatening and disabled bodies as not complying,[20] how does one not fear for one's safety, integrity, and right to just be? How do we give more attention to this issue without requiring more tragic events? As a Black disabled person who has been through interactions with the police, these are questions I ask myself often. But more than that, I felt the need to be out there, looking more closely at one of my biggest fears. Six months after moving to Montreal, a Black woman was brutally arrested by the police for talking and laughing too loudly on Boulevard Saint-Laurent[21] at 10:00 a.m., a few blocks from my workplace. When her white boyfriend questioned the officers, he was violently arrested too. This triggered the sensation of being policed and surveilled in public spaces constantly. I have been laughing loudly in the street quite often, and the outcome of this encounter with the police would have had a dangerous turn as a disabled person. Taking all this into account, I wanted to contribute to the discussion around the experiences of Black disabled people facing, addressing, or protesting police violence.

For this initiative to be a communicative performance and intervention, I needed to combine three core elements: public space that is open and accessible, performativity that poses oppositional logic through embodiment, and intervention that changes the normal course of thing—even just a little bit, just enough to learn differently. An impossible idea started to grow in me, becoming almost inevitable over the years. On Saturday, April 2, I performed with my Black disabled body and the building of the Canadian Armed Forces to shape each other by force. I am not able to put my left hand behind my back, which is a well-known order coming from the police. I applied contact and pressure between my body and the Canadian Armed Forces building to get to that dangerous and painful position and present my reshaped body to the building of the police. The transformation of the buildings is invisible and symbolic; the transformation of my body is visible and concrete. Exposed to the gaze, my body is not only the medium but also the performance. My performing body in public space could raise questions such as "What happened to you?"[22] "What are you doing?" "Why is it happening here?" I used that moment to evoke what police violence can do to me. Preparing for this performance, I thought about contacting four artists and friends to assist me with cameras. I quickly realized that having five Black people near the police station with cameras was not the best idea, and I switched to two white people and two Black people. I gave my ID documents to a white friend and made them stand with cameras closer to me. With my four camera assistants, I established my own surveillance setup at a well-surveilled crossroad. A few passersby stopped to look at my performance, took pictures and videos, and sometimes intervened to disrupt. But most of them walked by as usual, except when one of these disruptions would occur and someone would tell them to leave me alone. Operating on the sidewalk of the buildings of the Armed Forces and the police in downtown Montreal, I was intervening in a very frequented area bringing together police and the armed forces as a reminder of the militarization of the police (Gerbet, Ouellette Vézina, Roberts, Wood).

In September 2022, I was invited to show the short video resulting from this performance: *Force and Form—Part II*, at While Black Montreal, for a projection night curated by Dominique Fontaine and Cécilia Bracmort at Maison de la culture Janine Sutto in my neighbourhood. It was an ideal occasion to make the performance live beyond the event and to share in a space of, by, and for Black people before opening it to a general audience.

Among the generous feedback I received, one comment from a friend and artist stuck with me for the rest of the night: "It's like a horror movie in slow motion that I needed to see." As much as I appreciated the warm positive comments, I knew that I would never screen this video in a theatre again. This dispositive worked for me only because it was a Black event; it would have been a totally different experience if the audience was in majority non-Black. I started to think about how to present the archive of the performance so its impact can live beyond the action but in a way that challenges the gaze of the viewer, knowing it would mostly be a white gaze still holding space for Black viewers. To counter the possibility of fast consumption of Black suffering and the non-engagement of the viewers, I needed to make a video installation that was performative and interactive. The archive had to be an art piece on its own. *Force and Form—Parts III & IV* are the final iterations of a series of performative interventions. The projects build on the intertwined fear, frustration, and defiance of dealing with the presence of the police in public space and the related discussions in private, the media, and the streets. I revisited the experience from memories and video footage. Despite the clear intention to address police brutality and surveillance in public space, this performance also brought me back in time, to when I was a little kid in the re-education section of the hospital. The area had a swimming pool and a physiotherapy space where I would remove my clothes and practice painful movements following the instructions of the white medical staff. I became hyperconscious of myself through these repeated traumatic micro-events. This experience was brought back during the performance, and I lived two parallel experiences. It exposed a connection with childhood memories of receiving an order from a holder of institutional power, the harmful consequence for one's dignity and integrity if executed, and the equally bad punishment if rejected. This internal experience became a wall behind which to encounter my fear of police brutality on my body because I knew how bad it could easily and quickly become. The body and its choreography were the medium through which we collectively practised and questioned gaze and surveillance. Using material from the first occurrence of *Force and Form* (physical and mental movements, documentary videos, and sound recordings), *Force and Form—Parts III & IV* are complementary multimedia installations that reshape and resize to explore the coexistence of contrasting elements. Super-presence of the body and dissociation of the mind. Pain and silence. Gaze and the absence of contact. Danger and slowness. Blurring the boundaries between surveillance and spectatorship. Surrounded by a multiplied, magnified, deformed, and disappearing body movement projected on walls and textile and vinyl screens, viewers watch this same choreography set in a policed environment through five synchronized videos to surveil me and bystanders. As both gazers and objects of the gaze, their role is extended in a control room where related news articles, reports, and research papers are arranged next to a monitor screen displaying a live video of the audience watching my intervention.

After these studio tests, I presented this project in the spring of 2023 for the exhibition *IGNITION 18*, curated by Michèle Thériault and Eli Kerr, at the Leonard and Bina Ellen Gallery at Concordia University (Montreal, Canada). A core element of my proposal for this project to be selected was to emphasize that the gallery is situated close to the crossroad where the intervention occurred, to geographically connect the performance that happened in a nearby public space and its archive installed in an art gallery. Visitors could feel this project in the gallery as its archive, and then in the street charged with the acts, a memory forever encrusted in these buildings. This concluded a cycle of iterations to engage with the discussion through artmaking involving action and its archive through performance and multimedia installation. On Friday, April 12, 2024, I participated in Writing as Sedition, a symposium organized by Dark Opacities Lab led by Pr. Balbir Singh at Concordia University. I presented the first draft of this paper for a workshop-style presentation to receive feedback and hold a discussion for a work in progress.

The symposium concluded with keynotes by generous guest speakers, Pr. Jakeya Caruthers and Dr. Malav Kanuga. In her exposé, Pr. Caruthers presented cases and patterns of Black women being brutalized by the police or the judicial system for exercising self-defence or for protecting a member of their community in cases of harassment, domestic violence, or sexual assault. She emphasized the policing of their response for doing the bare minimum, sometimes even barely the minimum. These Black women were read as automatically excessive and not eligible for protection. Their protective response is read as excess, and this excess is criminalized. Their actions and emotions had to be calculated to respect a hidden and very narrow window in terms of nature, timing, and amount. Pr. Caruthers pointed out the monitoring of their muchness and how they were set up for the abuse-to-prison pipeline. I immediately felt the resonance of what she was articulating for us, and I intuitively thought about this Black woman being arrested close to my workplace for laughing too loudly. She was too much by barely doing anything. As a Black disabled gender queer person read as woman, I was thinking about all of us being constantly too much, having to monitor our nature, timing, and amount, trying to avoid being pushed into some known but often concealed pipeline.

Doing interventionist performance art is a necessity for me as an artist. I sit with this muchness for doing the minimum or almost nothing and authorize myself to be mad.[23] This rage is charged with information and creative and transformative energy, and I can feel some freedom in this release. While still negotiating with the co-presence of power, vulnerability, risk, and agency, I try to move beyond muchness, intentionally step into too-muchness, and embrace it. I am moving with my mad ideas—that are sense-making and that give me agency—to intervene through performance by doing too much and not much at the same time. Intervening in specific space, time, and audience (context) allows me to return the gaze, create an oppositional logic, and create an opportunity to understand differently and collectively, beyond automatic intellectualization, thanks to the rage. *Force and Form* consolidated an artistic and activist methodology with an embodied and em-minded approach for a performative and installation practice on which I base further research and creative projects. And as I unsuccessfully try to conclude this chapter, new names are taking over my social media feeds: Nicholas Nembhard (Canada) and Sonya Massey (United States).

Video References of the Work

"Po B. K. Lomami Discusses Performance Art Piece *Force and Form*." *The Concordian*, April 19, 2022. YouTube. https://www.youtube.com/watch?v=1EACbvEjnRs.

"*Force and Form—Parts III & IV* (1/2)." Po. B. K. Lomami, January 11, 2023. YouTube. https://www.youtube.com/watch?v=1DkiDRxPtMk.

"*Force and Form—Parts III & IV* (2/2)." Po. B. K. Lomami, January 11, 2023. YouTube. https://www.youtube.com/watch?v=sRoGxLsGgdI.

Selected References

Abenchuchan, Alex. "Black Disabled Lives Matter March & Protest in Detroit." YouTube, Deaf News, June 18, 2020. https://www.youtube.com/watch?v=oC8_PahiMVs.

Bernard, Léonel, and Christopher McAll. "La mauvaise conseillère" [A Bad Adviser]. 2010. *Revue du CREMIS* 3: 12–13. http://www.cremis.ca/docs/Revue%20du%20cREMIS%20vol.%203%20no%201%2002-03-16%2072%20dpi.pdf.

Bruce, La Marr Jurelle. *How to Go Mad without Losing your Mind: Madness and Black Radical Creativity*. Duke University Press, 2021.

Connelly, Eileen AJ. "Overlooked No More: Brad Lomax, a Bridge between Civil Rights Movements." *New York Times*, July 8, 2020. https://www.nytimes.com/2020/07/08/obituaries/brad-lomax-overlooked.html.

CRARR. "Walking While Black: Black Woman and Her White Boyfriend Violently Arrested and Fined $444 Each for Talking 'Loud' in the Plateau." CRARR. https://www.crarr.org/?q=node%2F19973.

Gerbet, Thomas. "Vague D'Achats de Fusils d'Assaut au Sein des Corps Policiers du Québec." Radio Canada, CBC/Radio Canada, May 15, 2018. https://ici.radio-canada.ca/nouvelle/1099783/armes-fusils-assaut-policier-quebec-canada-policiers-patrouille-spvm-sq-laval-longueuil-grc-toronto.

Green, Tahirah Alexander. "Our Calls to Action against Anti-Black State Violence Cannot Be Ableist." The Black Youth Project, June 12, 2020. http://Blackyouthproject.com/our-calls-to-action-against-anti-Black-state-violence-cannot-be-ableist/?fbclid=IwAR3G_CIFIYZuXAny3F3r145xCFoGWVGHaoYl3CFwEtc2nO2oz_VvmcnGYxk.

Ibrahim, Dyna. "Public Perceptions of the Police in Canada's Provinces, 2019." Statistics Canada, Government of Canada, November 25, 2020. https://www150.statcan.gc.ca/n1/pub/85-002-x/2020001/article/00014-eng.htm.

Kim, Sarah. "We Can't Erase Disability in the Black Lives Matter Movement." *Teen Vogue*, July 3, 2020. https://www.teenvogue.com/story/black-disabled-lives-matter.

Lau, Rachel. "Disabled, Anglophone Black Man's Rights Violated by Montreal Police: Quebec Human Rights Commission—Montreal." Global News, May 23, 2019. https://globalnews.ca/news/5307734/disabled-anglophone-Black-man-rights-violated-montreal-police/.

The Library of Contress. "This Little Light of Mine: The Legacy of Fannie Lou Hamer." August 5, 2015. https://www.loc.gov/item/2021689857.

Marcoux, Jacques, and Katie Nicholson. "Deadly Force." CBC News, CBC/Radio Canada, 2018. https://newsinteractives.cbc.ca/longform-custom/deadly-force.

McCauley, Erin J. "The Cumulative Probability of Arrest by Age 28 Years in the United States by Disability Status, Race/Ethnicity, and Gender." *American Journal of Public Health* 107, no. 12 (2017): 1977–1981.

Ouellette Vézina, Henri. "Armes D'assaut: Le SPVM Veut Augmenter sa Force de Frappe." *Journal Métro*, November 29, 2019. https://journalmetro.com/actualites/montreal/2402352/armes-dassaut-le-spvm-veut-augmenter-sa-force-de-frappe/.

Perry, David M., and Lawrence Carter-Long. *The Ruderman White Paper on Media Coverage of Law Enforcement Use of Force and Disability*. The Ruderman Family Foundation, 2016.

Roberts, Konrad. "Militarization of Police." Public Safety Canada, Government of Canada, June 17, 2020. https://www.publicsafety.gc.ca/cnt/trnsprnc/brfng-mtrls/prlmntry-bndrs/20200930/034/index-en.aspx.

Salerno, Alisha C. "Police Response to Development Disability." Master's thesis, York University, 2017.

Singh, Inayat. "2020 Already a Particularly Deadly Year for People Killed in Police Encounters, CBC Research Shows." CBC News, CBC/Radio Canada, July 23, 2020. https://newsinteractives.cbc.ca/fatalpoliceencounters/.

Tate, Julie, et al. "998 People Have Been Shot and Killed by Police in 2018." *Washington Post*, January 25, 2019. https://www.washingtonpost.com/graphics/2018/national/police-shootings-2018/?utm_term=.f62945024587.

Teddy. "Black Disabled Lives Matter, Join Us Monday June 11th." Disability Power, September 9, 2020. https://www.detroitdisabilitypower.org/post/Black-disabled-lives-matter-join-us-monday-june-11th.

Thompson, Vilissa. "Disability Solidarity: Completing the 'Vision for Black Lives.'" *HuffPost*, September 8, 2016. https://www.huffpost.com/entry/disability-solidarity-completing-the-vision-for-Black_b_57d024f7e4b0eb9a57b6dc1f.

Thompson, Vilissa. "Understanding the Policing of Black, Disabled Bodies." Center for American Progress, February 10, 2021. https://www.americanprogress.org/article/understanding-policing-Black-disabled-bodies.

Thomson, Rosemarie Garland. "Staring Back: Self-Representations of Disabled Performance Artists." *American Quarterly* 52, no. 2 (2000): 334–338.

White-Johnson, Jennifer. "How the Black Disabled Lives Matter Symbol Took on a Life of Its Own." Eye on Design, November 11, 2020. https://eyeondesign.aiga.org/how-the-Black-disabled-lives-matter-symbol-took-on-a-life-of-its-own/.

Wood, Lesley. "Militarisation et Privatisation de la Police au Canada et à L'Étranger." Ligue des Droits et Libertés, July 11, 2019. https://liguedesdroits.ca/militarisation-privatisation-de-police-canada-a-letranger/.

Wortley, Scott, et al. *Use of Force by the Toronto Police Service: Final Report* (July 2020). Ontario Human Rights Commission.

Notes

1 Green, "Our Calls to Action against Anti-Black"; Kim, "We Can't Erase Disability"; Thompson, "Disability Solidarity."
2 Lau, "Disabled, Anglophone Black Man's Rights."
3 Tate et al., "998 People Have Been Shot."
4 Perry and Carter-Long, *The Ruderman White Paper*.
5 McCauley, "The Cumulative Probability of Arrest," 1978.
6 Singh, "2020 Already a Particularly Deadly Year."
7 Ibrahim, "Public Perceptions of the Police."
8 Singh, "2020 Already a Particularly Deadly Year."
9 Marcoux and Nicholson, "Deadly Force."
10 Wortley et al., *Use of Force by the Toronto Police*.
11 Wortley et al., *Use of Force by the Toronto Police*.
12 Bernard and McAll, "La mauvaise conseillère."
13 Salerno, "Police Response to Development Disability."
14 Ibrahim, "Public Perceptions of the Police."
15 White-Johnson, "How the Black Disabled Lives Matter."
16 The Library of Congress, "This Little Light of Mine."
17 Connelly, "Overlooked No More."
18 White-Johnson, "How the Black Disabled Lives Matter."
19 Abenchuchan, "Black Disabled Lives Matter."
20 Thompson, "Understanding the Policing of Black," par. 8.
21 CRARR, "Walking While Black."
22 Thomson, "Staring Black," 334.
23 Bruce, *How to Go Mad*.

CREATIVE REFLECTIONS

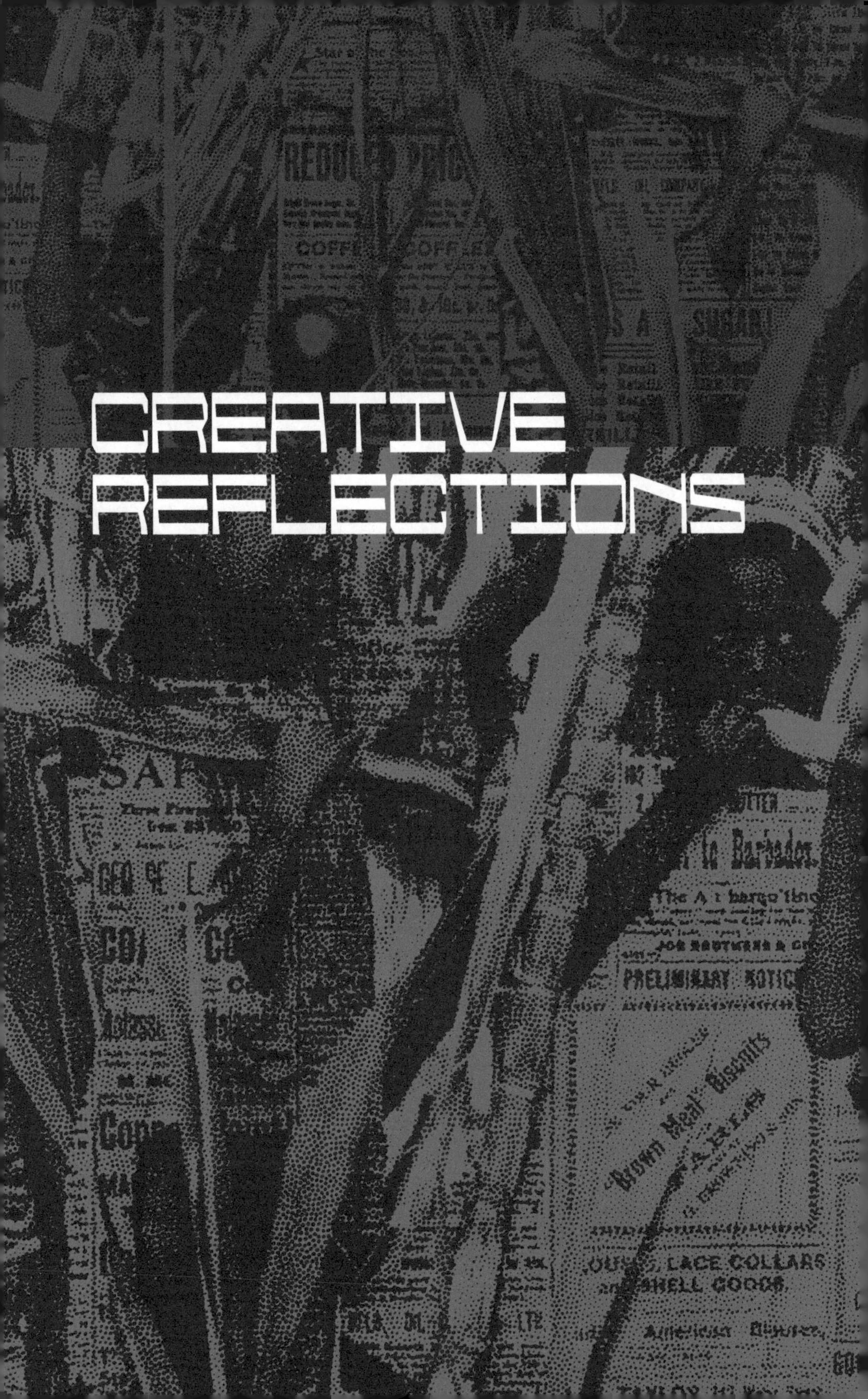

What follows are creative reflections in the spirit of encyclopedic entries by five Black artists: Simone Elizabeth Saunders, Theodore Walker Robinson, RYAN AD, Janine Carrington, and Natalie Wood.

THE FOUR QUEENS

by **Simone Elizabeth Saunders**

FOUR INDIVIDUAL WORKS, *QUEEN OF DIAMONDS*, *QUEEN of Clubs*, *Queen of Hearts*, and *Queen of Spades*, but one series: The Four Queens, 2020.

"The Four Queens are a celebration of Black womanhood. I created these colourful hand-tufted textiles to illuminate our essence: a connection to a universal sisterhood of femininity, leadership, power and joy. My research is fuelled by advocacy and perseverance toward racial liberation. And most of all; belonging. Through my textiles I uplift Black excellence, give contribution to Black culture and remain proud of my heritage and where I come from."

OPPOSITE: Simone Elizabeth Saunders, The Four Queens, 2020. Clockwise from top left: *Queen of Diamonds*, *Queen of Clubs*, *Queen of Hearts*, and *Queen of Spades*. Courtesy of the Artist.

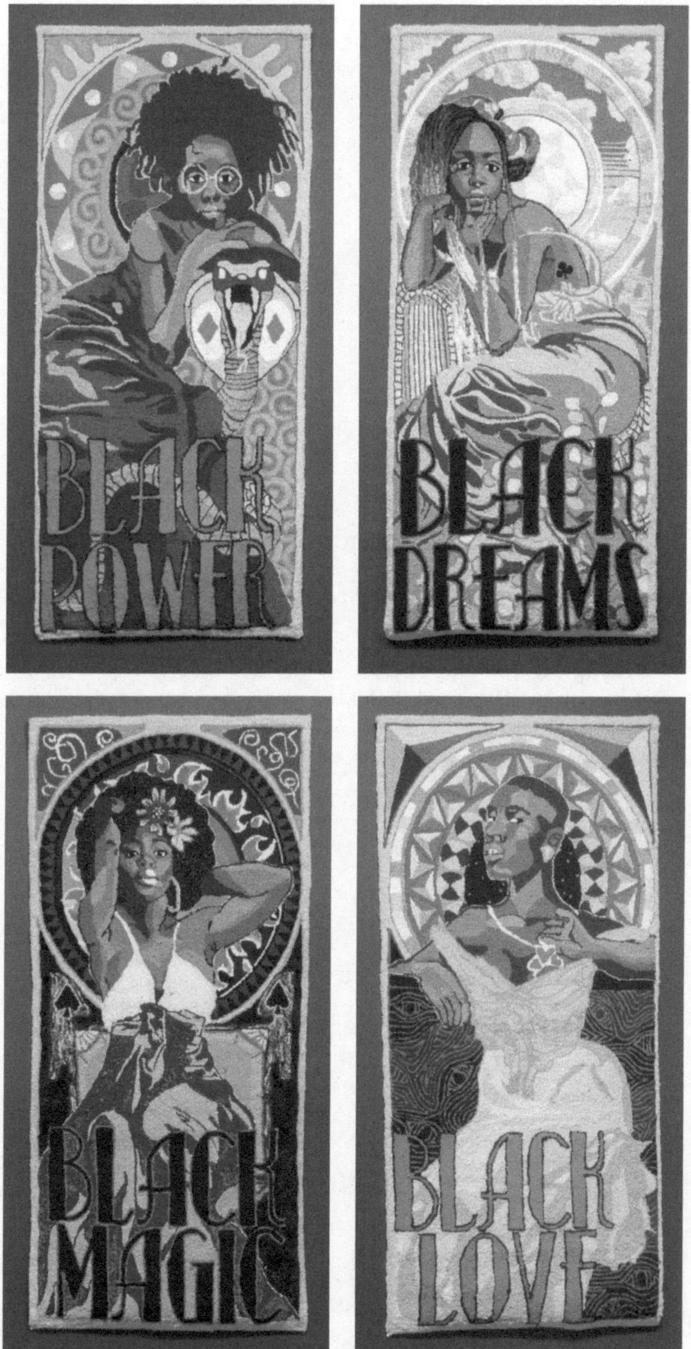
BLACK POWER
BLACK DREAMS
BLACK MAGIC
BLACK LOVE

MAROON CHILD

Mobility of Imagination

by **Theodore Walker Robinson**

I WAS BORN WITH SEVERE MYOPIA, WITH LESS THAN 10 percent of normative visual acuity in addition to congenital nystagmus, profound hearing loss, and undiagnosed neurodivergence, and I was raised in a God-fearing household of Black Caribbean immigrants who were caught up in the wave of Caribbean migration to Toronto in the 1970s. The narrative placed before me at the outset of my life was painted with lamentation, spiritual scapegoating, and anxiety. During a Sunday church service, I recall the preacher reading from the gleaming gilded-edged pages of a King James Bible: "And his disciples asked him, saying, Master, who did sin, this man, or his parents, that he was born blind? Jesus answered 'Neither hath this man sinned, nor his parents: but that the works of God should be made manifest in him.'"

The words of Jesus, read from the golden pages, secretly lifted me, while my parents remained steadfast in the words of his disciples. At our home on Silverthorne Crescent in Mississauga, Ontario, at the kitchen table, over tea with friends, family, or strangers, my mother would assuredly tell them (and remind me as I pressed my good ear up against my bedroom door, struggling to hear the kitchen conversations) that I was "born Black, assigned female at birth and disabled: my future was to pick up a trade."

I often struggled with feelings of being pathologically flawed and limited within my scope of potential. I learned to mask low vision and hearing and prioritize the limited imaginations and comfort of those around me. I was quiet and compliant and internalized the belief that the only life worth living in the world is one that is seeing, hearing, and neurotypical. In a Christian household, I had no language for my gender or sexuality.

Behind my eyes, I saw a blurry and constantly moving world; my imagination made me prone to chronic dreaming and innocent delusions of grandeur as an escape from the capture of the malicious kitchen prophecies. My Maroon Jamaican blood boiled, and I prepared to escape into the jungle to live with self-sovereignty. As I sat in the back of my parents' Dodge Spirit, watching the world smear colours past me during a drive home from a family trip to Ottawa, I envisioned the olive-green carpet of the House of Commons underneath my feet. I would hear my voice call out: "Mr. Speaker, with all due respect…!" In my mind, I saw boundless social and economic mobility for myself.

Behind my eyes, I mentally rebelled against constructs of lack and limitation. I journeyed into the world to obtain academic degrees, run in a federal election, socially transition and obtain several corporate banking roles in human resources. I travelled and lived alone in Palestine. I took vows as a Buddhist monastic in Thailand. Maroon by blood, I strived to outrun those malicious kitchen prophecies. I saved myself by imagination and trusted the intuition of Disability. I understood Liberation as a practice of mobility of mind. For me, it was the pursuit of my full potential through embodied visioning. I wanted to experience all that this world had to offer through the creative practice of mind.

« PHANTASY NO. 3 »

by **RYAN AD**

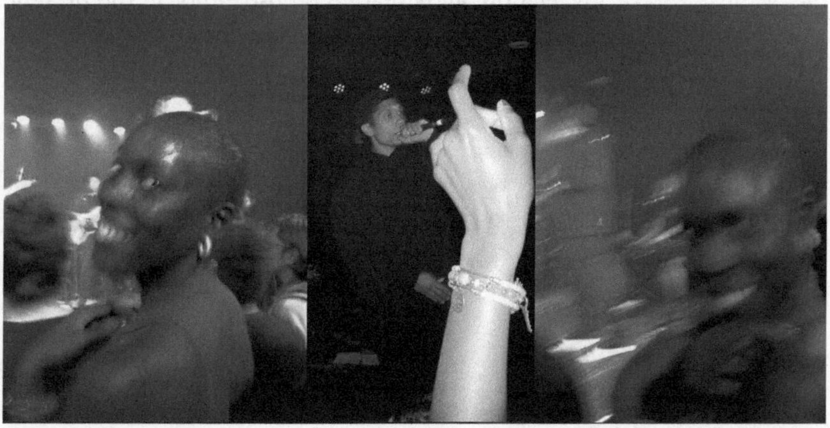

Ryan AD, *« PHANTASY No. 3»*, triptych, digital photograph on archival pigment print, 2019. Courtesy of the Artist.

ARTWORK CREATED IN AUTUMN 2019, FIRST EXHIBITED IN July 2020 on Treaty 1 Territory (Winnipeg, MB), as a part of Window Winnipeg's exhibition, *Joy is More Than Just a Feeling*. Ryan AD created « PHANTASY No. 3 » as an expression of life, contemporary Black leisure and unrestricted imagination (phantasy) as a means of youth resistance. In « PHANTASY No. 3 », joy, imagination, and youthful revelry stand at the forefront as revolutionary necessities to lean into the present moment and endure and overcome the intense, specifically anti-Black violence that pervades and continues to pervade Northern Turtle Island society. These cyclical horrors reached a landmark moment of explosion in the summer of 2020.

Historical points of dread and violence require, maybe more than other times, as much of a focus on care through laughter, dance, and other rituals of fun and unrestricted play within oneself and one's community as possible. As one recalls the past and documents the present horrors of systemic colonial oppression, one must also document how we find elation and make space for necessary leisure time. By investing in leisure, we push against capitalism and colonialism's consistent sapping away of this time for folks outside its ruling classes. This is something that we see today, with struggles here in Turtle Island as well as in more extreme cases abroad, in Congo, Gaza, Haiti, and Sudan, among other bastions of revolutionary liberation struggles. Revolution is struggle but it is not only struggle; it must also be joy, elation, and creative repose, if not in the present, then in a timeless space of imagination for better futures.

ICE CREAM DREAMS

by **Janine Carrington**

"ICE CREAM DREAMS" IS A DIGITAL ILLUSTRATION BY Canadian artist Janine Carrington. It depicts two Black children lost in laughter holding an oversized ice cream cone and lollipop. Buildings in the background suggest an urban setting while a warmly coloured haze suggests summer's heat. The children in the work are fictional. They face the same direction with eyes closed and heads tilted; mouths open in laughter. The girl who is positioned on the left side of the image rests her hand lightly on the boy's shoulder giving the air of a recently told joke. Their skin tones fall in the middle of the spectrum of Black skin, and their hair textures range from wavy to coily. The figures have an illustrative quality marked by the visible dark outline around their arms and facial features while their light-coloured shirts blend into the bright and colourful haze. Areas of chromatic aberration are used to emphasize the dreamlike quality of this piece. This work was intended to speak to the literary movement of the late twentieth and early twenty-first century that is characterized by an explosive growth of literature for and about Black children. It is emblematic of the artist's endeavours to aggressively counteract the oversupply or trauma-inspired Black imagery prevalent at the time by creating ethereal, joyous, peaceful, light-infused drawings for children. The goal of this work and others of the same milieu is to engender a positive association with Blackness as part of the campaign to dismantle white supremacist, colonialist systems of oppression.

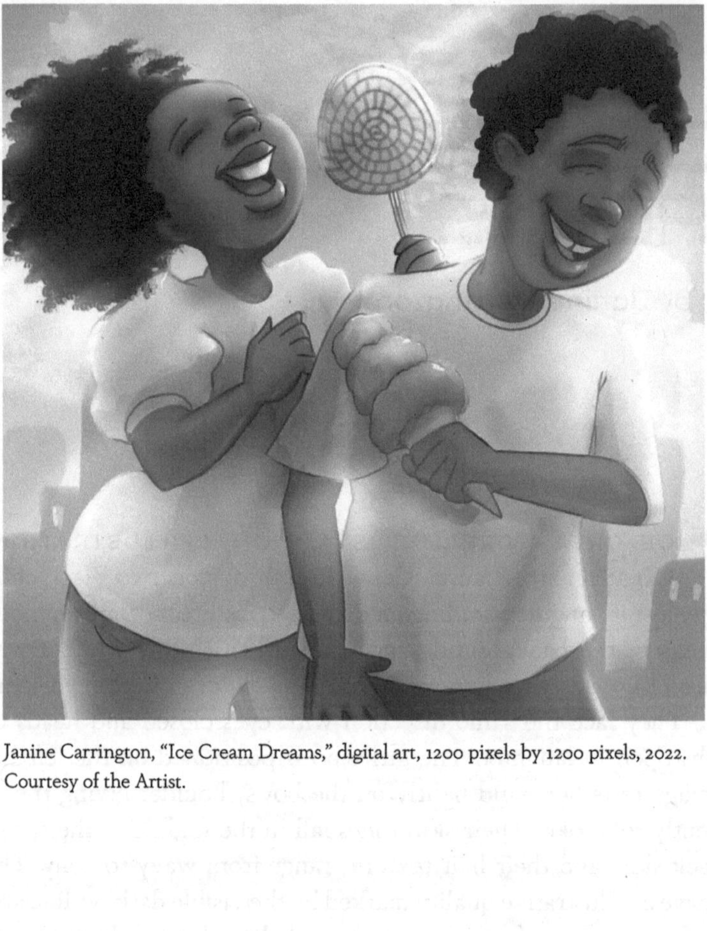

Janine Carrington, "Ice Cream Dreams," digital art, 1200 pixels by 1200 pixels, 2022. Courtesy of the Artist.

THEY SAY WE CAN'T BREATHE UNDERWATER

by **Natalie Wood**

This reflection considers an exhibition at A Space Gallery September 2022 that I created and co-curated with Geneviève Wallen.

IN 2021, I DEVELOPED ASTHMA, A CONDITION THAT WAS exacerbated by the very real terror and precarity of living Black lives. For the month-long solo exhibition that I created entitled *They Say We Can't Breathe Underwater*, I acknowledged that there have been structural attempts at Black suffocation on a large scale. Fuelled by this reality, I asked two main questions: a) How do we as Black people learn to breathe in unbreathable circumstances? and b) What abolitionist strategies champion collective care? I created the works for this exhibition drawing on the figure of Yemayá—the African deity who is mother of the oceans and of life and a powerful deity reconstituted in the diaspora who cares for the sick and traumatized.

I staged the three-part installation—a three-part video exhibit—to mirror a devotee's journey to connect to Yemayá. The first installation in the exhibition, *Undrowned in the Black Atlantic*, a meditative video projection, encouraged visitors to "breathe underwater" by synchronizing their breathing with the video's breath sounds. Visually, they were taken to the bottom of the Atlantic Ocean where they encountered Yemayá and a shipwreck teeming with aquatic life. In the second installation in the exhibition, *Rise Up!*, a fifteen-foot carnival costume depicting Yemayá was presented in a semi-devotional manner alongside two short videos, *Yemayá's Carnival Journey* and *Breathing Lessons*, exploring diasporic breathwork, resistance, and joy through carnival and playing mas. In front of this installation were two *Carnival Chairs* painted and decorated with sequins and feathers where visitors sat, performed, and "jumped up" to soca songs of their choosing. These performances activated a rebirthing process moving from Black suffocation to a space of Black joy, caring, and community.

Finally, *Dismantling Patterns: Abolition Dreams*, showed four stages of deconstructed cardboard ships with abolitionist lifeboats attached. These waxed paper lifeboats had stripped the cardboard, leaving patterns as reminders that we know what is needed to dismantle white supremacy and racial capitalism. Visitors left reminded we have tools of collective creativity, mas making, care, joy, and abolition to overthrow the terror of Black precarity.

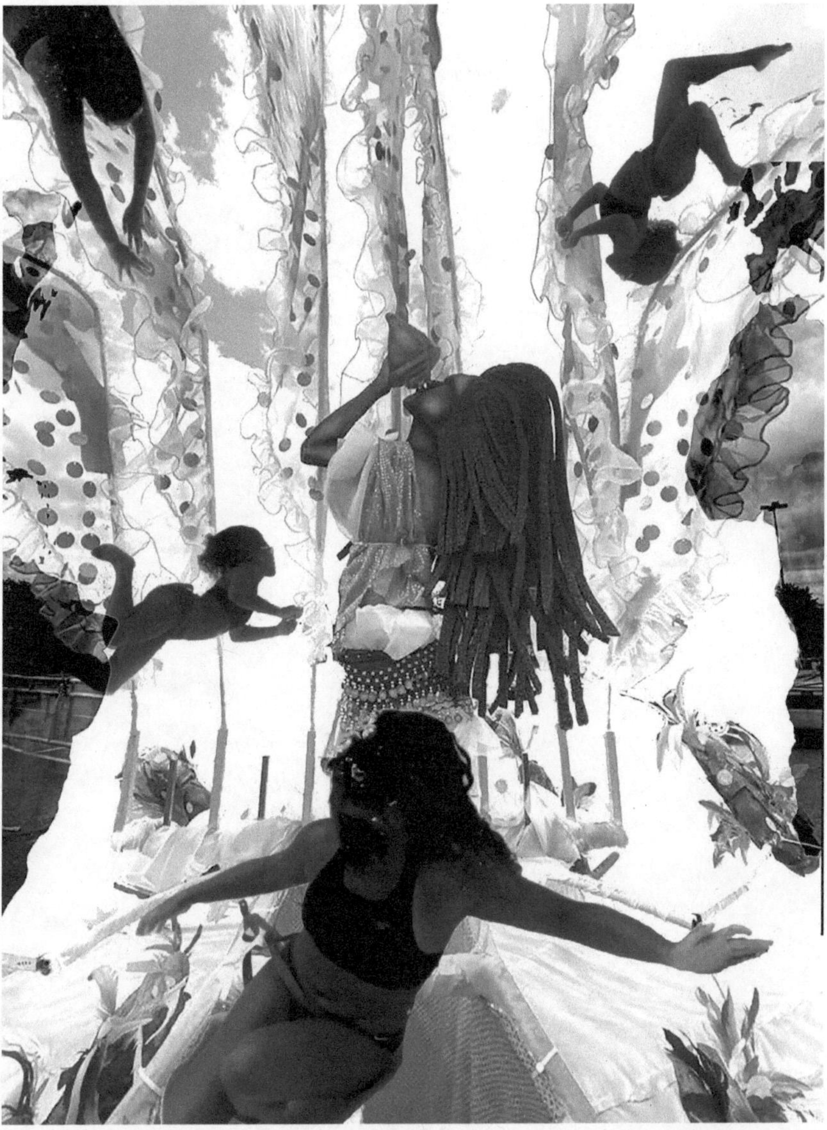

Natalie Wood, They say we can't breathe underwater, 2022. Courtesy of the Artist. Photo-based digital inkjet print that combines stills from *Undrowned in the Black Atlantic and Breathing Lessons*. edition of 5 + A/P 10 ½ x 14 ¼ inches (image size), 20 x 16 inches (sheet size) Paul Petro Contemporary Art.

[illegible] digital [illegible]
[illegible] Contemporary Art.

CONCLUSION

by **Dr. Syrus Marcus Ware**
Dr. Ra'anaa Yaminah Ekundayo (ABD)
Dr. d'bi.young anitafrika

WHAT WOULD IT MEAN TO PRACTICE THE FUTURE TOGETHER in ways that birthed new possibilities, offered new portals to transformed worlds shaped by our care? The chapters and artworks in *Free To Be More: Creative Activism in the Era of Black Lives Matter* offer insights into some of the unsung creative practitioners who have been bridging art and activisms and ushering in a freer abolitionist future for all Black people since the first sparks of uprisings began here in Northern Turtle Island and have been ongoing since 2013, and since long before. The artists in this collection are helping us practice our pre-figured futures together through artwork, practice, and healing justice—all stemming from their deep commitment to systems change and revolutionary struggle.

Activism and the arts have always been intrinsically linked: creative approaches make mobilizing more fun and can provide a clear and cohesive message through threads sewn tight or with paint splattered across a banner. And artistic practice is made infinitely more beautiful and powerful by connecting it to justice and changemaking. They amplify and ameliorate each other, like intertwined halves of the same coin. Art is activism is art. The authors in this edition are using their practices to bring community together, to topple old monuments of slavery and colonialism, sometimes literally, and to build a strong base for community to thrive together.

As artists, we've been interested in the creative possibilities linked to change making and are moved by the tremendous revolutionary and activist aesthetics being developed in this moment of upheaval and transformation. We are living in revolutionary times—for revolution is not a one-time event but rather a process that is ongoing. We are thankful for the many artists and creatives who are helping us manage life in the present, while dreaming into freer futures. We are stepping to the future, rolling to the future, together and in community. From conversations with the Montreal Steppers to poetry to Kim Ninkuru to scholarly reflections on monuments toppled, these creative projects are shaping a new world for us all. We move in the rhythm of change making, beat boxing and rhyming together. To move into creative space together, we move and dance together.

We want to close with some creative reflections from our collective of editors—sparks for future changemaking.

Offering One: A Manifestation of a Garden of Black Flowers and of a Future Teeming with Black Life

last night, while I slept
my heart slowly pushed its way
upwards

imperceptibly
through the surface of my skin
to rest
on top my chest

like time-lapse photography of plants
slowly curling upwards and shaking off their heavy soil
to reach upwards towards the sun
to taste the water

and so today I covered over my heart with soil
with deep Black earth
slowly spread across delicate parts

(rough fingers moving gently across tissue-thin membranes)
and then

I will purchase as many fritillaria persica bulbs as I could buy
on Roncesvalles Avenue
to plant tomorrow, as intentions
before this dark winter

knowing full well, that in the spring
my garden
will awaken

bulbs will slowly make tiny cracks
in their hard shells
bursting open
ever so slowly

imperceptibly

pushing their life
upwards

Making together
a sea of Black flowers
a garden of Blackness

and every petal will be so soft
that to brush your hand
across the surface

will be like touching g-d
will be like
touching the beginning of time
stirring up atoms
molecular regeneration
making life begin

and I know that with each caress
my heart will
embrace this Black soil
curl back inwards
burrowing
beneath

a reversal process
time-lapse footage
in the other direction

and it will sink back through my skin
almost imperceptibly
into the beautiful darkness

and while I sleep
it will whisper to the universe

I'm home
I'm home
I'm home

In the beautiful darkness, possibility is revealed. Through these pages, we have a chance to reflect on movements for Black lives globally with a focus on Northern Turtle Island, and what we are left with is how many small actions by individuals and collectives can weave together to form a network of changemaking that is ultimately helping us believe that we can "win," as Assata Shakur suggested, and that helps us get there through work, struggle, and creative inspiration.

Offering Two: A Chrysalis for a New Future

> It is in shedding our deepest sorrows and pains that we are truly born anew

Unburdened,
Unbound,
Unbothered by what has been

The fleeting kiss of life brushes our being
The richness of existence

It is here   I am still
                I am seen
                I am sound

Memories not forgotten
But forgiven

For living
For learning
For leaving what's left behind

Hidden for so long
Cocooned in the abyss
Engulfed in sorrow and terrifying bliss

But from the pits of despair, crawl the way out
Hold close to our hearts
The hearth of our home

In growth, we embrace
A child deep within
Bare and adrift, clad in confusion

It is pain
It has passed
It is the past shaping the present

Protecting what was and what will be
Look back look forward ceaselessly

Presence
A gift of the universe

Who are you becoming?
Who have you been?
Who has been chosen to lead the life you live?
Revelations realizations
Diffidence indifference
On an infinite loop

Look out
Look in
Believe in what you know

Shed the fears
Uncertainty
And darkness from below

Let it go
          Let it go
                    Let it go

I am weightless
Free to choose
No longer tethered to the gaze

Free to win and free to lose

But grounded
In clarity and in delights
A mirror to reality inverted on my self

I am transformed
A bountiful butterfly
Wings spread breath deep and eyes open wide

Everlasting change
Eternal growth

Everything dreamed of and desired the most

Here on the horizon
Our solace arrives
Warm and familiar, but reborn inside

Come forth
Come witness
As seasons change

On the cusp of greatness
I find my way home

Metamorphosized
I return

As seasons change, and we move further into this new period of human activity on Earth—in a moment plagued by climate crisis and many challenges related to racial injustice and intersecting systems of oppression—remain committed to the power of creative strategy for helping us, and importantly for helping others around us to envision and picture a tangible and changed future. For those who are having trouble imagining the "winning" that Assata Shakur described (Shakur 2018), or who need help with practising the future (Palahniuk et al. 2024), the conceptual and hands on work of making, drawing, sewing, performing, stepping, drumming, writing, and dreaming together is a roadmap for getting to where we need to go. Artists literally help us paint a picture of where we are going and help us practice the steps to get there together. Activists have long shown the power of prefiguring our futures, and artists are working in the now to support these efforts. We are thankful for the chance to turn toward each other through struggle and build together in ways that transform our world and ourselves—like butterflies moving from their gooey chrysalis into an expansive free post-cocoon life flying in the sunshine. We root into hope through these changes and water the seeds of possibility for a better, more just world.

Offering Three: Meditations on a Black Creative Future

inna di Black future we dance
past di dutty
past di corrupt
past di greedy
we shimmy we skank we boogie
we dance on the remains of headquarters
no more policing pirates of prisons and puncture

inna di Black future we laugh
past di white wickedness of racism
past di lateral violence of internal hate
past di pollution of di yes-people who climb
imaginary towers of power

inna di Black Black future
di Black(w)hole of we
across di event horizon, transphobia
trans-formed into a garden of infinite possibilities
on the spectrum of gender, sexuality, ability
on the spectrum of everything
because everything is a spectrum

oh, dat future
dat Black future
of clean water
shining pon wi
skin radiant like revolution
sunshine fertile with seeds
that can grow fruits and vegetables

cuz inna di Black future
di water ways are our spiritual highways
sharing and caring with our animal kin
with our plant kin
loving di skin wi in
inna di Black future

We dream forward into a future where we and our plant kin are both loving our skin and celebrating our creative magic. The artists in this collection have helped us better understand the ways that Black arts practice intertwines with the land, with community, and with mobilization toward structural change in our world. We continue to dive deep into pools of poetic text to help us communicate with future generations about this moment of revolutionary zeal in the 2010s and 2020s.

In these poetic works, we, too, are taking up the tools of our craft to help usher forward a future that is imbued with an inherently valuable Black life. We are tapping into our movement-building and activism and offering forward some art of Black activism—dreams of a new Black-affirmed set of communities around the world.

Selected References

Palahniuk, Chuck, Invisible Monsters, and adrienne maree brown. "April Anson." *The Existential Toolkit for Climate Justice Educators: How to Teach in a Burning World* (2024): 170.

Shakur, Assata. "To My People." *Women's Studies Quarterly* 46, no. 3 & 4 (2018): 217–221.

ACKNOWLEDGEMENTS

To the village of artists, activists, and artivists who contributed to this book: you provided us with magical mirrors that reflect infinite Black creative radiance. We say ase and thank you for your bountiful beingness, love, care, and brilliance. Thank you for trusting in us and this vision. Thank you to the team at URP, especially Rachel Stapleton, and to Ali McDonald at 5 Otter Literary. Thank you to Mila Mendez, whose early brainstorming with Syrus led to the creation of the first prospectus for this project.

ABOUT THE CONTRIBUTORS

Aisha Sasha John is a performer, choreographer, and poet. Recent works include The Pool (Toronto Dance Theatre, 2025) and the poetry collection *total* (McClelland & Stewart, 2025). Aisha is interested in the power of reception as creative methodology and in choreographing performances that occasion real love.

Anna Jane McIntyre is a visual artist–parent with a practice combining listening, drawing, thinking, doing, looking, breathing, sharing, telling, being, non-being, shape-shifting, $5-improv-benevolent-capitalism, and microactivism. Anna's work investigates how people perceive, create, and maintain their notions of self, belonging, and culture through behaviour and visual cues. Anna's work acknowledges the past-present-future, in joyous response to Dr. Martin Luther King Jr.'s question of *Where Do We Go from Here: Chaos or Community?*

TonyXTones (Anthony Gebrehiwot) is a multiple award–winning visual artist, photographer, and community leader whose creative lens re-visions photography as an ongoing dialogue of social change between subject and society.

Born and raised in Kingston, Ontario, Britta Badour, better known as **Britta B**, is an award-winning artist, public speaker, voice talent, and poet living in Toronto. She is the author of the poetry collection and audiobook *Wires that Sputter*, published by McClelland & Stewart.

Charmaine Nelson is a Provost Professor of Art History and the founding Director of the Slavery North Initiative, which supports research and research creation on the study of Canadian slavery and slavery in the American North. Prior to this appointment in 2022, she was a professor of Art History and a Tier 1 Canada Research Chair in Black Diasporic Art and Community Engagement at NSCAD University in Halifax, Canada (2020–2022), where she founded the Institute for the Study of Canadian Slavery, the first-ever research centre focused on the overlooked 200-year history of Canadian participation in transatlantic slavery.

Elicser Elliott is a Toronto-based aerosol artist whose creations adorn the cultural landscape here and abroad. As an integral part of downtown Toronto's street-art community for over a decade, he has been recognized for his artistry and praised by both street and fine art collectors all over the world. His work has been featured in a multitude of publications, hung in prestigious galleries like the Art Gallery of Ontario, and for a number of years he had his own installation in the Royal Ontario Museum.

Erica N. Cardwell is a writer, art critic, and educator based in Toronto. She is the recipient of a 2021 Andy Warhol Foundation Arts Writers Grant for her book, *Wrong is Not My Name: Notes on Black Art* (Feminist Press, 2024). Her writing has appeared in *ARTS.BLACK*, *Art in America, Frieze, Bomb*, the *Brooklyn Rail, C Magazine*, the *Kenyon Review*, and other publications. She has written exhibition and catalogue essays for artists such as Crystal Z. Campbell, Rico Gatson, Samantha Box, Chitra Ganesh, Sandra Brewster, and Amanda Williams. Erica is an assistant professor of creative writing at the University of Toronto Scarborough.

Isak Vaillancourt is a multidisciplinary artist, activist, and filmmaker based in N'Swakamok (Sudbury, ON). His work explores identity, Black healing, and decolonization through vibrant visual storytelling. He is also Co-Founder and Director of Black Lives Matter–Sudbury and holds an MA in Media Production from Toronto Metropolitan University.

jamilah malika abu-bakare is a writer, artist, and educator meditating on sound (art) as refusal and refuge. Her works have appeared via Sweden, Los Angeles, and Chicago as well as across Canada, including the Galt Museum and Archives, Two Rivers Gallery, and EspacePop! Her writing has appeared in *CBC Arts Online*, *Canadian Art Magazine*, and *Active Cultures Digest*, and her interviews can be heard on the *Hush Harbours*, *A Kind of Healing*, and *Constellations* podcasts.

Janine Carrington is an illustrator who specializes in BIPOC-centred Black-affirming children's books and comics. Born in Toronto, Ontario, and taught the basics of drawing by her father, she went on to study art in high school and at the Ontario College of Art and Design. She is currently inspired by her wonderful son to create art that uplifts all children, especially those of colour.

Kanika Gordon is an Afro Indigenous artist and storyteller engaging with memoir. Her practice involves exploring the body as a reservoir of ancestral knowledge. Her work is driven by a deep sense of loss from the horrors of colonization and, yet, an acknowledgement that this force extends beyond longing for our obfuscated truths—it is also about the deep connections that still exist and the innate knowing we possess.

Kayode Jonathan Akande is a multimedia artist, born in Nigeria but now thriving in Sudbury, Ontario. His creations focus on the uplifting representation of BIPOC individuals, vivid emotions, and bright colours, with surreal modern twists. His works often revolve around narratives of his experiences and those surrounding him.

Kim Ninkuru is a multimedia artist who was born in Bujumbura, Burundi. She has been living and working in Montreal and Toronto since 2009. Using video and sound performance, storytelling, and installation work, she creates pieces that explore and express rage, love, desire, beauty, or pain in relation to her own body, mind, and soul. While her art is very personal, she is committed to speaking out about the liberation of Black women and femmes everywhere.

King Kxndi (Kendi Tarichia) is an artist, a medium for/to/of feelings. Through words, imagery and curated spaces, King Kxndi explores what it means...to be of Earth, on Earth, with Earth, from Earth.

Kyisha (Keisha) Williams is a Tkaronto-born Black nonbinary femme dreamer, writer, actor, director, and health equity consultant. Kyisha fuses public health and digital media by creating socially relevant content that discusses health and promotes healthy sexuality and consent culture. Kyisha works to highlight the experiences of people who experience marginalization at many intersections, including Black, queer, and criminalized communities. They are deeply committed to Black and Indigenous joy, health, and freedom.

Mohammed A. Odusanya is a graduate of McGill University's Faculty of Law. Before pursuing his legal studies, he earned a Joint Honours degree in Art History and Gender, Sexuality, Feminist, and Social Justice Studies from the same institution.

Montreal Steppers

Kayin Queeley is the founder and director of the Montreal Steppers, which was formed in 2019, and has since connected with more than 15,000 participants and offered more than 500 workshops in schools across the country. He has created and produced several original productions that explore Black diasporic life and resilience in Canada in the afterlife of slavery. He is also a Case Manager in Crisis Response in the Office of the Dean of Students at McGill University and has worked to support students in his various roles at McGill as well as other institutions over the past ten-plus years.

Natasha "Tashe" Clery is a mother, daughter, sister, and friend who was born and raised in Montreal, Quebec, Canada, to exceptional St. Lucian parents. She has twenty-two years of experience at the McGill University Health Centre in Montreal, with administration experience in the clinical, medical, surgical, and finance departments. She was the first to initiate the stepping art form in Canada at Vanier College in 1991 and is currently a member of the exceptional Montreal Steppers team, serving on the Board of Directors for the organization.

Natalie Wood is an award-winning Trinidadian-born, Tkaronto-based visual and media artist. Her multimedia artwork cohabits the areas of popular culture, education, and historical research, and explores her fascination with counter-narratives, Caribbean folk tales, healing cultures, and icons that liberate Black and queer communities. Her practice includes painting, drawing, printmaking, photography, video, and performance, and extends into her work as a curator, educator, and community-based queer activist. She is presently completing a research-creation project for her PhD focused on Black Queer Resistance in the performance of Blue Devil mas.

Natasha "Courage" Bacchus, from Toronto, Ontario, is both an award-winning athlete and actor, combining her athleticism with her physicality in theatre. She is the recipient of numerous medals in track and field including gold and silver from the World Games for the Deaf, Bulgaria (1993) and gold from Denmark (1997); silver from the Pan Am Games for the Deaf, Venezuela (2007); and Master Track Breaking Records in Track and Field (2014–2015). Performance highlights include her debut as Shaw TV talk show host, BC (2014), Verse Festival ASL storyteller, BC (2014), and ASL poet, Women of Colour, Sisters in Motion, Quebec (2017–2018).

Po B. K. Lomami (Pauline Batamu Kasiwa Lomami) is an indisciplinary and interventionist artist. They are a Congo-descendant (DRC) from Belgium currently based in Tiohtià:ke-Mooniyang-Montreal, Canada. Lomami's practice initially emerged from urgency, strategy, and reclamation of space-time. Their art is a continuation that cultivates intrusion, interference, and introspection.

Ravyn Wngz, "The Black Widow of Burlesque," is a Tanzanian, Bermudian, Mohawk, Two Spirit, queer, and Transcendent empowerment storyteller. Ravyn is an abolitionist and co-founder of ILL NANA/DiverseCity Dance Company. She is a Canadian best selling author, one of the Top 25 Women of Influence in Canada (2021), and a co-founder of Black Lives Matter Canada.

Rodney Diverlus is a Haitian-Canadian multi-hyphenate artist who works in dance, theatre, film, multidisciplinary performance, and public arts–based political interventions.

RYAN AD is an interdisciplinary artist, curator, and cultural worker currently working between Kanien'kehá:ka and Treaty 1 territory, the latter on the land of the Cree, Anishinaabeg, Dakota, and Métis peoples. He/they have a self-taught practice, which is in constant search of the intangibles existing somewhere between the heart, the brain, and the digital and analogue worlds. Ryan AD's work reaches beyond and bends conventional notions of space and time.

Based in Toronto, **Sandra Brewster** works in drawing, video, photo-based works, and installation. Her themes focus on identity and representation, and movement in the depiction of gesture resulting in a re-presentation of the portrait. She uses specific landscapes as metaphors and manipulates old photographs to centre the people within them.

Simone Elizabeth Saunders (she/her) is an award-winning Canadian textile artist whose powerful tapestries have attracted the attention of galleries, media, and prominent collectors from around the world. Using a punch needle and tufting machine, she carefully hand weaves each canvas with a strong focus on emulating Black womanhood, uplifting their joys, strength, and resilience. Her colourful textiles highlight motifs and iconography from her Jamaican heritage and engage with sociocultural factors reclaiming power from oppressive ideologies.

Theodore Walker Robinson is a Black, low-vision, hard-of-hearing, nonbinary broadcaster, scholar, fashion designer, and multidisciplinary artist. Theodore was born to parents of Maroon Jamaican and Afro Chinese Trinidadian descent who settled in Toronto, Ontario, Canada, in the early 1970s. Theodore is subject-matter expert in West African woven kente and Malian Mud Cloth textiles.

Dr. Winsom Winsom is a Maroon Canadian artist with a decades-long career marked by bold colours, dynamic brushstrokes, and themes of movement and energy. Born in Jamaica, she studied at the Jamaica School of Art (1965–1968). Her work has been widely exhibited across Canada, the United States, and the Caribbean, earning numerous awards and grants.

Yung Yemi (Adeyemi Adegbesan) is a Toronto-based multidisciplinary artist whose practice aims to examine the cultural intersectionalities within Black identity. Reflecting on Black cultural ideologies from precolonial,

colonial, present day, and future timelines as well as across regions, religions, varying levels of income, and political lines, Adegbesan examines the dichotomy of the richness of Black experiences with the imposed societal homogeneity of "Blackness." Through his work, Adegbesan pulls from these cultural inspirations to create Afrofuturist/Afrosurrealist portraits that embody themes of history, fantasy, speculative futures, and spirituality.

ABOUT THE EDITORS

Dr. Syrus Marcus Ware is an assistant professor at the School of the Arts, McMaster University. His research-creation practice spans drawing, installation, and performance, and considers social justice frameworks and Black activist culture. His work has been shown widely, including solo shows at Tangled Art + Disability in 2022 (*Random Access Memory*), Grunt Gallery in 2018 (*2068: Touch Change*), and Wil Aballe Art Projects in 2021 (*Irresistible Revolutions*). His work has been featured as part of the inaugural Toronto Biennial of Art in both 2019 and 2022 in conjunction with the Ryerson Image Centre (*Antarctica*; *Ancestors, Do You Read Us?: Dispatches from the Future*; and *MBL: Freedom*), as well as for the Bentway's *Safety in Public Spaces* initiative in 2020 (*Radical Love*).

Syrus's recent curatorial projects include *And the Spaces Between Us Smiled* for Nuit Blanche, central zone (City of Toronto, 2024), *That's So Gay* (Gladstone Hotel, 2016–2019), *Re:Purpose* (Robert McLaughlin Gallery, 2014), and *The Church Street Mural Project* (Church-Wellesley Village, 2013). Syrus was co-curator of *The Cycle*, a two-year disability arts performance initiative of the National Arts Centre (NAC) with Dr. Sarah Garton Stanley. He is part of the inaugural curatorial team for the NAC's National Creation Fund.

Syrus is a co-founder of Black Lives Matter Canada and co-founder of Wildseed Centre for Art & Activism. He is the innovator of the Wildseed Black Arts Fellowship, the Put Your Roots Down Residency, and the

Black August Residency. Syrus is a past co-curator of Blackness Yes!/Blockorama (2004–2022), the largest and longest-running programming at the Pride Toronto Festival.

Syrus has won several awards, including the Mayworks Labour Award (2017) and the TD Diversity Award (2017). Syrus was voted "Best Queer Activist" by *NOW Magazine* (2005) and was awarded the Steinert and Ferreiro Award (2012). He is a board member for the Tegan and Sara Foundation and board treasurer for Wildseed Centre for Art & Activism. Syrus holds a doctorate from York University in the Faculty of Environmental Studies. He is the co-editor of the best selling *Until We Are Free: Reflections on Black Lives Matter in Canada* (University of Regina Press, 2020), *Abolition is Love* (Triangle Square/Penguin Random House, 2023), *Marvellous Grounds: Queen of Colour Formations* (Between the Lines, 2018), and *Queering Urban Justice* (University of Toronto Press, 2018).

Dr. Ra'anaa Yaminah Ekundayo (ABD) is a Tiohtià:ke (Montreal, QC)–based emerging multimedia visual activist scholar. Their work explores the intersection of art and activism, particularly contemplating the entanglement of Black identity, community, and futurity. Co-founder and chair of Black Lives Matter–Sudbury, Ra'anaa strives to actively decolonize every facet of their life, supporting calls to defund the police, to abolish the prison industrial complex, and for liberation in our lifetime.

A cultural curator, Ra'anaa works with various communities and mediums, exploring radical love, self-care, and joy as an act of resistance and means of liberation. Most recently, they curated Love is the Antidote (Wildseed Centre for Art & Activism, 2024) and Effervescence (Galerie du Nouvel–Ontario, 2025). Since 2018, they have worked alongside Up Here: Urban Arts Festival, supporting the works of national and international installation and mural artists. Ra'anaa's written work is featured in *A Thousand Tiny Awakenings* (Latitude 46, 2025) and *Queer Country Crossroads* (Caitlin Press, 2025), and as co-editor of *The Arts of Black Activism: Black Cultural Politics in Northern Turtle Island 2020–Present* (University of Regina Press, 2026).

They produced the award-winning short documentary *Collective Resistance* (2023) and are a co-creative lead, writer, and actor for the forthcoming short film *Can You Feel It Now* (2025). Ra'anaa was a 2022 STEPS Public Art CreateSpace Artist-in-Residence, a 2022–23 Barry Pashak Social Justice Graduate Fellow, and a 2023–24 Wildseed Centre for Art &

Activism Black Arts Fellow. They hold a master's degree in Architecture and are currently pursuing their SSHRC-funded doctorate in Art History at Concordia University, exploring the emergence of Black activist public art in N'Swakamok (Sudbury, ON). A LEGO lover and world-builder at heart, Ra'anaa believes in accessible art that dreams, disrupts, and invites us all to imagine new worlds.

We're not free until we're all free.

Dr. d'bi.young anitafrika is an internationally celebrated biomythicist, theatre-maker, and decolonial pedagogue whose work spans performance, scholarship, and arts leadership across four continents. Laureate of the 2025 Johanna Metcalf Performing Arts Prize, they have shaped contemporary theatre and performance training through their pioneering methodology, the Anitafrika Dub Praxis—a system integrating the Anitafrika Method, Critical Dub Pedagogy, the Biomyth Three R Process, Dubography and Dubology.

d'bi.young has authored 12 plays, released 7 dub poetry albums, published 4 poetry collections, and headlined festivals and theatre seasons worldwide. Their contributions have been recognised with numerous honours, including three Dora Awards, the KM Hunter Theatre Award, the Canadian Poet of Honour Award, a Siminovitch Playwrights Prize Finalist, and a Global Leader in Theatre and Performance distinction from Arts Council England. Their PhD–*Personhood, Practice, and Pedagogy in Black Womxn Theatre*–is a groundbreaking dubography that theorises Black womyn's theatre-making and addresses critical research gaps in Canadian performance scholarship.

A sought-after educator, d'bi.young has lectured at Addis Ababa University, Rose Bruford College of Theatre and Performance, London South Bank University, University of Toronto, and the University of Victoria, where they received the 2025 Innovative Course Design Award for their decolonial pedagogy. Founding Artistic Director of the Black Theatre School and Spolrusie Press, and Principal Researcher of Canada's first Black Womyn in Theatre Archive, d'bi.young is currently developing their doctoral dissertation into a literary publication.

